MANAGING KNOWLEDGE

MANAGING KNOWLEDGE

Perspectives on
cooperation and competition

edited by
Georg von Krogh and Johan Roos

SAGE Publications
London • Thousand Oaks • New Delhi

Preface, introductory material, editorial selection and
Chapters 2, 5 and 11 © Georg von Krogh and Johan Roos
1996.
Chapter 1 © John Harald Aadne, Georg von Krogh and
Johan Roos 1996
Chapter 3 © Kenneth Wathne, Johan Roos and Georg von
Krogh 1996
Chapter 4 © Marjorie Lyles, Georg von Krogh, Johan Roos
and Dirk Kleine 1996
Chapters 6 and 7 © Georg von Krogh, Johan Roos and
Thorvald Hærem 1996
Chapter 8 © Georg von Krogh, Johan Roos and Kenneth
Slocum 1996
Chapter 9 © Salvatore Vicari, Georg von Krogh, Johan
Roos and Volker Mahnke 1996
Chapter 10 © Georg von Krogh, Johan Roos and George
Yip 1996

First published 1996

 SAGE Publications Ltd
6 Bonhill Street
London EC2A 4PU

SAGE Publications Inc
2455 Teller Road
Thousand Oaks, California 91320

SAGE Publications India Pvt Ltd
32, M-Block Market
Greater Kailash – I
New Delhi 110 048

British Library Cataloguing in Publication data

A catalogue record for this book is available from
the British Library.

ISBN 0 7619 5180 6
ISBN 0 7619 5181 4 (pbk)

Library of Congress catalog card number 96-069872

Typeset by Photoprint, Torquay, Devon
Printed in Great Britain at the University Press, Cambridge

Contents

Contributors

John Harald Aadne is doctoral candidate and research assistant at the Institute of Management (IfB) at the University of St Gallen in Switzerland. He received his Master of Business and Economics from the Norwegian School of Management in 1995, and graduated as Master of Science with Honors in International Marketing and Strategy at the Norwegian School of Management in 1995. He has worked as research assistant in strategic management and teaching assistant in finance at the Norwegian School of Management. His present research interests are strategy development processes, strategic management practices in emerging industries, cooperative processes, and knowledge management and learning in organizations.

Thorvald Hærem is a PhD student at the Norwegian School of Management and the Copenhagen Business School and holds a Master of Science degree in International Marketing and Strategy. He is leading the research project 'Companies Unlimited' at the Norwegian School of Management. The research project concerns issues such as new organizational forms, knowledge transfer and new developments in information technology. He has worked as researcher and consultant with companies such as Norwegian Telecom, Digital Equipment Corporation and Philips.

Dirk Kleine is research assistant and doctoral candidate at the University of St Gallen, Switzerland. He holds a Bachelor degree from Berufsakademie Mannheim and an MBA from Lancaster University. He has been working on different European projects with major multinational companies. He is participating in the research project 'Cooperation and Knowledge Management' at the University of St Gallen and his current research addresses the role of organizational argumentation processes on knowledge transfer and development in cooperative settings.

Marjorie Lyles is Associate Professor of Strategic Management at Indiana University's School of Business. She is also Director of the Indiana University Center on Southeast Asia and a member of the American Management Association's International Advisory Council. Her research centers on global strategies and industry analysis, strategic decision making, organizational learning, planning systems and cooperative alliances. She has presented and authored over 50 articles on strategic management and consulted with numerous organizations, including Westinghouse, DEC, and Lilly.

Volker Mahnke is a doctoral student at the University of St Gallen and holds a Master of Science degree in International Finance and Marketing. He is participating in the research project 'Cooperation and Knowledge Management' at the University of St Gallen. The research project concerns issues such as new epistemology, knowledge transfer and knowledge management. He has worked as researcher and consultant with international companies such as Ernst & Young, Volvo, SAS and Wieland-Werke AG.

Johan Roos is a professor at the International Institute for Management Development (IMD) and an expert on how companies become, and remain, healthy enough to keep adapting. Related areas of expertise include managing knowledge, strategy processes and cooperative strategies. He is currently involved in several research projects in close cooperation with companies, and has consulted widely on these issues for both US and European corporations and associations. He is the author, or co-author, of a range of articles published in *Strategic Management Journal, Management Science, Advances in Strategic Management, International Business Review, Personnel Review, Industrial Marketing Management, Irish Marketing Review, Journal of International Management Review, Journal of Organizational Change Management, European Management Journal, Long-Range Planning*, and *Financial Times*. He has published seven books and is a frequent speaker on various conferences in the management realm.

Kenneth R. Slocum is Senior Vice President of SENCORP, a privately held, US-based corporation with businesses in a variety of world markets. For the past 13 years, Slocum has been leading research, development and implementation of new management concepts that integrate knowledge development in an organization with the management of existing operation. Slocum's business experience includes executive management positions in both private and public multinational companies. He holds a Bachelor's degree in Electronic Engineering and an MBA from the Harvard Business School.

Salvatore Vicari is Professor of Business Administration at Bocconi University, Milan, and the Director of Human Resources Development at SDA Bocconi, the Graduate School of Business Administration. He has published extensively in the fields of strategy, marketing and organization theory. His current research interests cover the new sciences as they apply to firms, among them autopoiesis theory and chaos theory. Professor Vicari is a member of several editorial boards and also an active management consultant in the areas of strategy and management.

Georg von Krogh is Professor of Management at the University of St Gallen and a member of the board of directors at the Institute of Management. He is also an active advisor to European and American firms in the area of corporate and competitive strategy. His present research interests are in the area of strategic management; cooperative strategies, strategic processes including knowledge and competence development, strategic management practices in emerging industries and the foundations of qualitative research in the field of strategy. He has published several books as well as some 30 articles in international scientific journals.

Kenneth Wathne is a researcher and doctoral student at the Norwegian Institute for Research in Marketing, Norwegian School of Management. His current research focuses on interorganizational relationship management. He earned his Master of Science degree in International Marketing and Strategy from the Norwegian School of Management.

George Yip teaches business strategy and international marketing at the University of California, Los Angeles, and is a former faculty member at the Harvard Business School and Georgetown University. A successful consultant to companies in the United States and abroad, he has also held management positions with major multinational companies. Yip is holder of a Master's degree in Economics from Cambridge University, a Master's from Cranfield School of Management, and an MBA and doctorate from the Harvard Business School.

Preface

This book is the outcome of more than five years of joint research and consulting practice on the issue of cooperative strategies and knowledge management. The book brings together contributions that attempt to shed more light on an increasingly important and visible dimension of cooperation – that involving knowledge and knowledge transfer.

The task of learning more about knowledge development and knowledge transfer in different cooperative settings, within and between companies, has been a challenging one. We have uncovered much conceptual ambiguity and many methodological traps. We approached this challenge by using *both* theoretical lenses that are well known *and* lenses unknown to most researchers as well as to most managers in the realm of strategic management and organizational studies.

Many of the chapters are conceptual in nature. This is not an accident, nor should it be surprising to the reader. The topics of organizational cooperation and knowledge development do suffer from a conceptual ambiguity that, in our opinion, often prevents 'breakthrough insights'. Still, it has been natural to first work with existing conceptual frames and empirically investigate those. As a complement, however, we have developed a new conceptual foundation from which we can see things differently and, indeed, we have seen new things!

We gratefully acknowledge the research efforts of our co-authors: John Harald Aadne, Thorvald Hærem, Dirk Kleine, Marjorie Lyles, Volker Mahnke, Ken Slocum, Salvatore Vicari, Kenneth Wathne, and George Yip. The mere number of co-authors indicates that this has been, and remains, a substantial research undertaking.

In addition to being one of the co-authors, Dirk Kleine has professionally managed this book project from the initial idea to its completion. He deserves all credit for *de facto* materializing the book.

Much of the conceptual and empirical research reported in this book is the outcome of a three-year research project (1993–5) funded by the Norwegian Research Council (NFR/NORAS grant no. 2151309). We gratefully acknowledge this financial support.

We thank the publishers who have granted permission to reprint four articles previously published in *Strategic Management Journal* (Chapter 8), *International Business Review* (Chapter 10) and *European Management Journal* (Chapters 7 and 11).

Introduction

Georg von Krogh and Johan Roos

This book is a result of a major research effort focusing on the important issue of managing knowledge within organizations and in cooperative strategies. As we move from the industrial age to the information age, knowledge is becoming increasingly critical for the competitive success of firms. In recent years economists and organizational theorists have claimed that the creation of wealth and profit is less dependent on the mechanistic control of resources than it has previously been. The key to success in today's business is the application and development of specialized knowledge and competencies. This raises questions about how to define and study knowledge and how organizations can develop and manage knowledge. These are the kinds of questions we will explore in this book.

Despite enormous attention in business and academia, it is fair to say little is still known about knowledge in organizations in general and about knowledge transfer and development in cooperative arrangements in particular. These research topics are relatively new and much contemporary research effort naturally goes into defining an area of investigation and developing a conceptual apparatus. The concept of knowledge is still ambiguous and gives rise to much confusion. We believe that it will take a while before a consistency emerges in the research on knowledge development and transfer within organizations and in cooperative strategies. However, as Ludwig Wittgenstein suggested, although the concept of 'knowledge' cannot be precisely defined, we should not refrain from using it.

This book addresses a wide area of issues concerning the management of knowledge, ranging from knowledge transfer and developments *between* organizations, e.g. acquisitions, alliances, joint ventures, to knowledge management *within* organizations. The purpose of this book is to provide new ideas regarding organizational cooperation and developing knowledge within organizations. In turn, we hope these ideas will give rise to new insights for all readers!

We want to point out that this book represents a 'status report' on the research on knowledge in organizations and knowledge transfer in cooperative strategies pursued by us and our fellow researchers. There is much to be discovered in the field of knowledge management and we are still on the very first steps of what appears to be a long ladder. We hope that this book will fuel debate on the concepts of 'knowledge' and 'knowledge transfer' among business researchers and practitioners. We also hope that both the research results and the practical implications presented in this book will be a stimulus for the advancement of managerial thinking and reflection in general.

An Organizing Framework for the Book

The book is arranged in two parts manifesting a fundamental conceptual distinction between two world-views:

Part I :   Representationism: Traditional Approaches to Viewing Know-
           ledge, Knowledge Transfer and Cooperative Strategies
Part II: Anti-Representationism: New Perspectives on Knowledge and
           Knowledge Transfer in Organizational Cooperation

The chapters in Part I 'Representationism: Traditional Approaches to Viewing Knowledge, Knowledge Transfer and Cooperative Strategies' are all based on the 'cognitivist' perspective. The fundamental assumption of this perspective is that the world is pre-given, and that the aim of this cognition is to create the most accurate or 'truthful' representations of this objective world. Representations, e.g. of people, companies or industries, can be stored and retrieved in knowledge structures and/or organizational memories. This perspective assumes an information processing model of human cognition whereby the brain employs logic in its processes of reasoning and solving problems.

Representationism or cognitivism has been the basis for the bulk of the contributions in the field of strategic management and organizational theory since Simon, March and Cyert's breakthrough research. In this school of thought, knowledge is often substituted with information and organizations are viewed as completely open systems that process information which is obtained from the environment. The contributions in Part I capture these assumptions. The concepts and models that we have developed in this part of the book are of great value to academics as well as managers because they shed light on a number of important issues that affect knowledge development between and within firms.

In Part II 'Anti-Representationism: New Perspectives on Knowledge and Knowledge Transfer in Organizational Cooperation' we take up a new and distinct perspective of knowledge management which is based on autopoiesis theory. This perspective goes far beyond conventional ways of perceiving and managing knowledge. Unlike the representationistic perspective, autopoiesis theory proposes that the world is not a pre-given state to be represented. The world is brought forth through the creative act of cognition. From this perspective knowledge and information are developed in the brain and in social systems. Developing information is simply to 'put data in form'. Knowledge is developed internally in a self-referential manner. Knowledge, therefore, is private and the organization is seen as a simultaneously open and closed system; it is open with respect to data but closed with respect to information and knowledge.

The innovative implications arising from this new perspective in the realm of knowledge management are presented in the second part of the book. We believe that this new line of thinking will have a significant impact on future research and progress in the field of knowledge management.

Figure A (p. 4) illustrates the overall structure of the book. We will repeat the appropriate parts of this figure in the introductions to Parts I and II in order to guide the reader through the book. As can be seen, Chapters 1 to 7 discuss various topics of knowledge management from the representationistic perspective and Chapters 8 to 11 address the topic area from the anti-representationistic perspective as seen through the lens of autopoiesis theory.

On the Contributions

In Chapter 1, we will form a basis for the representationistic stream of thinking and research. We will argue that at the heart of existing literature on cooperative strategies there is the idea of perceiving knowledge as representing a pre-given world. Consequently, managers involved in cooperative strategies are advised to focus on issues like the protection of knowledge, knowledge acquisition, joint planning, conflict resolution and formal agreements. However, in our opinion although this stream of research provides many insights on how knowledge is developed in a cooperative context, many questions still remain open. In fact, several of the problems faced by managers involved in cooperative strategies are related to this lack of conceptual clarity. John Harald Aadne is co-author of this chapter.

Chapter 2 explores the role of imitation in the context of knowledge development. A major theme in strategic management thinking and practice is that imitation limits the sustainability of a firm's competitive advantage. Theories of the sociology of knowledge are merged with selected contributions from the strategic management literature in order to better understand the process of imitating knowledge. We will develop a conceptual model including four concepts with direct and indirect causal influences on the effectiveness of knowledge imitation.

In Chapter 3, we develop and test a model of knowledge transfer in cooperative strategies. Building on the strategic management literature and the sociology of knowledge, we examine how actors from different social contexts develop a common stock of knowledge in cooperation. This is done by a cross-sectional field study of cooperative relationships of Nordic companies. Focusing on the management of cooperation, the empirical findings complement previous research, underscoring the importance of openness, defined by trust and richness in channels of interaction. This chapter was written together with Kenneth Wathne.

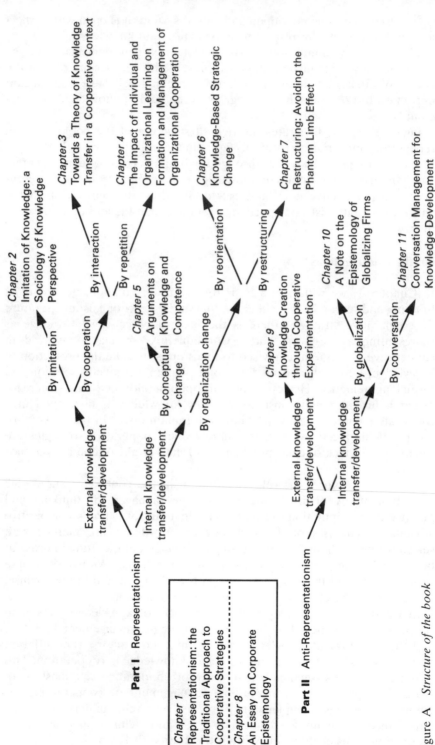

Figure A　*Structure of the book*

In Chapter 4, we will argue that traditional approaches to the formation and management processes of cooperative arrangements ignore the issues of individual and organizational learning as factors that have an impact on how, why and in what way a firm will enter a cooperation. It is envisioned that individual and organizational learning is a critical variable influencing the strategic decision-making process of determining whether a new cooperation will be formed or not. The crucial question explored is the extent to which managers and organizations have learned from previous processes, how learning has been transferred, and the extent to which this influences actions taken in the future. Written with Marjorie Lyles and Dirk Kleine, Chapter 4 draws heavily on previous work of Marjorie Lyles.

The objective of Chapter 5 is to uncover managers' 'espoused' concepts and theories on competence and knowledge. As in our daily speech the concept of competencies is often used to code a broad range of our experience related to craftsmanship, specialization, intelligence and problem solving. Based on an analysis of how managers in ten companies argue about these issues, it is clear that competence is an 'experience-near' concept that needs further conceptual clarification if it is to serve the purpose of either theory building or managerial practice.

Chapter 6 addresses the issue of strategic change processes within organizations as determined by information and knowledge transfer. The chapter builds on an ethnographic study carried out within the Digital Corporation in Norway. We argue that a 'knowledge gap' is a critical stage in the strategic change process. We will discuss how the relation between the knowledge gap and the knowledge transfer process determines the direction of future strategic change in the organization. A model will be developed that provides an analytical tool to improve the understanding of the influence of knowledge and information on the strategic change process and vice versa. Chapter 6 was written in conjunction with Thorvald Hærem.

Although corporate restructuring is a much-studied area in management literature, divestitures have not yet been discussed from the perspective of their negative effects on knowledge transfer and corporate performance. In Chapter 7, we examine this phenomenon in relation to the competence base of the firm and suggest means by which corporate management can overcome the potentially negative outcomes of 'phantom limb' effects. Thorvald Hærem is co-author of this chapter, which is based on an article previously published in the *European Management Journal*.

Chapter 8 forms the basis for the anti-representationistic perspective. By elaborating on corporate epistemology, we will develop a new perspective on strategic management by outlining a new theory of organizational knowledge. We will focus on how managers can understand and guide knowledge development processes in organizations. The use of autopoiesis theory assists us in viewing strategic management and cooperative strategies differently. This chapter was previously published as an article in the *Strategic Management Journal* in 1994 and includes Ken Slocum as a co-author.

The purpose of Chapter 9 is to demonstrate that the theory of autopoiesis provides a new understanding of strategic learning in organizational cooperation. Our aim is to highlight a select number of topics from the theory in order to show how these ideas may improve the understanding of knowledge development in a cooperative context. The implications of the approach for strategic learning will be discussed and a new concept – management of strategic experiments in cooperative settings – is presented. It will be shown that cooperative strategies are not just an alternative to internal growth: they are also a way of exploring possible learning and development hypotheses in relation to new opportunities. Chapter 9 was written together with Salvatore Vicari and Volker Mahnke.

Chapter 10 aims to contribute to a theory of knowledge for globalizing firms. In the first section, we discuss how knowledge has been dealt with in the literature of globalizing firms particularly in light of a conventional epistemology. It is argued that studies have provided much insight into knowledge *per se* in globalizing firms, but have revealed very little about *how* knowledge actually develops in globalizing firms. Building on Chapter 8 we elaborate on the two concepts of language games and self-similar processes to better understand the process of knowledge development in globalizing firms. Chapter 10 was written with George Yip and was published in *International Business Review* in December 1994.

The main line of argument in Chapter 11 is that language is the currency for knowledge development in a management team. A distinction between strategic and operational conversation is made to better understand why managers have difficulties in discussing future strategies. The concept of conversation management refers to a systematic process that stimulates 'languaging' throughout the company. Practical advice is given to managers who are involved in strategy development. Chapter 11 is based on an article that was previously published in the *European Management Journal* in December 1995.

Part I

Representationism: Traditional Approaches to Viewing Knowledge, Knowledge Transfer and Cooperative Strategies

The contributions of the first part of this book are all based on the assumptions that the world is pre-given and that the aim of cognition is to represent this objective world. Thus, learning means being increasingly better at mirroring this world. The bulk of research in management and organizational studies rests firmly on these assumptions. Therefore, the objective of the seven chapters in Part I is to incrementally develop new distinctions in the areas of knowledge, knowledge transfer and cooperative strategies from the representationistic perspective. The first part of the book is structured as in Figure B overleaf.

Chapter 1 explores the cognitivist assumptions in the context of cooperative strategies. This chapter should sensitize the reader to the assumptions made in the representationistic perspective and therefore provide a better basis for an understanding of the remaining chapters of Part I. The next step is to discuss knowledge development/transfer both internally, i.e. within the organization, and externally, i.e. between organizations. The issue addressed in Chapter 2 is *imitating* knowledge. Both Chapter 3 and Chapter 4 focus on knowledge management in different *cooperative* settings. Whereas Chapter 3 is concerned with knowledge transfer through *interaction* between partner companies, Chapter 4 explores the impact of learning experiences on formation and management of organizational cooperations when firms *repetitively* enter alliances. These two chapters are linked to each other as well as to Chapter 1.

Having discussed the issues related to external knowledge development/ transfer mentioned above, we will then focus on internal aspects in the remaining three chapters. As can be seen in Figure B, the first distinction we make refers to *conceptual change* versus *organizational change*. Chapter 5 explores the managerial perception of the *concepts* of knowledge and competence, and illustrates how a change in the understanding of these concepts may impact on knowledge development. In the context of *organizational change*, Chapter 6 discusses the impact of knowledge on *organizational reorientation* and Chapter 7 its role in *organizational restructuring*.

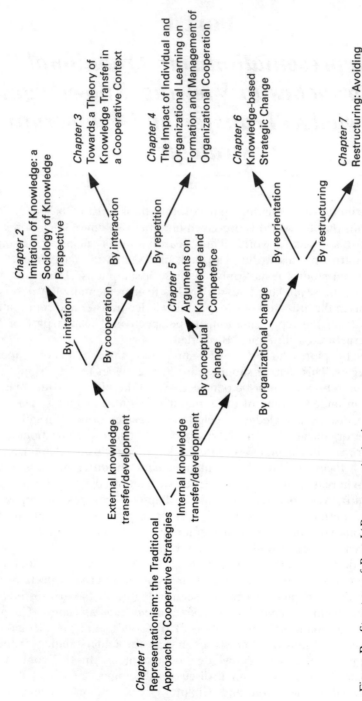

Figure B   *Structure of Part I 'Representationism'*

1

Representationism: the Traditional Approach to Cooperative Strategies

John Harald Aadne, Georg von Krogh and Johan Roos

Whatever you think about an alliance, it is always on the move to
something else. I will be disappointed if what I believe will happen
tomorrow, today, is what will happen.

Erik Tønseth, President CEO, Kværner AS

Cooperative Strategies and Knowledge

Over the last decade, cooperative strategies have become an essential
feature of companies' overall organizational activity. More and more
companies have realized that competitive advantage increasingly depends
not only on their internal capabilities and industry characteristics, but also
on the way they cooperate with other companies. Cooperative strategies
can be defined as intended horizontal and vertical strategic connections
between firms which share compatible goals, strive for mutual benefits, and
acknowledge a high level of mutual interdependence. Furthermore, joint
efforts aim at results that each firm would find difficult to achieve by acting
alone (this definition is inspired by Mohr and Spekman, 1994). By using
such a broad definition we want to incorporate every type of strategic
cooperative activity into our discussion, ranging from more informal
strategic agreements to joint ventures, networks and acquisitions that have
a strategic character.

However, many companies and managers have learned, to their regret,
that cooperative activity is not an easy way to do business. A high degree of
frustration and substantial 'failure rates' related to different types of
cooperative relationship seem to be prevalent (Porter, 1987; Geringer and
Hebert, 1991; Bleeke and Ernst, 1992; The Economist Intelligence Unit,
1994).

Today, most businesses face faster changes in technology, more competitive environments, strategic behavior among firms, vanishing industry
boundaries and increased interfirm competition, forcing them to rethink
their way of looking at strategy, performance, survival, success etc. In this
world of 'creative destruction' (Schumpeter, 1942) more and more
researchers and practicing managers argue that knowledge is the most

critical resource for sustaining high performance. Firms increasingly compete on a differentiated stock of knowledge (Arthur, 1990; Stinchcombe, 1990; von Krogh and Roos, 1995b), and management of the firm's knowledge base has emerged as a major challenge for firms that want to stay on the competitive edge (Spender, 1993). According to Badaracco, competitive firms 'succeed by developing, improving, protecting and renewing knowledge' (1991a: 1).

Traditionally, cooperative strategy activities were mostly concerned with pure product–market potentials. Recently, however, companies like IBM, Sega, Nestlé, Coca-Cola, Dyno, AT&T, and Apothekernes Laboratorium have seen the enormous potential of forming 'knowledge links' (Badaracco, 1991a) and have exploited the potential found in complementary knowledge and mutual knowledge development. Gary Hamel, for example, argues in the following way: 'The traditional "competitive strategy" paradigm (e.g. Porter, 1980), with its focus on product–market positioning, focuses on only the last few hundred yards of what may be a skill-building marathon' (1991: 83). Moreover, Hamel argues that competitiveness to a large extent will be determined by the firm's pace, efficiency, and extent of knowledge accumulation. Badaracco (1991a) even claims that the increased importance of knowledge in the business society may partly be a consequence of the emerging dense web of cooperative relationships, because such relationships speed up the global migration or transfer of knowledge. The research and managerial focus on knowledge and its role in strategic management in general, and cooperative strategies in particular, however, is still in its infancy. In their introduction to a recently published special issue on new thinking within the strategy field, the editors C.K. Prahalad and Gary Hamel (Prahalad and Hamel, 1994) emphasize knowledge development and cooperative strategies as two of the most important and promising areas for further research and development.

Several different approaches to cooperative strategies can be found in the literature originating from various areas of the management field, e.g. strategic alliances (Harrigan, 1985; Contractor and Lorange, 1988; Lorange and Roos, 1992), virtual corporations (Davidow and Malone, 1992), networks (Benson, 1975; Thorelli, 1986; Jarillo, 1988), distribution channels (Stern and El-Ansary, 1992), relationship marketing (Arndt, 1979; Hunt, 1983; Webster, 1992), and mergers and acquisitions (Weston et al., 1990; Haspeslagh and Jemison, 1991; von Krogh et al., 1994b). These contributions paint a comprehensive picture of different aspects of cooperative strategies. However, this literature has to a large extent one major commonality: arguments and lines of reasoning are strongly influenced by what we would call 'conventional cognitivistic assumptions' about management and organization.

In this chapter we will address the role of knowledge and knowledge development in cooperative strategies, and how it is described in the existing literature. At the heart of this literature, we argue, is the idea that knowledge represents a pre-given world. A comprehensive literature review will be presented, and some of the managerial implications from a representationist view of knowledge are discussed. Finally, we will discuss the existing literature and managerial implications in the critical light of representationism. We will argue that the existing streams of research do not shed sufficient light on how knowledge develops in a cooperative context.

A Representationistic View on Knowledge

Friedrich Hayek started his seminal article about the use of knowledge in society with the following claim: '*If* we possess all the relevant information, *if* we can start out from a given system of preferences and *if* we command complete knowledge of available means, the problem which remains is purely one of logic' (1945: 519). Even though this assumption is both familiar and still widely applied, Hayek questions whether it is relevant or will provide any answer to the problems which society faces. For the representationist or cognitivistic view on knowledge, however, Hayek's question has never been the most dominating.

The ideas and line of reasoning developed by cognitive science researchers about the mind and the functioning of the mind in the 1950s have had substantial impact on several fields of research (Varela et al., 1992; von Krogh, Roos and Slocum, Chapter 8 in this volume). From this perspective, called the 'cognitivist' perspective by Varela (1992), two major assumptions about cognition can be identified. First, cognition is seen as a representation of a pre-given world. This implies that reality, be it objects, events, or states, resides outside the cognizing subject, and is objectively given for everyone. Further, in multiple ways the mind has the ability to create inner representations which more or less correspond to this given reality. Thus, knowledge can be seen as a mirror of reality. Consequently, from this point of view, the fundamental criteria or goals for any cognitive system are those of adequacy, accuracy, and truth itself (Lyotard, 1984: viii). Second, cognition can be seen as information processing and rule-based manipulations of symbols (Varela et al., 1992; von Krogh and Roos, 1995a). The central idea behind this is that intelligence, human intelligence included, is to a large extent comparable to the essential characteristics of computation, where computation 'is an operation that is carried out or performed on symbols [on elements that represent what they stand for]' (Varela et al., 1992: 40). Thus, human beings are transparent to information from the outside, which then is processed and subsequently used to build mental representations that can be stored in the mind. Similar to the role of logic in computation, logic is thought of as a human competence that allows us to reveal the *truth* about phenomena observed, that is, logic is a vehicle for human beings to attain knowledge. Additionally, because of the potential complexity of objects, events, or states to be represented, and the time constraints on the observations, the human brain is assumed to have some kind of competence at probability judgments and heuristics. These two competencies combined are essential for the ability to make increasingly better representations (von Krogh and Roos, 1995a). From this perspective, learning means to improve representations through assimilating new experiences, and to further develop competence in logic and competence in probability judgments.

To summarize, the representationist view is based on the following general assumptions about knowledge:

- Knowledge represents a pre-given world.
- Knowledge is universal and objective.
- Knowledge results from information processing.
- Knowledge is transferable.
- Knowledge enables problem solving.

Knowledge and Cooperative strategies: a Literature Review

Several authors have proposed cooperative arrangements as a powerful way of accessing and transferring organizationally embedded knowledge (e.g. Kogut, 1988; Badaracco, 1991a; Hamel, 1991). It is argued that some types of knowledge are rather explicit, articulated and packaged, and thus relatively easy to transfer between firms. Consequently, such knowledge will migrate in the business community, and be accessible for most companies regardless of their cooperative activity. However, some knowledge can be highly firm-specific and less diffusible across the boundaries of the firm. Residing in individual and social relationships in the firm, this knowledge is seen as tacit and personal (Polanyi, 1962), and the only possible way to reveal and transfer this knowledge is to establish a closer and more interactive relationship with the one possessing it.

One of the first and most quoted publications drawing attention to knowledge or learning issues related to cooperative strategies was Lyles (1988). Drawing on Fiol and Lyles (1985), she refers to organizational learning as 'the development of insights, knowledge and associations between past actions, the effectiveness of those actions, and future action' (1985: 811). Lyles (1988) argues that learning has to be reflected in structural elements and outcomes, which means that learning is both action outcomes and changes in the state of knowledge. More recently, the organizational knowledge and learning perspectives have directed considerable attention to different aspects of transaction and transfer. However, they differ fundamentally from other transaction- or transfer-oriented research approaches, like transaction cost economics (Williamson, 1975; 1985). The organizational learning literature emphasizes organizational and cognitive factors rather than derivatives of opportunism under uncertainty and asset specificity as explanatory factors (Kogut, 1988).

From the literature on cooperative strategies, at least four issues seem to be of substantial importance for understanding and managing knowledge transfer: motives, openness, prior experience, and internalization.

Motives

The literature regarding the formation of cooperative arrangements emphasizes the utmost importance of understanding both your own motives and the motives of potential partners. For a company thinking about involvement in cooperative strategy activity, specification and understanding of motives will have significant impact on the choice of partner, which activities to include, and the form of the relationship (Badaracco, 1991a). Gray argues that the overarching theme that unites different types of strategic alliances is that 'each needs the others to advance their individual interest' (1989: 6). Several authors have contributed to different types of categorization of motives or explanations for involvement in cooperative strategies (e.g. Berg et al., 1982; Harrigan, 1986; Kogut, 1988; Borys and Jemison, 1989; Oliver, 1990; Badaracco, 1991a; Singh, 1993; Heide, 1994).

Kogut (1988), for example, distinguishes between three different types of motives for joint ventures: transaction costs, competitive positioning, and organizational learning. In the merger and acquisition literature, a strong community of researchers has addressed financial motives and the handling of possible principal–agent issues as crucial (Copeland and Weston, 1988; Singh, 1993). Recently, however, a stronger emphasis on distinguishing knowledge and learning motives from other types of motives has been more dominant.

Badaracco (1991a) pinpoints the difference between what are called product links and knowledge links. The former focus primarily on issues like cost and risk reduction, market access and flexibility, while the latter may be of substantial importance for building strengths for future competitiveness. Further, in his analysis of international joint ventures, Hamel (1991) argues that knowledge transfer is rare when a clearly communicated learning motive is lacking. Thus, learning in the case of cooperative strategies took place by 'design' rather than by 'default'. Hamel's study also addresses the importance of understanding not only your own motives, but the motives of your partner companies as well. Hamel argues: 'The competitive consequences of skills transfers, as well as the actual migration of skills, were often unintended, unanticipated and unwanted by at least one of the partners' (1991: 92).

Hamel has identified the following indicators which influence the strength of the knowledge transfer motive. First, cooperative strategies seen as a temporary vehicle for improving competitiveness relative to the partner and others may indicate a stronger motive for knowledge transfer than a long-term collaboration. Second, if a company faces a lack of resources compared to the requirements for achieving its corporate and competitive ambitions, knowledge transfer is seen as a powerful route. Third, when knowledge that can be potentially transferred is of a kind that can be leveraged into and exploited in several different businesses (core competencies), its attractiveness is higher than knowledge limited to a more narrow range of businesses. Finally, positive learning outcomes may be associated with an asymmetry in power between the partners. Any balance of power may bring instability into the relationship. This is often experienced in cooperations involving Japanese firms. In Japanese society, dependence plays a significant role, and the analogy of parent–child is often applied (Hamel, 1991).

Openness

As seen above, a knowledge transfer motive is emphasized in the literature as a basic requirement for any learning to take place in cooperative strategies. However, even if a firm has a clearly defined and communicated learning motive, the potential for learning is highly determined by the openness of the partner (Hamel, 1991) or an appropriate atmosphere (Haspeslagh and Jemison, 1991). In this case, openness can be seen as willingness to share knowledge, and to interact closely with a partner. Stata (1989), for example, defines openness as the partners' willingness to put all cards on the table, eliminate hidden agendas, make their motives, feelings, and biases known, and invite other opinions and points of view. Within the context of cooperative strategies this means, for example, access to technologies, laboratories, project review meetings, libraries etc. Hamel (1991) using the concept of 'transparency', argues that this is a determining factor for the learning potential in cooperative strategies. Managers involved in Badaracco's study of strategic alliances claimed consistently, and with conviction, that open communication is invaluable for successful alliances. Badaracco argues: 'Openness is paramount in knowledge links because much of what the parties are trying to learn from each other or create together is so difficult to communicate. It is often embedded in firms' practices and culture, and it can only be learned through working relationships that are not hampered by constraints' (1991a: 142).

In their analysis, both Badaracco (1991a) and Hamel (1991) distinguish between different types of knowledge. Hamel (1991) argues that one type of knowledge is of a rather explicit and discrete type, residing in, for example, technical drawings or patents. Another type of knowledge is more tacit, and of a more systemic kind. Consequently, the latter type is seen as more difficult to transfer than the former. Hamel illustrates this by arguing that a more specific technology, like microprocessor chip design, is more transparent than the underlying competencies or skills. In the same way, market intelligence may be easier to transfer than knowledge related to leading edge manufacturing. Similarly, Badaracco (1991a) distinguishes between 'easily encodable' or 'decodable' knowledge characterized by a high degree of transferability, and tacit knowledge characterized by a high degree of embeddedness. Transfer of embedded knowledge is heavily restrained because it resides to a large extent in more complex social relations. Hamel (1991) also refers to the extent to which knowledge is context-bound, however, mainly referring to the difference in contextuality between occidental cultures and others. For example, several Western companies expressed frustration over the problem of distinguishing between form and content, ritual and substance when they cooperated with Japanese companies. A similar frustration was not identified among Japanese managers.

However, a positive causality between high transparency and substantial transfer of knowledge can also be disputed. Harrigan (1985) claims the following will occur when transparency in a joint venture is high: (1) less transfer of knowledge to the venture company will take place; (2) the difficulties associated with preventing technological transfer (bleed-through) will be exacerbated; and (3) the joint venture relationship will be unstable.

Several authors argue that discussions of openness have to be located in the ongoing interaction between individuals and small groups rather than on a firm-to-firm level (Hamel, 1991; Badaracco, 1991a; Ring and Van de Ven, 1994; Wathne, Roos and von Krogh, Chapter 3 in this volume). This indicates that structural issues, be they legal, governance or task oriented (Harrigan, 1988; Killing, 1983; Tybejee, 1988) only have a limited influence on the relationship between the partners. Wathne, Roos and von Krogh (in this volume) emphasize the role which the channel of interaction between the partners plays, and argues that 'media richness' (Daft and Huber, 1987) is a determinant of the extent to which knowledge may successfully be transferred. Going even further in this direction, Hamel (1991) views the potential for knowledge transfer as the outcome of a series of micro-bargains through the day-to-day interaction between the operating employees of the partners. In these micro-bargains, factors such as operational effectiveness, fairness and bargaining power will be of crucial importance for the possibility to 'win' and thereby attain access to the partner's knowledge. These micro-bargains are both implicit and explicit.

Contrary to Hamel's rather 'win–lose' view on the interactive dynamics between cooperating partners, other authors (Badaracco, 1991a; Ring and Van de Ven, 1994; Wathne, Roos and von Krogh in this volume) include trust as a substantial determinant for openness or perceived openness in the relationship. Firms and employees involved in cooperative arrangements have a tendency to hold their 'cards' as close as possible (Badaracco, 1991a). Consequently, if the interacting parties are not able to develop trust over time, not only may the fragile managerial and economic cooperation be threatened, but the potential for knowledge transfer and learning may be rather limited (Faulkner, 1993; Wathne, Roos and von Krogh in this volume). When trust increases, confidence about future expectations grows, and the partners tend to interact as if the future were more certain. Thus, the partners predict behavior based on their attempt to understand the other in terms of acts, dispositions and motives. Regarding knowledge links, Badaracco has the following comment: 'Studies have confirmed that when the parents of a joint venture trust each other, they are more inclined to grant substantial autonomy to managers, enabling them to respond more quickly to problems and opportunities and thereby raising the venture's chances of success' (1991a: 142).

Prior Experience

In both the strategic management and cooperative strategy literatures, one of the fundamental assumptions is that successful firms learn from their past experiences by transforming experiences into useful knowledge. They store this in the organizational memory, and finally retain it as a part of their ongoing decision-making processes (e.g. Huber, 1991; Lyles and Schwenk, 1992; Lyles, 1994). Wathne, Roos and von Krogh (in this volume) argue that diversity and depth of knowledge are among the fundamental determining factors for knowledge transfer in cooperative strategies. Building on Cohen and Levinthal (1990), diversity is seen as a robust basis for learning, because it enhances the probability that incoming information may relate to what is already known. Further, the ability to acquire and exploit new knowledge will also be influenced by in-depth knowledge within specific fields and 'discrimination skills' (Lyles, 1988; Lyles and Schwenk, 1992). A discrimination skill is defined by Lyles (1988) as the ability to discriminate between different decision situations, and to select the actions that might be the most appropriate. Consequently, the richness (breadth and depth) of the existing knowledge structure will influence both the assimilation and the exploitation of external knowledge.

Lyles (1988; 1994) focuses on the relationship between joint venture experience and memory, and its influence on other joint venture formation processes. This is described in depth in Chapter 4. She argues that learning takes place by people and their sharing of experiences and their development of organizational stories, and by development of management systems. Further, the top management of the firm plays an important role in this transfer of knowledge. Through its role of overseeing all the different cooperative activity the firm is involved in, it becomes the medium for collection and sharing of lessons learned, by communicating to and socializing with managers.

Westney (1988) raises the question of whether, or to what extent, experience in managing linkages in one context can be effectively trans-ferred to other types of linkages. She admits that it may be intuitively obvious that extensive experience in cooperative strategies enhances the chance of successful management of new linkages. However, instead of necessarily being generally cumulative, she argues that learning curves may be cumulative only in very specific contexts, like certain firms, types of organizations, industry segments or products. Based on this argument, she distinguishes between two types of learning curves: management of relations between the partners and transfer of learning within the firm. Effective transfer of learning could then contribute to added value in production, services and processes. Further, this latter type of learning is seen as more likely to be cumulative across contexts, because your own organizational structures and processes are more established and independent of the specific contexts where cooperative activity takes place.

Finally, experience with a specific partner may also contribute to the cooperative climate and the potential for knowledge transfer (Inkpen, 1992). A prior relationship contributes to a faster and more efficient development of the particular cooperative arrangement, because some of the initial uncertainty is overcome (Ring and Van de Ven, 1994; Wathne, Roos and von Krogh in this volume). Ring and Van de Ven further argue: 'Increases in trust between parties, which are produced through an accumulation of prior interactions that were judged by the parties as being efficient and equitable, increase the likelihood that parties may be willing to make more significant and risky investments in future transactions' (1994: 101).

For more discussions concerning the importance of prior experience in organizational cooperation, see Chapter 4.

Internalization

Given that motive is the desire or willingness to learn, and openness is the opportunity to learn, internalization is concerned with, or determines, the partners' ability or capacity to learn (Hamel, 1991). This part of the knowledge transfer process may be divided into two aspects: receptivity and dissemination. In the cooperative strategy literature, researchers have mainly used this distinction in delineating the difference between individual learning and collective or shared learning. For the former, the existing stock of knowledge and prior related experience have the main impact. Hamel (1991), for example, experienced that the partner possessing the greatest need to learn had the highest barriers to receptivity. It may have had problems not only in understanding what the partner was doing, but also in understanding or tracing the process leading to the partner's knowledge development. In fact, if the gap in knowledge is substantial, knowledge transfer may even be almost impossible. A similar pattern was seen by Crossan and Inkpen (1992) in their study of joint ventures between American and Japanese firms. American firms especially had difficulties in learning, even if they had almost unhindered access to their Japanese partners. The main problem was that they failed to appreciate their partners' dedicated knowledge. Thus, inability to absorb information need not be consistent only with low transparency. Hamel (1991) also draws on traditional organizational learning literature (e.g. Hedberg, 1981; Nystrom and Starbuck, 1984; Argyris and Schön, 1978) when he argues that the organization's ability to absorb knowledge depends on both the process of altering existing perceptual maps and replacing old status quo behavior with new improved behavior.

The second feature of internalization is to distribute relevant knowledge throughout the parent organization, and finally exploit its potential. Hamel (1991) argues for a two-step process for transforming individual learning into collective learning. There have to be mechanisms integrating fragmented knowledge gained by single individuals, and learning has to be distributed to all those that potentially could benefit from it. This task could be achieved through establishment of cross-functional teamwork and interbusiness coordination. Crossan and Inkpen (1992) denote this type of organizational system as 'artifactual facilitation'. Other mechanisms belonging to the same category may be: rotation of managers, regular meetings between venture and parent management, plant visits and tours by parent managers, and senior management involvement in cooperative activities (Crossan and Inkpen, 1992). In addition, Crossan and Inkpen (1992) argue for two other possible mechanisms which may promote the sharing of knowledge received. First, a leader, or influential person, could foster the integration of the different individual schemata into shared understanding. Second, the individuals involved could engage in processes aimed at sharing common ground themselves. These alternatives are not mutually exclusive.

Management of Knowledge

Above, we have comprehensively described the main concepts and lines of reasoning on knowledge and knowledge transfer in the traditional litera-ture on cooperative strategies. To serve as a background, the concepts presented were not discussed according to their degree of influence by representationism. In this section, we will more specifically highlight management of knowledge from a representationistic point of view.

Badaracco emphasizes the following main responsibilities for managers engaged in cooperative strategy activity: 'Managing alliances, particularly knowledge links, is at bottom a process of learning, creating, sharing, and controlling knowledge. As executives manage the boundaries of their firms, they are determining when and how knowledge and skills will move into and out of their organizations' (1991a: 129). Thus, managing the flow of knowledge within and between the companies is a major managerial responsibility. The distinctions between motive, openness, and internaliza-tion made in the literature review above also illustrate that several of the knowledge-related concepts seen in the cooperative strategy literature can be traced to some aspect of the flow of knowledge. Motive is mainly concerned with the flow between a firm and its partners. It influences the knowledge transferred to the cooperative context, and the type and amount of knowledge expected to be transferred from the cooperative context. Openness directs focus towards the specific cooperation, and how the continuous interchange of knowledge takes place between the partners. Finally, internalization addresses the flow of knowledge within the firm. The three different flows of knowledge are illustrated in Figure 1.1. Based on this, at least three different management responsibilities can be identified: controlling the flow of knowledge, managing the knowledge transfer context, and managing internalization.

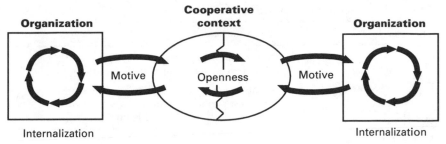

Figure 1.1   *The different flows of knowledge*

Controlling the Flow of Knowledge

We will divide control of the flow of knowledge into two parts. From a managerial point of view, one important part is to protect yourself from transferring core and company-specific knowledge. A second aspect is the assessment of the knowledge possessed by potential partners. In the case where the major motive of both partners is to access the other's knowledge, a highly unstable relationship may be the result. Hamel et al. (1989), for example, argue that cooperation where one partner is focused on learning and the other has no ambition beyond investment avoidance may often be the most smooth running. This does not mean investment avoidance as such, but rather a pure focus on access to products, or reducing the costs and risk of entering new markets, and no interest in learning and knowledge transfer. However, several companies and researchers believe that it is possible to manage the balance between learning and protection. To protect important knowledge and competence, firms have to build a 'Chinese wall' around it (Lewis, 1990), or create 'a black box' (Lorange and Roos, 1992). Hamel et al. (1989) argue that specification in formal agreements is one possibility to limit unintended knowledge transfer. In a contract, the scope of cooperation may be limited to a single technology rather than a whole range, one or few products rather than the entire line, one or few markets, and a more specific period of time. Lorange and Roos (1992) argue that the easiest way to do this in practice is not to give away or involve unique or critical knowledge in the cooperative activity at all. In this case, one solution is to perform these functions on behalf of the alliance rather than to share it. Another alternative is to bundle many discrete activities into an integrated 'package'. Then the systematic totality may be more difficult to understand, and any attempt to break up specific parts may threaten the whole relationship. Table 1.1 shows some guidelines for managing protection of knowledge.

The boundaries between core 'know-how' (Lewis, 1990), or 'core competencies' (Hamel, 1991) and less sensitive areas, however, cannot be regarded as static. Parents will provide their children with 'pieces of technology incrementally as the knowledge becomes less proprietary or as the firm gains confidence in working with its partners in the joint venture.

Table 1.1   *Protection of knowledge*

Knowledge	When to share
Core	Never disclose May share application results
Important non-core	Combined value well exceeds separate worth Can trust partner to protect Limit scope of use to avoid harm

Source: based on Lewis, 1990

This will be done because they have no other satisfactory way to protect appropriable knowledge that gives them bargaining power' (Harrigan, 1985: 82).

Assessment of partner knowledge is seen as a crucial part of the considerations leading up to involvement in knowledge-focused cooperative arrangements (Badaracco, 1991a; Hamel, 1991; Hamel et al., 1989). Establishing partnerships is a cumbersome and time-consuming process, and may considerably limit your future menu of partner alternatives. Consequently, firms should be highly focused on their own strategic motive, and be concerned about what knowledge the company needs to meet its long-term strategic goals, and what relationships are vital to bring the necessary knowledge into the company. However, the 'terror balance' between the cooperative partners' competencies should not be exaggerated. Harrigan points out: 'Managers recognized that bleedthrough [transfer of knowledge and technology] problems were created by pooling information, but they regarded this phenomenon as being more helpful to collegiality than harmful for its damage to competitive advantage' (1985: 354). In many cases there were more problems with encouraging transfer of technology than discouraging it. This organizational inertia or unwillingness to learn is similar to some of the findings of Crossan and Inkpen (1992).

Managing the Knowledge Transfer Context

This is the second management responsibility often emphasized in the literature. Whether the motive is aggressive 'out-learning' of the partner, or sharing knowledge in a 'win–win' situation, managers have to create an atmosphere that fosters knowledge transfer. Hamel, for example, introduces the concept 'collaborative membrane' as something that determines learning, and 'through which flow skills and capabilities between the partners' (1991: 100). Several authors argue that effective transfer of knowledge requires a high degree of closeness to the partner (e.g. Badaracco, 1991a; Helleloid and Simonin, 1994; Wathne, Roos and von Krogh, Chapter 3 in this volume). This is especially the case where the demanded knowledge is highly complex and embedded in social relations. Thus, cooperation aimed at R&D and other types of activity involving extensive knowledge development may require cooperative arrangements with ongoing and close interaction, such as joint ventures and acquisitions. In the same way, ongoing and close interaction may be the most appropriate context for firms having a strong learning motive as well.

After the initial connections between the partners are made, the development of trust has been seen as instrumental for common value creation and transfer of knowledge (Zajac and Olsen, 1993; Ring and Van de Ven, 1994; Wathne, Roos and von Krogh in this volume). However, as long as trust development is so highly interlinked with other interpersonal and interorganizational factors, trust management is not an isolated and easy definable management task. Nevertheless, the coevolution of cooperation, communication and trust has been seen as important for how managers assess the outcome of their interorganizational activity (Anderson and Narus, 1990; Inkpen and Birkenshaw, 1994). In these studies, communication has been defined as formal and informal transfer of meaningful and timely information. Mohr and Spekman (1994) go further and propose three aspects of communication behavior as essential for cooperative strategies: communication quality, information sharing, and participation. The first aspect refers to such factors as accuracy, timeliness, adequacy, and credibility of the information exchanged between the partners. Information sharing focuses on the extent to which critical and firm-specific information is communicated between the partners. Finally, Mohr and Spekman emphasize the role of participation in joint planning and goal setting to match expectations and specify efforts.

Congruency is seen by several authors as necessary for cooperative arrangements to be successful. Westney (1988) argues that organizations working closely together may be subject to an 'isomorphic pull'. In other words, organizations may realize that interactions will run more smoothly and effectively if they start to develop or move towards similar structures and processes. Effective learning and transfer of learning, for example, may be achieved by the creation of structures within the boundaries of the firm which are parallel or analogous to those developed together with the partner. An example from Hamel's (1991) study may illustrate this. One partner assembled a 'collaborative team' to observe, interpret and apply the knowledge of their partner. To increase their possibility to learn, the different types of skills present in the team were composed as parallel as possible to those possessed by their partner. Similar arguments are presented by Ring and Van de Ven (1994) on a more specific level. They argue that for two cooperating firms, the sense of purpose, the values and the expectations have to be congruent or even identical over time. As an example, they propose that congruent expectations may include areas such as common agreement on norms, work roles, the nature of work itself, social relationships, and security needs (Ring and Van de Ven, 1994).

Managing Internalization

Finally, the third management responsibility is managing the internalization of knowledge transferred. Helleloid and Simonin (1994) argue that a key principle for the management of learning is the substitution of individual memories by organizational memory. This view is supported by Lyles (1994), who argues that in their memory, or organizational knowledge structures, organizations store belief systems, memories of past events, stories, frames of reference and values. Thus, the organizational memory serves as a basis for influencing future actions. Helleloid and Simonin argue that the transition from individual to organizational memory can be done by increasing the redundancy of information, through replication of experiential knowledge and duplication of knowledge bases existing in the organization, for 'A multiplicity of depository agents will help assure that the knowledge can be accessed at a later time' (1994: 225). Further, for knowledge to be accessible and disseminated in the organization some mechanisms have to be established that can inform members about its existence and how it can be retrieved. If such a coordinating mechanism does not exist, those needing the knowledge may be aware of neither its presence in the organization, nor how it can be accessed. Finally, Lyles (1994) argues for organizational story-telling as a powerful way of sharing experiences.

To summarize, several authors see knowledge as transferable. For managers involved in cooperative strategies, control of this transfer is one of the main responsibilities. By managing the flow of knowledge, you can control the amount and quality of knowledge transferred to your partner, and consequently you can influence the knowledge development of your partner. Additionally, several of the contributions discussed here conclude that partners have 'similar', 'congruent', or 'identical' knowledge, assuming that knowledge has an objective nature and exists independently of the single firm or individual. These characteristics are typical footprints of representationism in use. In the next section we will discuss some of these aspects in more depth.

Discussion

The structured description above captures the main arguments about knowledge transfer and related concepts seen in the cooperative strategy literature. Several of these concepts and their application by different authors, however, have, to a large extent, one thing in common: they are rarely defined, and, most of the time, are taken for granted. On a walk down the 'cooperative strategy lane' you quite often stumble on concepts like knowledge, technology, skills, competence, capabilities, information and learning used both interchangeably and as distinct and mutually related (see Table 1.2 for a brief overview). Consequently, cumulative development and distinctive use of concepts are clearly lacking within this field.

Several authors recognize that the degree of transferability may be dependent on different types of knowledge. Badaracco describes migratory knowledge in the following way: 'Some knowledge is capable of moving quickly because it can be packaged in a formula, a design, a manual, or

Table 1.2 *Different concepts in use in the cooperative strategy literature*

Author	Study[1]	Knowledge	Technology	Competence	Capabilities	Skills	Information	Learning
Harrigan, 1985; 1986	Survey	✓	✓				✓	
Lyles, 1988; 994	Cases							✓
Westney, 1988	Conceptual	✓						✓
Lewis, 1990	Cases	✓	✓					✓
Badaracco, 1991a	Cases			✓	✓	✓		✓
Hamel, 1991	Cases			✓		✓		✓
Haspeslagh and Jemison, 1991	Conceptual			✓	✓	✓		✓
Lorange and Roos, 1992								
Crossan and Inkpen, 1992	Cases			✓		✓		
Powell and Brantley, 1992	Survey	✓	✓					✓
Vicari, 1994	Conceptual	✓						✓
Deiser, 1994	Conceptual						✓	✓
Helleloid and Simonin, 1994	Conceptual	✓	✓	✓			✓	✓
Tyler and Steensma, 1995	Survey	✓		✓	✓	✓		✓
Wathne, Roos and von Krogh (Chapter 3 in this volume)	Survey	✓						

[1]The different studies are rather broadly categorized using only three categories: conceptual, cases and survey. However, the methods applied in the empirical studies range from experience-close methods like grounded theory development (Hamel, 1991) to rather experience-distant and heavy quantitative studies applying structural equation modeling (Wathne, Roos and von Krogh in this volume).

a book, or because it can be contained in one person's mind or incorporated in a piece of machinery' (1991a: 35). Further, he argues that receiving this type of knowledge is only dependent on the receiver's capability to unpack and extract it. Because of the general knowledge development in society, more and more companies and nations have this capability. Thus, transfer of migratory knowledge is seen as uncomplicated. Hamel (1991) and Badaracco (1991a) emphasize that embedded and tacit knowledge, by its very nature, is more difficult to transfer. This type of knowledge resides in social relations, and is highly context and history dependent. However, even though these authors stress the difficulties of transfer, this type of knowledge is not seen as impossible to transfer. Badaracco explains: 'The boundaries of firms can either impede or hasten the slow movement of embedded knowledge. The type of alliance I have called a knowledge link . . . is a way in which companies can learn embedded knowledge from other organizations' (1991a: 79). Hence, some flavor of representationism is present even when tacit and embedded knowledge is referred to in the cooperative strategy literature, although not to the same extent as when migratory knowledge is described.

The impact of explicit and implicit use of cognitivist assumptions and the information processing literature on cooperative strategy has been substantial. However, only a few authors (e.g. Lyles, 1988; 1994; Thomas and Trevino, 1993; Helleloid and Simonin, 1994) apply ideas and concepts from the information processing literature on a broader scale. Of the concepts used, either independently or combined, acquisition, gathering, processing, storage and retrieval are certainly the most common. Helleloid and Simonin, for example, argue that 'once knowledge has been processed in light of a context or problem, meaning is extracted which may be directly utilized by the organization and/or stored away for future use' (1994: 225). Here, knowledge is seen as the result of information processing. Moreover, knowledge is related to a context or problem, but its meaning is at the same time seen as objective and universal. A similar view on knowledge can be found in Lyles (1994). She argues that: 'once the key decision makers have determined that the change challenges the core elements of the knowledge structure, they make changes in the knowledge structure and communicate these changes to others in the organization' (1994: 460). All these elements are fully in accordance with the representationistic view on knowledge. The organization is seen as an input–output device, where information about the environment is picked up, processed, and finally stored and retrieved in organization-wide knowledge structures (von Krogh and Roos, 1995a).

At the heart of the information processing point of view is the need for reducing uncertainty through information gathering and information processing (Thomas and Trevino, 1993). The underlying assumption of this thinking is that when managers and decision makers face uncertainty, they in fact lack some amount and/or type of information. Consequently, the way to reduce this 'information gap' is to gather more information (Daft and Lengel, 1986). Thomas and Trevino (1993) further argue that this type of information can be seen as objective and task-related input for rational decision-making processes. The strong emphasis on transfer and sharing processes and the importance of protection seen in the cooperative strategy literature shows several similarities with the 'information gap filling' argument. Several authors argue for example that increased communication and information sharing reduce the uncertainty in the relationship, and consequently improve the cooperative atmosphere (e.g. Hamel, 1991; Mohr and Spekman, 1994; Inkpen and Birkenshaw, 1994; Wathne, Roos and von Krogh in this volume). Further, a typical argument is that the effectiveness of this communication and information distribution is highly dependent on the establishment of appropriate structures and routines (e.g. Lyles, 1988; Hamel, 1991; Crossan and Inkpen, 1992). Thus, information processing is seen as a central mechanism in the organization. Information and knowledge can easily be distributed or transferred both throughout and between organizations, as long as appropriate information handling infrastructures are established. Implicit in this point of view is an assumption about neutrality of knowledge and information. Both knowledge and information are seen as independent of the specific situation, context, organization and individual. Thomas and Trevino (1993) provide a worthy illustration. They describe one of their cases as a *'data worshipping* environment where the gathering, analysing, and dissemination of data through written documents was a highly-valued behaviour' (1993: 806). The top manager in this company applied an underlying assumption that information was 'facts', and based his activity on the rule that 'facts speak for themselves'. Thus, the handling of information was seen as processing of information primarily in written form, and every problematic situation was met by more processing of information. The possibility of multiple interpretations was never taken into account. This view on information and information handling is fully in line with the assumptions of the representationistic perspective on knowledge.

Most publications on cooperative strategies focus on organizational levels that go far beyond the specific cooperative arrangement and its operating activity. Normally, discussions are mainly concerned with the parent company, the relation between parent and venture, the relation between parent companies cooperating, or ventures in general. In addition, several authors address these relationships from the viewpoint of the top managers. Consequently, much of the cooperative strategy literature has a rather unitary view on organizations; they are seen as one entity, executing the organization's common goals and activities. Hamel et al. argue that: 'Knowledge acquired from a competitor-partner is only valuable after it is diffused through the organization. Several companies we studied had established internal clearinghouses to collect and disseminate information . . . [The collaborations manager] identified what information had been collected by whom and then passed it on to appropriate departments' (1989: 139). Badaracco (1991a) raises the question of how a firm remembers what it knows. Drawing on the work of Cyert and March (1963), he answers that firms remember 'through a "memory" that consists of its standard operating procedures, the formal and informal routines its members use to get their work accomplished' (1991a: 88). Badaracco also asks in what sense a firm thinks. This time he draws on Chester Barnard (1968), and says: 'Organizations "think" and "decide" by processing – transmitting, altering, refining, elaborating, ignoring, and combining – both hard and soft information' (1991a: 89). Finally, Badaracco emphasizes the contributions made by Herbert A. Simon and Kenneth Arrow in conceptualizing the firm. Simon describes the firm as an information processing system, where the focus is directed 'upon the flows and transformations of symbols' (1945: 292), and Arrow describes the firm as an 'incompletely connected network of information flows' (1973: 19). Here, we see that Badaracco strongly draws on the 'founding fathers' of the cognitivistic information processing literature in his description of the firm and its role as an embodiment of knowledge. Concepts with a strong representationistic flavor, like 'memory', 'processing', 'information' and 'information flows', are recurrent in this section of Badaracco's discourse.

The underlying assumptions about knowledge driving such a view are not very sophisticated. Knowledge is seen as a rather static asset, highly distributed, and with an objectively given content. However, even some of the more recent contributions within the field of information processing question this approach. Thomas and Trevino (1993) argue that information processing to reduce equivocality is essential for cooperative arrangements. By equivocality they mean ambiguity and the existence of multiple and conflicting interpretations (Weick, 1979; Daft and Weick, 1984). Because cooperative strategies involve multiple parties possessing differing goals, different cultural backgrounds and interpretations, the people in these organizations have to be involved in discussion and communication aimed at equivocality reduction and shared meaning (Thomas and Trevino, 1993; Daft and Weick, 1984). This line of reasoning redirects the focus from the organization as a whole towards individuals and groups. Organizations are the embodiment of actions taken on behalf of both the organization and the individuals (Ahrne, 1994). However, everything done in organizations is enacted by the individuals representing it (Weick, 1979). A similar view is presented by Badaracco (1991a) and Hamel (1991), when they address the importance of the individual and the daily ongoing activity in the cooperative arrangement. Badaracco, for example, argues that 'cooperative arrangements are not fundamentally links between one firm and another . . . Such firm-to-firm abstraction does not exist. Only individuals and small groups can establish relationships. Hence, the success of collaboration depends on whether specific individuals in separate organizations can work together and accomplish joint tasks' (1991b: 15). However, Badaracco (1991a) and Hamel (1991) do not focus more particularly on how knowledge transfer or knowledge development may take place, or on what the 'collaborative membrane' looks like and how the 'series of micro-bargains' takes place (Hamel, 1991).

Inspired by the recent development of the resource-based view of the firm (e.g. Wernerfelt, 1984; Conner, 1991) and competitive advantage (e.g. Barney, 1991; Amit and Schoemaker, 1993) much of the cooperative strategy literature focuses primarily on imitation or replication of existing knowledge possessed by the partner rather than development or creation of new knowledge. Hamel et al., for example, argue that: 'Successful companies view each alliance as a window on their partners' broad capabilities. They use alliance to build skills in areas outside the formal agreement and systematically diffuse new knowledge throughout their organization' (1989: 134). Similarly, Lewis argues that 'learning from another organization can be a powerful tool: it shows how things actually work' (1990: 45). One of the few extending beyond this view is Badaracco (1991a). In addition to seeing knowledge focused collaboration as a way to attain socially embedded knowledge, he emphasizes its utmost possibility for renewing and reshaping core capabilities and creating new knowledge. Vicari (1994) is even more explicit than Badaracco on the role and importance of knowledge development. First, he views the firm as a social system where individuals enter into relations with one another to achieve their objectives, 'through a process of creating knowledge to use available knowledge to produce new knowledge' (1994: 342). Further, he argues that because of significant increases in dynamism, fragmentation, and coexist-ence of contradictory phenomena, managers face an increasing com-plexity. To cope with these challenges, Vicari proposes that firms should involve themselves purposely in cooperative arrangements focused on experimentation with new hypotheses and possible new development projects. In this way, the firm emphasizes knowledge development as a strategy for improved adaptation and strategic flexibility. More specific-ally, Vicari argues in the following way: 'Technological progress . . . requires enterprises to show a great capacity in the continuous experi-mentation of new technological solutions. This capacity is obtainable through acquisitions and alliances which form networks of enterprises, joined together through processes of technological exchanges' (1994: 347). Other areas for experimentation may be the globalization process and the breakdown of barriers between markets (Vicari, 1994). However, neither of these contributions investigates the processes of knowledge creation and development and their role, characteristics and possibilities within the context of cooperative strategies.

Our findings from these discussions are summarized below:

- Knowledge is rarely defined, and is often used interchangeably with several other concepts.
- Knowledge is seen as transferable within and between organizations.
- Knowledge is seen as objective representations of a pre-given world, rather than subjective and observer dependent.

- Discussions of knowledge are related to the organization level, rather than to group and individual levels.
- Discussions in traditional literature focus on imitation and replication of knowledge, rather than knowledge development.

Final Comments

The discussion above addresses some of the weaknesses seen in the existing literature on cooperative strategies. However, we believe that the potential for a thorough investigation of these issues drawing on the traditional approach and assumptions may be of only a partial type. We believe that the starting point for a new research agenda for cooperative strategies should be of a more fundamental nature. For even though knowledge and knowledge development have been addressed as the imperative for future competitiveness, only a few authors have a consistent and considered view on knowledge and knowledge-related questions such as: how individuals and organizations come to know; what counts as knowledge; what drives and impedes knowledge development; and whether knowledge can be transferred. As seen in our presentation of the representationist assumptions and their strong influence on the existing literature on cooperative strategies, these sorts of questions are not brought to the surface. However, we aim to shed more light on these questions in Part II of the book.

References

Ahrne, G. (1994). *Social Organizations: Interaction Inside, Outside and Between Organizations*. London: Sage.

Amit, R. and Schoemaker, P.J.H. (1993). Strategic assets and organizational rent. *Strategic Management Journal*, 14: 33–46.

Anderson, J.C. and Narus, J.A. (1990). A model of distributor firm and manufacturer firm working partnerships. *Journal of Marketing*, 54 (January): 42–58.

Argyris, C. and Schön, D. (1978). *Organizational Learning*. Reading, MA: Addison-Wesley.

Arndt, J. (1979). Toward a concept of domesticated markets. *Journal of Marketing*, 43 (Fall): 69–75.

Arrow, K.J. (1973). *Information and Economic Behavior*. Stockholm: Federation of Swedish Industries.

Arthur, W.B. (1990). Positive feedback in the economy. *Scientific American*, February: 80–85.

Badaracco, J.L. (1991a). *The Knowledge Link: How Firms Compete through Strategic Alliances*. Boston, MA: Harvard Business School Press.

Badaracco, J.L. (1991b). Alliances speed knowledge transfer. *Planning Review*, March/April: 10–16.

Barnard, C.I. (1968). *The Functions of the Executive*. Cambridge, MA: Harvard University Press.

Barney, J. (1991). Firm resources and sustained competitive advantage. *Journal of Management*, 17: 99–120.

Benson, J.K. (1975). The interorganizational network as a political economy. *Administrative Science Quarterly*, 20: 229–49.

Berg, S.V., Duncan, J. and Friedman, P. (1982). *Joint Venture Strategies and Corporation Innovations*. Cambridge, MA: Oelgeschlager, Gunn & Hain.

Bleeke, J. and Ernst, D. (1992). *Collaborating to Compete*. New York: Wiley.

Borys, B. and Jemison, D.B. (1989). Hybrid arrangements as strategic alliances: theoretical issues in organizational combinations. *Academy of Management Review*, 14: 234–49.

Cohen, M. and Levinthal, D. (1990). Absorptive capacity: a perspective on learning and innovation. *Administrative Science Quarterly*, 35: 128–52.

Conner, K. (1991). A historical comparison of resource-based theory and five schools of thought within industrial organizational economics: do we have a new theory of the firm? *Journal of Management*, 17, 1: 121–54.

Contractor, F.J. and Lorange, P. (eds) (1988). *Cooperative Strategies in International Business*. Lexington, MA: D.C. Heath.

Copeland, T.E. and Weston, J.F. (1988). *Financial Theory and Corporate Policy*. Reading, MA: Addison-Wesley.

Crossan, M.M. and Inkpen, A.C. (1992). Believing is seeing: an exploration of the organizational learning concept and the evidence from the case of joint venture learning. Working Paper, Western Business School, The University of Western Ontario, Canada.

Cyert, R.M. and March, J.G. (1963). *A Behavioral Theory of the Firm*. Englewood Cliffs, NJ: Prentice-Hall.

Daft, R.L. and Huber, G. (1987). How organizations learn: a communication framework. *Research in the Sociology of Organizations*, 5: 1–36.

Daft, R.L. and Lengel, R.H. (1986). Organizational information requirements, media richness and structural design. *Management Science*, 32: 554–71.

Daft, R.L. and Weick, K.E. (1984). Towards a model of organizations as interpretation systems. *Academy of Management Review*, 9(2): 284–95.

Davidow, W.H. and Malone, M.S. (1992). *The Virtual Corporation*. New York: Harper Business.

Deiser, R. (1994). Post-acquisition management: a process of strategic and organisational learning. In G. von Krogh, A. Sinatra and H. Singh (eds), *The Management of Corporate Acquisitions*. London: Macmillan. pp. 359–90.

Faulkner, D. (1993). International strategic alliances: key conditions for their effective development. PhD dissertation, University of Oxford.

Fiol, C.M. and Lyles, M.A. (1985). Organizational learning. *Academy of Management Review*, 10(4): 803–13.

Geringer, J.M. and Hebert, L. (1991). Measuring performance of international joint ventures. *Journal of International Business Studies*, 22(2): 249–64.

Gray, B. (1989) *Collaborating: Finding Common Ground for Multiparty Problems*. San Francisco, CA: Jossey-Bass.

Hamel, G. (1991). Competition for competence and interpartner learning within international strategic alliances. *Strategic Management Journal*, 12: 83–103.

Hamel, G., Doz, Y.L. and Prahalad, C.K. (1989). Collaborate with your competitors – and win. *Harvard Business Review*, January–February: 133–39.

Harrigan, K.R. (1985). *Strategies for Joint Ventures*. Lexington, MA: Lexington Books.

Harrigan, K.R. (1986). *Managing for Joint Venture Success*. Lexington, MA: Lexington Books.

Harrigan, K.R. (1988). Joint ventures and competitive strategy. *Strategic Management Journal*, 9: 141–58.

Haspeslagh, P.C. and Jemison, D.B. (1991). *Managing Acquisition: Creating Value through Corporate Renewal*. New York: Free Press.

Hayek, F.A. (1945). The use of knowledge in the society. *The American Economic Review*, xxxv (4): 519–30.

Hedberg, B.L.T. (1981). How organizations learn and unlearn. In P.C. Nystrom and W.II. Starbuck (eds), *Handbook of Organizational Design*. London: Oxford University Press. pp. 3–27.

Heide, J.B. (1994). Interorganizational governance in marketing channels. *Journal of Marketing*, 58(1): 71–85.

Helleloid, D. and Simonin, B. (1994). Organizational learning and a firm's core competence.

In G. Hamel and A. Heene (eds), *Competence-Based Competition*. London: Wiley. pp. 213–39.

Huber, G. (1991). Organizational learning: the contributing process and the literature. *Organization Science*, 2: 88–116.

Hunt, S.D. (1983). General theories and the fundamental explanada of marketing. *Journal of Marketing*, 47 (Fall): 9–17.

Inkpen, A.C. (1992). Learning and collaboration: an examination of North American–Japanese joint ventures. PhD dissertation, University of Western Ontario.

Inkpen, A.C. and Birkenshaw, J. (1994). International joint ventures and performance: an interorganizational perspective. *International Business Review*, 3(3): 201–17.

Jarillo, J.C. (1988). On strategic networks. *Strategic Management Journal*, 9: 31–41.

Killing, J.P. (1983). *Strategies for Joint Venture Success*. New York: Praeger.

Kogut, B. (1988). Joint ventures: theoretical and empirical perspectives. *Strategic Management Review*, 9: 319–32.

Lewis, J.D. (1990). *Partnerships for Profit: Structuring and Managing Strategic Alliances*. New York: Free Press.

Lorange, P. and Roos, J. (1992). *Strategic Alliances: Formation, Implementation and Evolution*. Cambridge, MA: Blackwell.

Lyles, M.A. (1988). Learning among joint venture sophisticated firms. *Management International Review*, Special Issue: 85–98.

Lyles, M.A. (1994). The impact of organizational learning on joint venture formation. *International Business Review*, Special Issue: 459–68.

Lyles, M.A. and Schwenk, C.R. (1992). Top management, strategy, and organizational knowledge structures. *Journal of Management Studies*, 29(2): 155–74.

Lyotard, J.-F. (1984). *The Postmodern Condition: A Report on Knowledge*. Minneapolis: University of Minnesota Press.

Mohr, J. and Spekman, R. (1994). Characteristics of partnership success: partnership attributes, communication behavior, and conflict resolution techniques. *Strategic Management Journal*, 15: 135–52.

Nystrom, P.C. and Starbuck, W.H. (1984). To avoid organizational crises, unlearn. *Organizational Dynamics*, 12(4): 53–65.

Oliver, C. (1990). Determinants of interorganizational relationships: integration and future directions. *Academy of Management Review*, 15(2): 241–65.

Polanyi, M. (1962). *Personal Knowledge: towards a Post Critical Philosophy*. London: Routledge.

Porter, M. (1980). *Competitive Strategy*. New York: Free Press.

Porter, M. (1987). From competitive advantage to corporate strategy. *Harvard Business Review*, May–June: 43–59.

Powell, W.W. and Brantley, P. (1992). Competitive cooperation in biotechnology: learning through networks? In N. Nohira and R. Eccles (eds), *Networks and Organizations: Structure, Form and Action*. Boston, MA: Harvard Business School Press. pp. 366–94.

Prahalad, C.K. and Hamel, G. (1994). Strategy as a field of study: why search for a new paradigm? *Strategic Management Journal*, 15: 5–16.

Ring, P.S. and Van de Ven, A.H. (1994). Developmental processes of cooperative interorganizational relationships. *Academy of Management Review*, 19(1): 90–118.

Schumpeter, J.A. (1942). *Capitalism, Socialism and Democracy*. New York: Harper and Row.

Simon, H.A. (1945). *Administrative Behavior*. New York: Free Press.

Singh, H. (1993). Challenges in researching corporate restructuring. *Journal of Management Studies*, 30(1): 147–72.

Spender, J.-C. (1993) Workplace knowledge. Paper presented at the Conference on Distinctive Competencies and Tacit Knowledge, IFAP/IRI, Rome, 15 April.

Stata, R. (1989). Organizational learning – the key to management innovation. *Sloan Management Review*, Spring: 63–74.

Stern, L.W. and El-Ansary, A.I. (1992). *Marketing Channels*. Englewood Cliffs, NJ: Prentice-Hall.

Stinchcombe, A. (1990) *Information and Organizations*. Berkeley, CA: University of California Press.

The Economist Intelligence Unit (1994). *International Mergers and Acquisitions*. London: EIU.

Thomas, J.B. and Trevino, L.K. (1993). Information processing in strategic alliance building: a multiple-case approach. *Journal of Management Studies*, 30(5): 779–814.

Thorelli, H.B. (1986). Networks: between markets and hierarchies. *Strategic Management Journal*, 7: 37–51.

Tybejee, T.T. (1988). Japan's joint ventures in United States. In F.J. Contractor and P. Lorange (eds), *Cooperative Strategies in International Business*. Lexington, MA: D.C. Heath. pp. 457–72.

Tyler, B.B. and Steensma, H.K. (1995). Evaluating collaborative opportunities: a cognitive modeling perspective. *Strategic Management Journal*, Special Issue, 16: 43–70.

Varela, F.J. (1992). Whence perceptual meaning? A cartography of current ideas. In F.J. Varela and J.P. Dupuy (eds), *Understanding Origins: Contemporary Views on the Origin of Life, Mind, and Society*. Dordrecht: Kluwer. pp. 235–64.

Varela, F.J., Thompson, E. and Rosch, E. (1992). *The Embodied Mind: Cognitive Science and Human Experience*. Cambridge, MA: MIT Press.

Vicari, S. (1994). Acquisitions as experimentation. In G. von Krogh, A. Sinatra and H. Singh (eds), *The Management of Corporate Acquisitions*. London: Macmillan. pp. 337–58.

von Krogh, G. and Roos, J. (1995a). *Organizational Epistemology*. London: Macmillan. New York: St Martins Press.

von Krogh, G. and Roos, J. (1995b). A perspective on knowledge, competence and strategy. *Personnel Review*, 24(3): 56–76.

von Krogh, G., Sinatra, A. and Singh, H. (1994). *The Management of Corporate Acquisitions*. London: Macmillan.

Webster, F.E. (1992). The changing role of marketing in the corporation. *Journal of Marketing*, 56 (October): 1–17.

Weick, K.E. (1979). *The Social Psychology of Organizing*. Reading, MA: Addison-Wesley.

Wernerfelt, B. (1984). A resource-based view of the firm. *Strategic Management Journal*, 5(12): 171–80.

Westney, D.E. (1988). Domestic and foreign learning curves in managing international cooperative strategies. In F.J. Contractor and P. Lorange (eds), *Cooperative Strategies in International Business*. Lexington, MA: D.C. Heath. pp. 339–46.

Weston, J.F, Chung, K.S. and Hoag, S.E. (1990). *Mergers, Restructuring and Corporate Control*. Englewood Cliffs, NJ: Prentice-Hall.

Williamson, O.E. (1975). *Markets and Hierarchies: Analysis and Antitrust Implications*. New York: Free Press.

Williamson, O.E. (1985). *The Economic Institutions of Capitalism: Firms, Markets, Relational Contracting*. New York: Free Press.

Zajac, E.J. and Olsen, C.P. (1993). From transaction cost to transaction value analysis: implications for the study of interorganizational strategies. *Journal of Management Studies*, 30(1): 131–45.

2

Imitation of Knowledge: a Sociology of Knowledge Perspective

Georg von Krogh and Johan Roos

The firm's competitive advantage represents its *raison d'être*. Therefore, an understanding of the basis for competitive advantage is the core of the strategic management field. A firm is said to have a competitive advantage when it implements a strategy that is not being simultaneously implemented by other competing firms (Barney, 1986; Porter, 1985). What a firm can do to create competitive advantage is a function not simply of the opportunities in the environment (industry) but also of what knowledge the firm can accumulate and the resources that it can assemble (Barney, 1991; Penrose, 1958; Wernerfelt, 1984),[1] or even of plain luck (Barney, 1986). However, because one firm's success will inspire competitors to respond with superior product features, lower prices, or both, time will ultimately render all advantages obsolete (Williams, 1992).

A firm sustains its competitive advantage if it resists erosion by competitors and thereby keeps a unique position that allows it to consistently outperform its competitors (Hofer and Schendel, 1978; Lippman and Rumelt, 1982; Porter, 1985). As discussed by Reed and DeFillippi (1990), the question of how long a 'sustainable' competitive advantage lasts is firm-specific, but one thing is clear – it will not last forever (Barney, 1991).

The main threat to the erosion of competitive advantages is *imitation* (Barney, 1991; Reed and DeFillippi, 1990). Thus, it is obvious that understanding imitability is perhaps the most critical issue, not only in the resource-based perspective, but within the whole strategic management dialogue. Nevertheless, the question as to *how* competitive advantages erode through imitation is still open. What appears to be clear, however, is that knowledge is the most important source of creating and sustaining competitive advantages. *The objective of this chapter is to shed more light on the process of imitating knowledge.*

This chapter consists of four sections. In the first section we will briefly address the recent focus on 'unique resources' in the strategic management literature, giving us a better understanding of the importance of imitation *per se*. Then, the term 'imitation' will be characterized and, based on the sociology of knowledge, the imitation phenomenon further explored.

In the second section, six concepts of knowledge imitation are identified and discussed. Each concept is discussed in terms of several indicators. This results, in the third section, in a conceptual model of knowledge imitation, which covers two contextual and two organizational concepts, their indicators, and proposed direct and indirect influences on the effectiveness of imitation.

Implications for research and the advancement of research are discussed in the fourth and final section.

Unique Resources

Contemporary strategic management literature focuses on the importance of developing, nurturing and protecting 'unique resources'. A traditional categorization of resources includes, for example, financial resources (cash flow, debt capacity, etc.), physical resources (plant, equipment, etc.), organizational resources (planning, control and total quality systems, culture), technology (high-quality production, low-cost plants, etc.), intangible resources (goodwill, brand name etc.), and human resources (in terms of various types of personnel). In the resource-based perspective of strategic management, if a firm has a sustainable competitive advantage and superior industry performance, its resources have four characteristics: (1) they are valuable, (2) they are rare among competition, (3) they are imperfectly imitable, and (4) there are no strategically equivalent substitutes for them (Barney, 1991). This points to the strategic value of resources for the firm and to their potential strategic value for competing firms. It is not surprising that this perspective inevitably leads to a focus on imitability of 'unique' resources.

Unique resources tend to be at least closely related to knowledge. Some examples found in the literature include: distinctive competencies (Andrews, 1971; Ansoff, 1965; Hofer and Schendel, 1978), invisible assets (Itami, 1987), core competencies (Hamel and Prahalad, 1990), managerial, resource-, transformation- , and output-based competencies (Lado, et al., 1992), core capabilities (Stalk et al., 1992), internal capabilities (Barney, 1986), skill and capability accumulation (Teece et al., 1990), embedded knowledge (Badaracco, 1991), absorptive capacity (Cohen and Levinthal, 1990), underlying capabilities (Williams, 1992), unique combinations of business experience (Huff, 1982; Prahalad and Bettis, 1986), corporate culture (Fiol, 1991), valuable heuristic processes (Shoemaker, 1990), and unique managerial talent (Penrose, 1958). Strategically managing the firm becomes an act of maintaining the *uniqueness* of the knowledge underlying products/services. The challenge lies in balancing the costs of obtaining this uniqueness with revenues from increased competitive advantage (Barney, 1986).

Because knowledge may fulfill the four characteristics previously mentioned (Barney, 1991), it is an important basis for creating sustainable competitive advantages. Therefore, it is only natural that knowledge is

constantly subject to processes of imitation, and is, in turn, an important
issue in strategic management.

In order to understand knowledge imitation it is critical to understand
the nature of knowledge. Because knowledge exists on both an individual
and a social level, we need to merge a micro-level concept of knowledge
(individuals) with a macro-level concept of knowledge (firms). According
to Berger and Luckmann (1967) and Schutz and Luckmann (1973; 1989),
the sociology of knowledge, based on the phenomenology of Alfred Schutz
(1970), accomplishes this merger. Schutz (1970) describes the interaction
of individuals in a social setting, and how the social setting influences
the way individuals conceive the world. Therefore, the individual and
social knowledge coevolve over time. The sociology of knowledge literature also helps us differentiate knowledge from the traditional meaning of
resources in many ways: knowledge takes many forms and shapes at a
given moment in time, it may be dynamic, it is hard to grasp theoretically,
and it is the underlying basis for forming competencies.

Imitation

Webster's Dictionary (1983) defines the verb 'imitate' (from Latin *imitor*, to
follow): (1) to try to act or be the same as, to follow the example of; (2) to
act the same as, to mimic; (3) to reproduce in form, color, etc., to make a
duplicate of, copy, counterfeit; and (4) to be or become like in appearance,
look like. Thus, according to this quite comprehensive definition, imitation
is an act when something is made to resemble something else, usually
something superior, genuine or original. Traditionally, imitation has a
rather negative connotation, which may be an important reason for its
partial neglect and the lack of interest in it as a subject for systematic
study.[2] The most simple form of imitation is when an observer reproduces
direct behavior. Recent theoretical and empirical works, however, focus on
more complex processes (e.g. Decker, 1980; Gioia and Manz, 1985). The
work by Gioia and Manz, based on recent developments in cognitive
psychology, suggests that modeling can be viewed as a process of acquiring,
developing, and altering cognitive schemes (scripts) for behavior.[3]

Many authors have focused on the requirement for imitation to *not* take
place, rather than on understanding the processes involved in successful
imitation. In the competitive strategy literature, extensive work has been
done on 'entry barriers' (Caves and Porter, 1977; Sölvel, 1987; Yip, 1982).[4]
Teece (1986) introduced the notions of 'complementary assets' and
'appropriate regime', resources that allow a firm to capture profits from an
innovation. The literature, however, does not provide us with a precise
definition of the barrier concept. In the absence of such a definition, Reed
and DeFillippi suggested that 'a barrier is the restraining or obstructing of
imitation by competitors' (1990: 94). Still, the imitation process appears to
be an extremely complex one that is not completely understood. Dierickx
and Cool may serve as an example: 'Sustainability of a firm's competitive

advantage hinges on how easy it is to replicate . . . the imitability of a resource (asset) is related to the characteristics of the process by which it may be accumulated' (1989: 1507). It is hard to see how this type of claim provides a better understanding of the imitation process. Also, it is difficult to see how existing concepts can be empirically studied or provide conceptual development in the strategic management field.

An intent to imitate could be the starting point for understanding knowledge imitation. Such intent is the premise for imitating in the first place. In order to characterize what we call an 'imitation intent", we refer to the work of Hamel and Prahalad (1989; Hamel, 1991). Hamel and Prahalad point out that the concept of strategic intent 'encompasses an active management process that includes: focusing the organization's attention on the essence of winning; motivating people by communicating the value of the target; leaving room for individual and team contributions; sustaining enthusiasm by providing new operational definitions as circumstances change; and using intent consistently to guide resource allocation' (1989: 64). According to Hamel, internalization intent refers to 'a firm's initial propensity to view collaboration as an opportunity to learn' (1991: 89). Thus, it appears that a notion of 'imitation intent' is both relevant and related to these concepts.

Further elaborating on Hamel and Prahalad's concepts, at least four variables determine imitation intent: competitive posture *vis-à-vis* partners, relative knowledge position *vis-à-vis* partners and other industry participants, perceived pay-off capacity to exploit knowledge in multiple businesses, and dependence on the knowledge in question.

Given a certain imitation intent, six concepts surface from the literature as particularly relevant in knowledge imitation. These are: (1) observational closeness, (2) imitability of knowledge, (3) externalization of knowledge, (4) internalization of knowledge, (5) objectivation of knowledge, and (6) legitimation of knowledge.

Observational Closeness

The first concept that surfaces from the literature as appropriate for understanding knowledge imitation is observational closeness. A theoretical example is provided by Nelson and Winter (1982), who distinguish between 'replication' and 'imitation'. Replication is a 'costly, time-consuming process of copying an existing pattern of productive activity' (1982: 118). The point is that if an existing pattern or routine can be closely observed, then it can serve as a template for the creation of new patterns or routines. In this way relatively precise copying is possible. In the case of imitation 'the target routine is not in any substantial sense available as a template. When problems arise in the copy, it is not possible to resolve them by closer scrutiny of the original' (1982: 123). Thus, the imitator replicates as much as possible, and then fills in the remaining gaps by independent effort.[5]

The behavior of the former head of ITT, Harold Geneen, is a practical illustration of the importance of understanding the social context for knowledge transfer. His response to the European subsidiaries of ITT was different if they made their request by teletype to him in New York versus talking face-to-face with him in Europe: 'In New York, I might read a request and say no. But in Europe, I could see that the answer to the same question might be yes' (Sproull and Kiesler, 1991: 40). Thus, Geneen's knowledge clearly changed dramatically when knowledge was conveyed to him in personal interaction rather than via an information system where he was observationally close to the agents of the problem. Given the latent nature of the social context dimension, indicators need to be identified. We suggest that the observational closeness can be described in terms of three different social contexts, which have strong implications for the effectiveness of knowledge imitation. Because a knowledge imitation process is likely to cover several of these contexts, all three may be seen as indicators of observational closeness.

The first context is the *coevolutionary context*. In this context, a firm member, A, observes the task resolution process of another, B, including trials and errors. B may convey immediate experiences, more stable knowledge and skills, through speech, body movement, or by using and producing tools and marks. A may also acquire knowledge interactively by inquiring, commenting, and discussing with B the nature of the task at hand, B's own judgment of the necessary skills for the task at hand, and the particular problems in applying the skills to resolve the task at hand. Subsequently, or in parallel, A may use personal observations of B's task resolution to develop A's own competence, e.g. by using information about B's task at hand, by trying solutions suggested by B, and by using tools or marks produced by B. A may observe what Schutz (1970) called a *spontaneous* process in which B is totally immersed in the task and has lost self-awareness.

The second context is the *differentiated context*. Here, knowledge is still conveyed from one firm to another through a process of personal interaction but there is temporal differentiation. A no longer observes the task and the task resolution process (including trial and error) of B. This has at least two implications for the evolution of competence in the firm. First, compared to the coevolutionary context, the knowledge received by A may be increasingly restricted due to legitimation; it may be presented so as to fit the firm's language, rudimentary propositions and initial definitions of various projects (e.g., Bower, 1970), to defend or conceal committed errors or violations of routines (Argyris, 1988; Argyris et al., 1985), or to minimize conflicts with the existing paradigms of the organization (Argyris and Schön, 1978).

Second, the knowledge conveyed may be restricted when compared to that of the coevolutionary context due to differences in task conceptions. As noted by Brown and Duguid (1991) and Bourdieu (1977), a task looks different to someone working on it from how it looks with hindsight when completed. The finished task tends to look neatly structured, and task resolution can be linked with a particular stream of actions. In retrospect, formulating a recipe for successful task resolution may 'smooth out' the (unexpectedly) changing conditions of work. For example, in this second context only finished tools are transferred to others, not the complete experience of a cumbersome, difficult and frustrating manufacturing process.

Moreover, individuals and groups in firms often differ in their conceptions of task content, task complexity, and task variability (see also Scott, 1981; Taylor, 1981). For example, to those working on a task, the task may seem highly complex and unique, while others observing the task performers may conceive of the tasks as enduring and less complex. Therefore, competence evolution in a temporally differentiated context is subject to possible misunderstandings of tasks. Nevertheless, this context allows for immediate clarification of conveyed knowledge in a dialogue between individuals.[6]

The third context is the *detached context*. In this context, the firm members are temporally and spatially differentiated in competence evolution. Knowledge is conveyed in books, drawings, photographs, faxes, tools, marks, tapes, etc., which in their subsequent use are spatially and temporally detached from their source of origin.

Here, we draw particular attention to an argument that organizational routine is the primary way firms effectively retain knowledge about successful behavior (e.g., Cohen, 1991; Cohen and Levinthal, 1990; Huber, 1991; Nelson and Winter, 1982). A routine may be given in the form of norms and 'theories of action' (Argyris and Schön, 1978) or more formally as a written procedure or rule (Cyert and March, 1963). Routines are normally regarded as relatively stable over time, but some flexibility can be secured through 'switching rules' that signal which of several tasks are to be performed under a given set of conditions (March and Simon, 1958). Consistent with organizational learning theories, routines may also be changed as a result of identification of experimental behavior in the firm (Hedberg, 1981; Hedberg et al., 1976). Regardless of their formality and flexibility, however, routines are normally spatially and temporally detached from their source.

In spite of their effective knowledge retention, organizational routines probably have at least three implications for knowledge imitation. First, the organizational routines may in themselves prevent *knowledge dissemination* by their legitimate directing of messages (Feldman and March, 1981; Huber, 1982). The competence development of individuals, groups or organizational units may be negatively affected in that social knowledge does not disseminate to task performers who could use it.

Second, organizational routines may *institutionalize* a particular competence. A history of successful task resolution may lead firms to connect tasks and knowledge on a routine basis. If the task at hand changes, or if social knowledge changes, however, a problem may arise. Knowledge that is enforced into a task that it does not fit may become an obstacle to successful task resolution (e.g., Brown and Duguid, 1991; Levitt and March, 1988).

Third, 'even directives that are in plain English often require interpretation that is quite specific to the organizational context' (Nelson and Winter, 1982: 102). However, unlike the two other contexts (like the Omicron example), simultaneous temporal and spatial differentiation does not allow A to inquire into and observe the context of knowledge acquisition and objectivation of B, in short, to find out 'what the devil [these others] think they are up to' (Geertz, 1983: 58). For example, lack of interaction may prevent A from observing and making inquiries into how the knowledge and directives of B connect with stories, myths, theories, language, etc., of the firm. The knowledge disseminated in directives may thus take many different forms and lead to (or fail to create) many different competencies throughout the firm.

Imitability of Knowledge

The concept of 'causal ambiguity' was developed by Reed and DeFillippi (1990) in an attempt to better understand the relationship between imitation barriers and sustainable competitive advantage. The conventional view is that competition and free entry will eliminate differences stemming from uncertainty, so that their persistence is an indication of market power or impeded entry. If the uncertainty, however, stems from a causal ambiguity in the relationship between actions and their effect, it may be impossible to fully identify the factors responsible for superior performance. At the extreme, the causal ambiguity may be so great that not even the firm itself understands the relationship between actions and output.[7]

The authors are concerned with situations where managers understand what factors are responsible for superior performance better than their competitors, and not with conditions of extreme ambiguity. Further, they assume that competitors have sufficient understanding to attempt imitation, so uncertain imitability does not exist. Uncertain imitability is when 'the creation of new production functions is inherently uncertain and when either causal ambiguity or property rights in unique resources impede imitation and factor mobility' (1990: 421). The uncertainty in the creation of new production functions explains the origin of efficiency differentials, and the uncertainty related to all imitative and entry attempts explains their persistence. The latter uncertainty also implies that entry might cease before industry profits are eliminated.

Focusing on competitive advantage derived from competencies, Reed and DeFillippi (1990) explore how causal ambiguity is generated by three 'asset characteristics': tacitness, complexity and specificity. They suggest that high degrees of tacitness, complexity and specificity produce high degrees of ambiguity. Maximum ambiguity, and therefore the highest barriers to imitation, is obtained through a three-way interaction effect that increases ambiguity beyond the simple sum of the individual effects of each characteristic.

Tacitness Building on Polanyi (1958), Wagner and Sternberg suggested that tacit knowledge is 'disorganized, informal and relatively inaccessible, making it potentially ill-suited for direct instruction' (1985: 439). Because of a high level of unawareness, even the skilled performer faces difficulties in trying to codify the underlying decision rules and protocols. Thus, the factors responsible for superior performance are even less understandable to competitors.

The importance of tacitness is also illustrated by Nelson and Winter (1982) who suggested that successful imitation is contingent on the situation. At one extreme, imitation will be feasible by reverse engineering because of little tacitness in the production process. At the other extreme 'the target routine may involve so much idiosyncratic and impacted tacit knowledge that even successful replication is problematic, let alone imitation from distance' (1982: 124). Reed and DeFillippi compare the latter situation of extreme tacitness with Lippman and Rumelt's (1982) notion of extreme ambiguity and factor immobility. In discussing the extent to which the partner's distinctive skills are encodable and discrete, Hamel (1991) also underscored the difficulties in extracting knowledge that is embedded in complex social relationships or as individual craftsmanship.

Thus, the degree of clarity and determination of an element of knowledge depends to a great extent on the possibility of reconstructing the original process. This in turn depends on the extent to which knowledge is *thematized*. To some extent, this is consistent with the treatment of knowledge by Nonaka (1991) and Badaracco (1991). Thematized knowledge is comparable with the notions 'explicit' (Nonaka, 1991), 'migratory' (Badaracco, 1991), and 'articulated' (Itami, 1987). This category of knowledge is formal and systematic, and thus it is easily communicated and shared. Typically, this kind of knowledge resides in formulas, manuals, books, or machines.

At the other end, the parallels to *non-thematized* knowledge used by Nonaka and Badaracco are 'tacit' and 'embedded' knowledge. This kind of knowledge 'resides primarily in specialized relationships, attitudes, information flows, and ways of making decisions that shape their dealings with each other' (Badaracco, 1991: 79).

The use of thematized and non-thematized knowledge adds at least one dimension to the concepts used by previous authors, namely the *historical* dimension. Every part of the stock of knowledge is based upon unique historical situations. If the knowledge is non-thematized, then it will be impossible to grasp this knowledge for a person unfamiliar with the original accumulation process even through observation and conversation! The notion of thematized knowledge underscores the challenges involved in trying to imitate knowledge. In fact, imitation of knowledge implies imitating a process which carries a certain history.[8] In sum, *tacitness* is a first indicator of the concept of the imitability of knowledge.

Complexity   Reed and DeFillippi suggest that complexity arises 'from a large number of technologies, organizational routines, and individual- or team-based experience' (1990: 88). This complexity makes it difficult, if not impossible, for a single individual to have sufficient breadth and depth of knowledge to understand underlying performance relationships (Nelson and Winter, 1982). These arguments are analogous to those of Barney (1985) and MacMillan et al. (1985), who concluded that the necessary combination of a large number of interdependent skills and assets causes product complexity. Thus, the potential for imitation by competitors, through observation, is limited. Thus, *complexity* is a second indicator of the concept of the imitability of knowledge.

Specificity   Specificity refers to 'the transaction-specific skills and assets that are utilized in the production processes and provision of services for particular customers' (Reed and DeFillippi, 1990: 89). The transactions are supported by investments in four categories of asset specificity: site, physical assets, dedicated assets, and human assets (Williamson, 1985). Over time these transaction-specific investments become difficult to supplant (Williamson, 1975) and the relationships between action and result become 'highly specific and interdependent with the firm's internal and external transactions partners' (Reed and DeFillippi, 1990: 92). Thus, *specificity* is a third indicator of the concept of the imitability of knowledge.

Externalization of Knowledge

The nature of the organizations involved in the imitation process is, of course, a fundamental factor. Here, the concept of externalization surfaces as appropriate. Externalization is an anthropological necessity; it is 'the outgoing outpouring of human being into the world, both in the mental and physical activity of men' (Berger, 1967: 4).[9]

The literature on cooperative strategies contributes to the understanding of externalization. Hamel, for instance, discusses the concept of 'transparency' as the 'knowability or openness of each partner, and thus the potential for learning' (1991: 90).[10] Grant (1991) connected transparency to imitability, and, more precisely, claims that imperfect transparency is the basis for Lippman and Rumelt's (1982) notion of 'uncertain imitability'. One important distinction between Hamel's and Grant's uses of transparency is that the former refers to it as skill as such, while the latter narrows it to organizational routines.[11] Although externalization seems to be important for understanding the nature of the organizations involved in knowledge imitation, it needs to be further manifested.

Hamel (1991) pointed to one important dimension of transparency, namely attitudes towards outsiders. This could also be seen as an indicator of externalization. The high loyalty or clannishness of employees associated with Japanese firms (see Ouchi, 1980) seems to have limited the possibilities for skills transfer in many alliances between Western and Japanese firms. Here, we view *openness* as the willingness to communicate with non-firm members. This is the first indicator of externalization of knowledge.

Barney suggests that a barrier to imitation exists when a firm's resources are 'very complex social phenomena' (1991: 110).[12] In most cases it is possible to identify how these socially complex resources add value to a firm. Thus, there is little or no ambiguity concerning the causal relationship between actions and results. This does not mean, however, that a firm without these resources can engage in systematic efforts to create them (see Dierickx and Cool, 1989). Most firms do not have the necessary capabilities to perform this kind of social engineering (Barney, 1986; Porras and Berg, 1978).[13] Although it is an abstract variable in itself, we view *social complexity* as a second indicator of externalization of knowledge.

Another point made by Barney (1991) is that the performance of firms cannot be understood independently of the idiosyncratic attribute of history. Firms' ability to acquire and exploit some resources depends on their place in time and space. Accordingly, the lack of a particular history can represent a barrier to imitation because a firm can implement 'value-creating strategies that cannot be duplicated by other firms, for firms without that particular path through history cannot obtain the resources necessary to implement the strategy' (1991: 108). Organizational culture often emerges in the early stages of the history of the firm and may be very difficult to imitate for firms founded in another historical period. Similarly, a firm's scientists may be in a position to create or exploit a significant scientific breakthrough because of the history-dependent nature of these scientists. Thus, *idiosyncrasy of history* is a third indicator of externalization of knowledge.

Internalization of Knowledge

Another variable is the capacity to absorb the knowledge that is being imitated. This is called internalization. The concept of internalization means the reappropriation by humans of the knowledge that has been externalized, 'transforming it once again from structures of the objective world into structures of the subjective consciousness' (Berger, 1967: 4).

The concept of 'absorptive capacity' was developed by Cohen and Levinthal to mean the 'ability to recognize the value of new information, assimilate it, and apply it to commercial ends' (1990: 128).[14]

Cohen and Levinthal (1990) point at prior related knowledge as the most important determinant of absorptive capacity. Knowledge acquisition is a self-reinforcing process, where 'the more objects, patterns and concepts that are stored in the memory [the firm], the more readily is new information about these constructs acquired' (Bower and Hilgard, 1981: 424). The performance of the internalization process is greatest when the object of the knowledge accumulation is related to existing knowledge. Thus, *prior related knowledge* is the first indicator of internalization of knowledge.

Another point made by Cohen and Levinthal (1990) is the role of diversity of knowledge. Because the potential useful knowledge may be connected with complexity and ambiguity, the firm's ability to acquire and exploit this knowledge is dependent on the depth and breadth of existing knowledge. Thus, the diversity of knowledge provides a better foundation for internalization, because it enhances the possibility that new knowledge relates to already existing knowledge. *Diversity* is a second indicator of internalization of knowledge.

Cohen and Levinthal (1990) also make a distinction between acquisition and exploitation. Firms are dependent not only on the interface which makes imitation of knowledge possible, but also on the transfer of knowledge within both groups and the whole firm. Not only the process of communication is important, but in addition awareness about 'who knows what, who can help with that problem, or who can exploit new information' (1990: p.133). Thus, the *communication network* is a third indicator of internalization of knowledge.

Objectivation of Knowledge

A theory of constructed knowledge assumes that knowledge in a group, a firm or an individual is dependent on the knowing subjects transmitting knowledge through social or cognitive processes. But since knowledge about 'true reality' is always questionable across different firms, groups and individuals (Daft and Weick, 1984; Hedberg, 1981; Hedberg et al., 1976; Fiol, 1991; Sackman, 1991; Smircich, 1983; Weick, 1979), one must address the question of subjects and levels of analysis, in short, 'who knows what'.

A stock of knowledge on the subjective level is tied to individuals (Berger and Luckmann, 1967) and allows the individual to observe, to understand, and to act in everyday life. Subjective knowledge may be bound to time and circumstances (Hayek, 1945; 1975) since the individual continuously acquires new experiences through facing new events.

The individual's stock of knowledge contains both a subjective and a social component, but subjective knowledge is not shared by other individuals (Habermas, 1984). For a stock of knowledge to evolve at the social level, however, the individual must share subjective knowledge with others. Schutz and Luckmann (1985) called this process 'objectivation'. Objectivation is the 'attainment of the products of [externalization] of a reality that confronts its original producers as facticity external to and other than themselves' (Berger, 1967: 4). Thus, objectivation is a complex and continuously ongoing process in which individuals account for the experiences of the other members of a group or firm (interpretation) and share their own experiences with others. In short, objectivation means creating an objective reality.

The objectivation process covers more than just communication. In firms, it generally makes use of at least three channels: language and signs, tools, and marks (Schutz and Luckmann, 1985). Each of these is an indicator of objectivation of knowledge.

First, individuals convey their subjective knowledge by talking and writing, i.e. using *language*. Since parts of an individual's stock of knowledge are more or less tacit, however, the knowledge may be impossible to convey linguistically (Polanyi, 1967). Individuals may not be aware of their knowledge, or possess an appropriate repertoire of words to express their knowledge and feelings. However, lacking a language and seeking to complement linguistic expressions, the individual may convey knowledge by other *signs*: gesturing, playing, evoking facial expressions, drawing, etc.

Second, individuals may also convey subjective knowledge to others through creating and applying *tools* to solve tasks. As individuals struggle to resolve a particular task they may attempt many different solutions using different tools at hand. The successful resolution of a task may be obtained by one tool in particular, with all other tools discarded in favor of the successful tool. In the process of completing the task, as well as upon task completion, the tool has helped to objectivate subjective knowledge (tools that work or do not work) to a possible observer.

Third, *marks* are 'the results of acts established by the one acting in order to hold onto a definite element of knowledge and to remind one of this' (Schutz and Luckmann, 1985: 274). As such, marks, akin to ribbons marking a path through a forest, may also objectivate subjective knowledge, as in knowledge acquired of the particular forest.

Legitimation of Knowledge

The objectivation of an individual's knowledge may be affected by the process of legitimation (Berger and Luckmann, 1967; Crozier, 1964; Forester, 1992; Habermas, 1971; Morgan, 1986). The process of legitimation is needed in order for the firm to: (1) prevent an individual's stock of knowledge from disturbing the continuity and regularity of its operation; and (2) provide a context in which to convey knowledge (Berger and Luckmann, 1967). Thus, legitimation gives answers to any question about the 'why' of the knowledge being imitated. As such, legitimation becomes a restrictive factor on the development of new social knowledge.

In a broad sense, individuals, groups, and firms find themselves in difficult situations in every moment of life. Typically, an advertising campaign is designed, the board of directors has a meeting, product development takes place, or you learn about a new person. Each of these situations is, to a great extent, interpreted and mastered according to experiences from related situations or the accumulated stock of knowledge. Thus, the stock of knowledge is related to situations (Schutz and Luckmann, 1973). However, in many situations there will be several limitations to a perfect understanding of all aspects of the situation. And these limitations have major implications for a thorough understanding of the processes of knowledge acquisition.

Drawing on the work of Berger (1967), and Berger and Luckmann (1967), we propose that subjective knowledge must be made legitimate on at least four dimensions in order to contribute to the creation of new social knowledge. Each of these four dimensions can be seen as an indicator of the concept of legitimation of knowledge.

First, subjective knowledge must be conveyed by using *language and signs, marks and tools* that are commonly acceptable to a group (Schutz and Luckmann, 1985; Walker, 1991). The means used may not necessarily be commonly known, however, as when introducing new words and concepts to facilitate a frame-breaking process (Schutz and Luckmann, 1989).

Second, subjective knowledge can be made legitimate by referring to or evoking *organizational stories, myths, proverbs, or maxims*. Third, firms have a set of standard *operating procedures* and other more or less formally espoused theories, like forecasting techniques, accounting principles, quality control statistics, etc. Individual knowledge may be made legitimate by making a reference to or concretely using or supporting these theories.

Fourth, firms, like all institutions, also have some continuity of *paradigms* which give meaning to everyday activity and experience. Such paradigms put 'everything in its right place' (Berger and Luckmann, 1967: 116). For example, they function as 'industry-specific recipes' for acceptable firm behavior (Spender, 1990), or they put the firm in a context of neoclassical economies where intrafirm competition is acceptable.

A Conceptual Model of Knowledge Imitation

The literature on strategic management, combined with the sociology of knowledge, has brought forward six concepts in knowledge imitation: (1) observational closeness, (2) imitability of knowledge, (3) externalization of knowledge, (4) internalization of knowledge, (5) objectivation of knowledge, and (6) legitimation of knowledge. Based on these six concepts, we will now propose a conceptual model of knowledge imitation.

The identified six concepts can be divided into two sets: contextual and organizational. The contextual concepts include *imitability of knowledge* and *observational closeness*, whereas organizational concepts include *externalization of knowledge* and *internalization of knowledge* (see Figure 2.1). Our conceptual model encapsulates propositions of direct and indirect causal effects between the four concepts. In fact, the model can be treated as a set of propositions on two levels of abstraction regarding causal relationships between contextual and organizational concepts.

The conceptual model illustrated in Figure 2.1 shows the six concepts derived from the literature and their proposed direct and indirect influences on the effectiveness of knowledge imitation. The first-level

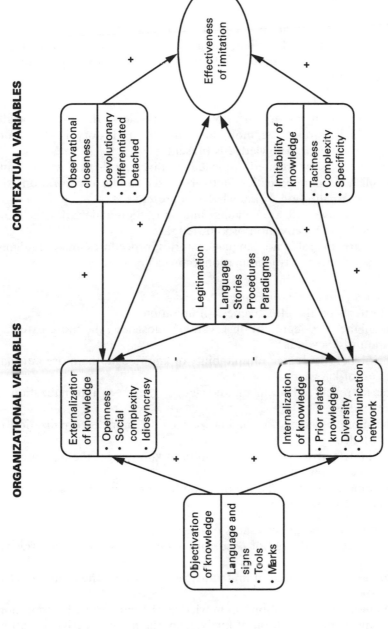

Figure 2.1 *Operationalized model of knowledge imitation*

causal relationships illustrate how the indicators form each concept[15] and the second-level causal relationships illustrate the proposed causal indirect and direct effects on effectiveness of knowledge imitation (indicated by the plus and minus signs on Figure 2.1).[16] The propositions encapsulated in the model are summarized below:

First-level causal relationships
Contextual variables:
1   The more the imitation situation is coevolutionary and the less it is differentiated and detached, the greater is observational closeness.
2   The more tacit, complex and specific is the knowledge, the less imitable it is.

Organizational variables:
3   The less open an organization is to outsiders, the more socially complex it is, and the more idiosyncratic its history is, the more externalization of knowledge is present.
4   The more prior related knowledge, diversity of knowledge and established communication networks exist in the organization, the more internalization of knowledge is present.
5   The more favorable are language and signs, tools and marks, the more favorable is objectivation of knowledge.
6   The more favorable are language, stories, procedures and paradigms, the less restrictive is legitimation knowledge.

Second-level causal relationships
Indirect effects on the effectiveness of imitation:
7   The higher the degree of observational closeness, the more externalization of knowledge.
8   The higher the degree of imitability of knowledge, the more internalization of knowledge.
9   The more objectivation of knowledge, the more internalization of knowledge.
10   The more objectivation of knowledge, the more externalization of knowledge.
11   The more restrictive the legitimation of knowledge, the less internalization of knowledge.
12   The more restrictive the legitimation of knowledge, the less externalization of knowledge.

Direct effects on the effectiveness of imitation:
13   The higher the degree of observational closeness, the more effective imitation.
14   The higher the degree of imitability of knowledge, the more effective imitation.
15   The more externalization of knowledge, the more effective imitation.
16   The more internalization of knowledge, the more effective imitation.

Implications for Research

The objective of this chapter was to shed more light on the knowledge imitation process. Imitating knowledge is not an easy task, nor is it a continuous and smooth process. The process of knowledge development in general can be seen as more or less discontinuous and iterative. Knowledge evolves through an endless process of trial and error. Along this process some amount of knowledge is related to every particular situation. Thus, every success and every failure has its own particular history. However, this knowledge is not necessarily accumulated in its totality. Through the accumulation process the most relevant and obvious knowledge is structured and partly thematized. Thus, for the persons, groups, or firms involved, the whole process seems in retrospect much simpler and easier to grasp than the original process (Bourdieu, 1977; Schutz, 1970; Schutz and Luckmann, 1973). We have tried to shed more light on this issue by developing a conceptual model of knowledge imitation, given an understanding of knowledge *as a process* combining the sociology of knowledge with strategic management theory.

Knowledge is critical to a firm's performance and survival because it provides perhaps the best basis for developing competitive advantage. The strategic management literature discusses firm performance in terms of the firm's ability to cope with strategic issues, including threats, opportunities, and stakeholder demands (Ansoff, 1980; Dutton and Jackson, 1987). In this sense, knowledge can have a particular strategic value.

Inspired by the perspective of knowledge outlined in this chapter, subsequent studies have the potential of uncovering more insights into the four core imitation concepts. In addition, some of the indicators of these concepts need further elaboration, e.g. legitimation. The most effective and/or most frequent means of conveying managerial experiences in creating social knowledge through imitation (in particular the role of face-to-face conversations on strategy) should be on the research agenda (see also discussions by Bowman, 1990; Priem, 1990; Schilit, 1990; Westley, 1990).

Strategic management theory and research should also be supplemented with a more precise outline of the context of imitation. For example, in the studies of strategic intrafirm cooperation, such as franchising, joint ventures, equity agreements, cooperative ventures, alliances and acquisitions, an emerging issue is whether or not it is possible to lose proprietary knowledge to a partner (Badaracco, 1991; Hamel, 1991). We have suggested that intrafirm and interfirm cooperation and competition must be studied in terms of observational closeness, each context having its own significance when it comes to certain opportunities and threats surrounding the protection of proprietary competencies. Future work should identify firms' modes of cooperating and/or competing in these three contexts, and then proceed to investigate how competence coevolves or evolves at different rates in the dyad of two firms.

The legitimation processes of each firm, mutual access to task resolution processes, personal interaction among firm members, the available means of conveying knowledge, and task complexity and variability, should all play an important role in these investigations. The emergence of an increasingly robust theory of knowledge imitation must pay attention to these factors.

Advancement of Research

The obvious implications for the advancement of research in strategic management stem from our attempt to advance the field by combining two theoretical streams. This resulted in both developing new meanings of existing concepts and identifying new key concepts.

Our conceptual model has two levels of abstraction. Thus, another implication for developing new research is to develop conceptual models, propositions, and hypotheses at various levels. It is sufficient to note that a research program aimed at advancing the understanding of knowledge imitation, e.g. by verifying or improving the propositions of this work, should first of all study the practices of some selected firms (Yin, 1984; see also Glaser and Strauss, 1967 on the constant comparative method). Starting from the recognition that social knowledge, though public, has its roots in individual thinking and actions (Holmes, 1990), such studies may allow for longitudinal mapping of individually and socially based knowledge imitations, including deliberating and inhibiting factors on knowledge evolution.

A major research output may be a list of further or different indicators of the concepts discussed in this chapter. Based on such indicators, then, the research program should proceed to empirically verify the relative importance of each concept. Appropriate, if not obvious, methodologies for studying relationships between latent variables are some of the 'second generation multivariate statistics' methods (Bollen, 1989; Fornell, 1982; Jöreskog and Wold, 1982; Wold, 1989), for instance maximum likelihood or partial least squares estimation of latent variables.

Finally, it should also be noted that an in-depth empirical examination of the concepts of this chapter, due to the volatility and the latency of subjective and possible social knowledge and possible differences in task conceptions, introduces measurement problems not easily handled by the above described methods (see also Donaldson, 1990; Fiol, 1991; Reed and DeFillippi, 1990). A methodology that takes seriously the challenge of studying the process of social knowledge construction, and thus the phenomenon of drifting competencies, is the 'interpretative interactionist approach' (Denzin, 1989; 1983; see also Denzin and Keller, 1981). This approach attempts to join traditional symbolic interactionist thought with participant observation, naturalistic studies, creative interviewing, and the case study method. In combining several research perspectives it gives the advantage of studying (and interpreting) the role of personal interaction and forms of expression in competence evolution, the interpretationprocesses of those observed, as well as the structures to competence development given by legitimation.

Notes

1   Rooted in evolutionary economics theory (e.g. Nelson and Winter, 1982), the resource-based approach has re-established the importance of the individual firm, as opposed to the industry, as the relevant unit of analysis (e.g. Barney and Ouchi, 1986). This perspective focuses on the firm's internal resources as the basis for creating competitive advantages (Barney, 1991; Dierickx and Cool, 1990; Penrose, 1958; Wernerfelt, 1984), and it goes far beyond the basic neoclassical assumptions of economic activity: that all parties have perfect and complete information, and that resources are completely mobile and divisible and, therefore, flow freely between companies. The core of this viewpoint was formulated by Rumelt: 'a firm's competitive position is defined by a bundle of unique resources and relationships' (1984: 557).

2   For instance, 'emulating pattern of another society has connotation of a lack of originality and even intellectual piracy. Copying is less estimable than inventing; imitation is less honorable than innovation' (Westney, 1987: 5).

3   The term 'imitation' is not commonly used in the latter context. In fact, these authors consider these complex behavioral models as going beyond imitation.

4   Although some barriers to imitation are higher than others, Porter (1985) argued that these barriers are never insurmountable. In fact, Ghemawat (1986) found that the potential for competitive advantage is greatest in industries where firms need large investments in specialized activities, skills and assets – a form of organizational commitment. Still, the more vigorous the barriers to imitation the more slowly competitors imitate competitive advantages.

5   One important distinction between Lippman and Rumelt and Nelson and Winter is that, while the former equate the 'production' of a production function with the creation of a new firm, the latter emphasize the advantage of existing resources (routines) in the replication and imitation process: 'a firm with an established routine possesses resources on which it can draw very helpfully in the difficult task of attempting to apply that routine on a large scale' (Nelson and Winter, 1982: 119).

6   Bourgeois and Eisenhardt (1987) give an excellent example of different task conceptions in their study of Omicron, a high-tech firm with financial problems. The task (as seen by the authors) was to improve the strategic position of the company, presumably a complex and unique task. To deal with this challenge, the Omicron management set up a strategizing session with its executives. To some of the executives the task was fairly simple: Omicron just needed to become better at implementing the existing strategy. Others conceived of the task as being substantially more complex and different in content: Omicron needed a totally new business strategy, as well as successful implementation. In this context, the group reached a common task conception after several tries. Subsequently, ground was prepared for conveying relevant knowledge for the task at hand.

7   The concept of causal ambiguity is comparable to the discussion of asymmetric information (Porter, 1985; Williamson, 1985; Barney, 1986). Although causal ambiguity and asymmetric information have several common properties, causal ambiguity goes beyond asymmetric information. As expressed by Reed and DeFillippi 'There is a fundamental difference between having information and understanding it' (1990: 94).

8   This can be illustrated by the case of Antonio Stradivari, which is so often alluded to (e.g. in Polanyi, 1958). Stradivari spent his life perfecting the Stradivarius violin. Through an endless number of trials and errors he incrementally improved the violin to what many experts would call 'perfection'. He had several apprentices who studied their master carefully, who, through the process of monitoring and communicating with Stradivari, had the possibility to exploit even the tacit dimension of his work. Nevertheless, none of them ever produced a violin as faultless as the original Stradivarius. Why? Because over time Stradivari had developed a substantial amount of situation-dependent thematized and non-thematized

knowledge. However, the problem for the apprentices was the lack of insight into the original knowledge accumulation process of their master! Without the opportunity to grasp this process the apprentices were always second best.

9 'Externalization' is taken from Hegel (*Entäusserung* and *Versachlichung*).

10 Many managers in Hamel's study preferred to make a distinction between 'transparency by design' and 'transparency by default'. One reason for this was that 'the competitive consequences of skills transfer as well as actual migration of skills, were often unintended, unanticipated, and unwanted by at least one of the partners' (Hamel, 1991: 92).

11 According to Hamel (1991), the degree of transparency ultimately depends on the day-to-day interaction, which he labeled 'the permeability of the collaborative membrane'. A positive causality between high transparency and substantial transfer of knowledge can be disputed. Harrigan (1985) claims the following relationships when transparency in a joint venture is high: (1) fewer transfers of knowledge to the venture company will occur; (2) the difficulties associated with preventing technological transfer (bleedthrough) will be exacerbated; and (3) the joint venture relationship will be unstable.

12 Note that social complexity should be distinguished from complexity in the framework developed by Reed and DeFillippi (1990), i.e. one of the indicators of imitability of knowledge.

13 In the context of imitation barriers, Barney (1991) distinguishes between complex physical technology itself and the exploitation of such technology. The former is by itself typically imitable whether it takes the form of machines, robots or information systems. The latter, however, often involves the use of socially complex resources. Although several firms may possess the same physical technology, only one of these may possess the social resources necessary to fully exploit this technology (Wilkins, 1989).

14 A somewhat related concept is 'receptivity', used by Hamel (1991).

15 The concepts can be seen as latent variables.

16 We will not discuss in this chapter how this performance measure can be manifested.

References

Andrews, K.R. (1971). *The Concept of Corporate Strategy*. Homewood, IL: Dow Jones Irwin.

Ansoff, H.I. (1965). *Corporate Strategy*. New York: McGraw-Hill.

Ansoff, H.I. (1980). Strategic issue management. *Strategic Management Journal*, 1: 131–148

Argyris, C. and Schön, D. (1978). *Organizational Learning*. Reading, MA: Addison-Wesley.

Argyris, C. (1988). Crafting a theory of practice: the case of organizational paradoxes. In R.E. Quinn and K.S. Cameron (eds), *Paradox and Transformation: Toward a Theory of Change in Organization and Management*. Beverly Hills: Sage. pp. 255–79.

Argyris, C., Putnam, R. and McLain Smith, D. (1985). *Action Science*. San Francisco: Jossey-Bass.

Badaracco, J.L. (1991). *The Knowledge Link: How Firms Compete through Strategic Alliances*. Boston, MA: Harvard Business School Press.

Barney, J. and Ouchi, W.G. (eds) (1986). *Organizational Economics*. San Francisco: Jossey-Bass.

Barney, J.B. (1985). Information costs and the governance of economic transactions. In Nacamali, R.D and Rugadini, A. (eds), *Organizations and Markets*. Milan, Italy: Societa Editrice it Milano. pp. 347–72.

Barney, J. (1986). Types of competition and the theory of strategy: toward an integrative framework. *Academy of Management Review*, 11: 791–800.

Barney, J. (1991). Firm resources and sustained competitive advantage. *Journal of Management*, 17: 99–120.

Berger, P. and Luckmann, T. (1967). *The Social Construction of Reality*. New York: Penguin.

Berger, P. (1967). *The Sacred Canopy*. Garden City, NJ: Doubleday.

Bollen, K.A. (1989). *Structural Equations with Latent Variables*. New York: John Wiley.

Bourdieu, P. (1977). *Outline of a Theory of Practice*. Cambridge: Cambridge University Press.

Bourgeois, L.J. and Eisenhardt, K.M. (1987). Strategic decision processes in Silicon Valley: the anatomy of a 'living dead'. *California Management Review*, Autumn: 143–59.

Bower, J. (1970). *Managing the Resource Allocation Process: A Study of Corporate Planning and Investment*. Boston, MA: Harvard University, Graduate School of Business Administration.

Bower, G.H. and Hilgard, E.R. (1981). *Theories of Learning*. Englewood Cliffs, NJ: Prentice-Hall.

Bowman, C. (1990). Shared understanding of strategic priorities. Paper presented at the Strategic Management Society Conference, Stockholm, 1990.

Brown, J.S. and Duguid, P. (1991). Organizational learning and communities-of-practice: toward a unified view of working, learning, and innovation. *Organization Science*, 2: 40–57.

Caves, R.E. and Porter, M.E. (1977). From entry barriers to mobility barriers: conjectural decisions and contrived deterrence to new competition. *Quarterly Journal of Economics*, 91: 241–62.

Cohen, M. and Levinthal, D. (1990). Absorptive capacity: a perspective on learning and innovation. *Administrative Science Quarterly*, 35: 128–52.

Cohen, M. (1991). Individual learning and organizational routine: emerging connections. *Organization Science*, 2: 135–40.

Crozier, M. (1964). *The Bureaucratic Phenomenon*. London: Tavistock.

Cyert, R.M. and March, J.G. (1963). *A Behavioral Theory of the Firm* London: Blackwell. Reprint 1992.

Daft, R. and Weick, K.E. (1984). Toward a model of organizations as interpretation systems. *Academy of Management Review*, 9: 284–295.

Decker, P.J. (1980). Effects of symbolic coding and rehearsal in behavioral modeling training. *Journal of Applied Psychology*, 65: 627–34.

Denzin, N.K. and Keller, C.M. (1981). Frame analysis reconsidered. *Contemporary Sociology*, 10: 52–60.

Denzin, N.K. (1983). Interpretive interactionism. In G. Morgan (ed.), *Beyond Method: Strategies for Social Research*. Newbury Park: Sage. pp. 129–47.

Denzin, N.K. (1989). *Interpretive Interactionism*. Newbury Park: Sage.

Dierickx, L. and Cool, K. (1989). Asset stock accumulation and sustainability of competitive advantage. *Management Science*, 35: 1514–30 .

Donaldson, L. (1990). A rational basis for criticism of organization economics: a reply to Barney. *Academy of Management Review*, 15: 394–401.

Dutton, J.E. and Jackson, S.E. (1987). Categorizing strategic issues. *Academy of Management Review*, 12: 76–90.

Feldman, M. and March, J.G. (1981). Information in organizations as signal and symbol. *Administrative Science Quarterly*, 26: 171–86.

Fiol, C.M. (1991). Managing culture as a competitive resource: An identity-based view of sustainable competitive advantage. *Journal of Management*, 17: 191–211.

Forester, J. (1992). Critical ethnography: On fieldwork in a Habermasian way. In M. Alvesson and H. Willmott (eds), *Critical Management Studies*. London: Sage. pp. 46–66.

Fornell, C. (ed.) (1982). *A Second Generation of Multivariate Analysis* (Vol 1–2). New York: Praeger.

Geertz, C. (1983). *Local Knowledge*. New York: Basic Books.

Ghemawat, P. (1986). Sustainable advantage. *Harvard Business Review*, 86(5): 53–8.

Gioia, D.A. and Manz, C.C. (1985). Linking cognition and behavior: a script processing interpretation of vicarious learning. *Academy of Management Review*, 10: 527–39.

Glaser, B.G. and Strauss, A.L. (1967). *The Discovery of Grounded Theory*. Chicago: Aldine.

Grant, R.M. (1991). The resource-based theory of competitive advantage: implications for strategy formulation. *California Management Review*, Spring: 114–35.

Habermas, J. (1971). *Knowledge and Human Interest*. London: Heinemann.

Habermas, J. (1984). *The Theory of Communicative Action*. Boston, MA: Beacon Press.

Hamel, G. and Prahalad, S. (1989). Strategic intent. *Harvard Business Review*, May–June: 63–76.

Hamel, G. and Prahalad, S. (1990). The core competence of the corporation. *Harvard Business Review*, May–June: 79–91.

Hamel, G. (1991). Competition for competence and interpartner learning within international alliances. *Strategic Management Journal*, 12: 83–103.

Harrigan, K.R. (1985). *Strategies for Joint Ventures*. Lexington, MA: Lexington Books.

Hayek, F.A. (1945). The use of knowledge in society. *American Economic Review*, 25: 519–30.

Hayek, F.A. (1975). Nobel memorial lecture: the pretence of knowledge. *Swedish Journal of Economics*, 432–42.

Hedberg, B. (1981). How organizations learn and unlearn. In P.C. Nystrom and W. Starbuck (eds), *Handbook of Organizational Design*. Vol. 1. New York: Oxford University Press.

Hedberg, B., Starbuck, W. and Nystrom, P. (1976) Camping on the seesaws: prescriptions for designing self-designing organizations. *Administrative Science Quarterly*, 21: 41–65.

Hofer, C.W. and Schendel, D. (1978). *Strategy Formulation: Analytical Concepts*. St. Paul, MN: West.

Holmes, R. (1990). Person, role and organization: some constructivistic notes. In J. Hassard and D. Pym (eds), *Theory and Philosophy of Organizations*. London: Routledge. pp. 198–219.

Huber, G. (1982). Organizational information systems: determinants of their performance and behavior. *Management Science*, 28: 135–55.

Huber, G. (1991). Organizational learning: the contributing processes and the literatures. *Organization Science*, 2: 88–116.

Huff, A.S. (1982). Industry influence on strategy reformulation. *Strategic Management Journal*, 3: 119–31.

Itami, H. (1987). *Mobilizing Invisible Assets*. Cambridge: Harvard University Press.

Jöreskog, K.G. and Wold, H. (1982). *Systems under Indirect Observation: Causality – Structure – Prediction* (Part I–II). Amsterdam: North Holland.

Lado, A.A., Boyd, N.G. and Wright, P. (1992). A competency-based model of sustainable competitive advantage: toward a conceptual integration. *Journal of Management*, 18: 77–91.

Levitt, B. and March, J.G. (1988). Organizational learning. *Annual Review of Sociology*, 14: 319–40.

Lippman, S. and Rumelt, R. (1982). Uncertain imitability: an analysis of interfirm differences in efficiency under competition. *Bell Journal of Economics*, 13: 418–38.

MacMillan, I., McCaffery, M.L. and Van Wijk, G. (1985). Competitors' responses to easily imitated new products – exploring commercial banking product introductions. *Strategic Management Journal*, 6, January–March: 75–86.

March, J.G. and Simon, H.A. (1958). *Organizations*. New York: Wiley.

Morgan, G. (1986). *Images of Organization*. Beverly Hills: Sage.

Nelson, R. and Winter, S. (1982). *An Evolutionary Theory of Economic Change*. Cambridge: Belknap Press.

Nonaka, I. (1991). The knowledge-creating company. *Harvard Business Review*, November–December: 96–104.

Ouchi, W.G. (1980). Markets, bureaucracies, and clans. *Administrative Science Quarterly*, 25, 129–41.

Penrose, E. (1958). *The Theory of the Growth of the Firm*. New York: Wiley.

Polanyi, M. (1958). *Personal Knowledge: Towards a Post Critical Philosophy*. London: Routledge.

Polanyi, M. (1961). *Personal Knowledge: Towards a Post-Critical Philosophy*. London: Routledge.

Polanyi, M. (1967). *The Tacit Dimension*. Garden City, NY: Anchor.

Porras, J. and Berg, P.O. (1978). The impact of organizational development. *Academy of Management Review*, 3: 249–66.

Porter, M.E. (1985). *Competitive Advantage*. New York: Free Press.

Prahalad, C.K. and Bettis, R. (1986). The dominant logic: a new linkage between diversity and performance. *Strategic Management Journal*, 7: 485–501.

Priem, R. (1990). Top management team group factors, consensus, and firm performance. *Strategic Management Journal*, 11: 496–78.

Reed, R. and DeFillippi, R (1990). Causal ambiguity, barriers to imitation, and sustainable competitive advantage. *Academy of Management Review*, 15: 88–102.

Rumelt, R.P. (1984). Toward a strategic theory of the firm. In R. Lanb (ed.), *Competitive Strategic Management*. Englewood Cliffs, NJ: Prentice-Hall. pp. 137–58.

Sackman, S.A. (1991). *Cultural Knowledge in Organizations: Exploring the Collective Mind*. Newbury Park: Sage.

Schilit, W.K. (1990). A comparative analysis of strategic decisions. *Journal of Management Studies*, 25: 435–61.

Schutz, A. (1970). *On Phenomenology and Social Relations*. Chicago: University of Chicago Press.

Schutz, A. and Luckmann, T. (1973). *The Structures of the Life-World*. Evanston, IL: Northwestern University Press.

Schutz, A. and Luckmann, T. (1985) [reprint 1973]. *The Structures of the Life-World*. Evanston, IL: Northwestern University Press.

Schutz, A. and Luckmann, T. (1989). *The Structures of the Life-World*. Vol. II. Evanston, IL: Northwestern University Press.

Scott, W.R. (1981). *Organizations: Rational, Natural, and Open Systems*. Englewood Cliffs, NJ: Addison-Wesley.

Shoemaker, P.J.H. (1990). Strategy, complexity and economic rent. *Management Science*, 36: 1178–92.

Smircich, L. (1983). Concepts of culture and organizational analysis. *Administrative Science Quarterly*, 28: 339–58.

Sölvell, Ö (1987). *Entry Barriers and Foreign Penetration*. Doctoral dissertation. Stockholm: Institute of International Business/Stockholm School of Economics.

Spender, J. (1990). *Industry Recipes*. New York: Wiley.

Sproull, L. and Kiesler, S. (1991). *Connections: New Ways of Working in the Networked Organization*. Cambridge, MA: MIT Press.

Stalk. G., Evans, P. and Schulman, L.E. (1992). Competing on capabilities: the new rules of corporate strategy. *Harvard Business Review*, March–April: 57–69.

Taylor, M.S. (1981). The motivational effects of task challenge: a laboratory investigation. *Organizational Behavior and Human Performance*, 27: 255–78.

Teece, D.J. (1986). Profiting from technological innovation: implications for integration, collaboration, licensing, and public-policy. *Research Policy*, 15: 285–305.

Teece, D.J., Pisano, G., and Shuen, A. (1990). *Firm capabilities, resources and the concept of strategy*. Working Paper. University of California at Berkeley.

Wagner, R.K., and Sternberg, R.J. (1985). Practical intelligence in real world pursuits. the role of tacit knowledge. *Journal of Personality and Social Psycology*, 49: 436–58.

Walker, T. (1991). Whose discourse?. In S. Woolgar (ed.), *Knowledge and Reflexivity: New Frontiers in the Sociology of Knowledge*. London: Sage. pp. 55–80.

Webster's Third New International Dictionary (1983). Chicago: Meriam–Webster.

Weick, K.E. (1979). *The Social Psychology of Organizing*. New York: Random House.

Wernerfelt, B. (1984). A resource-based view of the firm. *Strategic Management Journal*, 5: 171–80.

Westley, F.R. (1990). Middle managers and strategy: microdynamics of inclusion. *Strategic Management Journal*, 11(5): 337–51.

Westney, D.E. (1987). *Imitation and Innovation: The Transfer of Western Organizational Patterns to Meiji Japan*. Cambridge, MA: Harvard University Press.

Wilkins, A. (1989). *Developing Corporate Character*. San Francisco: Jossey-Bass.

Williams, J.R. (1992), How sustainable is your competitive advantage? *California Management Review*, Spring: 29–51.

Williamson, O.E. (1975). *Markets and Hierarchies*. New York: Free Press.

Williamson, O.E. (1985). *The Economic Institutions of Capitalism*. New York: Free Press.
Wold, H. (ed.) (1989). *Theoretical Empiricism*. New York: Paragon House.
Yin, R.K. (1984). *Case Study Research*. Beverly Hills: Sage.
Yip, G. (1982) *Barriers to Entry: A Corporate Strategy Perspective*. Lexington, MA: Lexington Books.

3

Towards a Theory of Knowledge Transfer in a Cooperative Context

Kenneth Wathne, Johan Roos and Georg von Krogh

Because of the increasing scale and pace of changes across markets, products, and technologies, the transfer and conversion of knowledge have become critical to both the survival and the advancement of organizations. In many situations, traditional governance structures have proved inadequate not only as a means of survival and keeping abreast of industry developments, but also (and more importantly) in exploiting knowledge in the setting of new standards. Several researchers have argued for the pursuit of cooperative strategies as a means of creating new knowledge or gaining access to knowledge and skills outside the firm's boundaries (e.g. Alter and Hage, 1993; Badaracco, 1991; Hamel, 1991; Kogut, 1988; Lyles, 1994; Parkhe, 1991; Powell, 1987; Prahalad and Hamel, 1990; Pucik, 1988; Westney, 1988). However, despite the emphasis on knowledge transfer as an important motive for pursuing cooperative strategies, the lack of theoretical integration and empirical research leaves many questions unanswered.

We address the issue of knowledge transfer and learning within cooperative arrangements, which has been treated mainly in conjunction with traditional reasons and conditions for cooperation such as risk reduction, economies of scale, and overcoming trade barriers (e.g. Contractor and Lorange, 1988). Much of the previous research has focused on partnership formation and the motives for cooperation, rather than factors influencing the processes within a cooperative relationship. Examining interpartner learning within international strategic alliances, Hamel (1991) argues for a shift from focusing only on the venture and task structure when attempting to account for partnership performance. He states that 'conceiving of an alliance as a membrane suggests that access to people, facilities, documents, and other forms of knowledge is traded between partners in an ongoing process of collaborative exchange' (1991: 100). Similarly, Badaracco (1991) holds that through the development of knowledge-linked cooperative arrangements, both migratory and embedded knowledge can flow between the cooperative partners.[1]

Hamel further states that 'conceiving of the firm as a portfolio of core competencies and disciplines suggests that inter-firm competition, as opposed to inter-product competition, is essentially concerned with the acquisition of skill' (1991: 83). Through the core competence concept, we also see the underlying change from product–market and static routines[2] toward dynamic competence development. In addition to refocusing from content to cooperative processes, the knowledge and skills exchanged between the partners are dealt with as dynamic assets. The latter perspective has been increasingly voiced within the resource-based view of the firm (e.g. Barney, 1986; 1991; Chi, 1994; Mahoney and Pandian, 1992; Rumelt, 1984; Wernerfelt, 1984). Authors have paid more attention to the process of asset accumulation (Dierickx and Cool, 1989) and exploring barriers to knowledge transfer (Teece et al., 1990). As the resources are not given to the firm, there is a need for access and development, be it internally, externally, or quasi-internally. The problem is that some resources are not tradable and are difficult to transfer (e.g. tacit knowledge: Polanyi, 1962), and some are combined in ways that are difficult to replicate because of causal ambiguity (Lippman and Rumelt, 1982; Reed and DeFillippi, 1990).[3]

Building on the strategic management literature and the sociology of knowledge, we developed and tested a model of knowledge transfer in cooperative contexts. More specifically, we examined how actors from different social contexts, in cooperation, develop a common stock of knowledge. We explored and tested selected key factors influencing the effectiveness of knowledge transfer. In basing our main arguments on human interpretations and conceptions, we took into account both partner-specific attributes and characteristics of the task activities performed.

First, we present the theoretical background and position our study in relation to previous work on cooperative strategies to establish the context of discovery and lead up to the model. We then develop our theoretical model, discussing the hypothesized effects of four factors that influence knowledge transfer between cooperative partners. Next, we describe our cross-sectional field study of cooperative relationships between Nordic companies. We use the data collected to test the relative importance of each hypothesized relationship in the model, thus addressing the normative questions surrounding the theory development process (what might be termed the context of justification). Finally, we discuss the results of our research and their implications for managers and researchers within the context of discovery.

Theoretical Background

Cooperative Strategies

Academic research on cooperative strategies has increased substantially in scope and amount, and diverse concepts have been used to describe cooperative arrangements. The diversity has not only created confusion about the meaning of the concepts, but also created problems in finding comparable studies on any given subject of analysis. Both the *terms* and the *forms* of cooperative arrangements are often loosely defined, and newer forms do not always fit neatly into the traditional classification schemes. One of the terms that has attracted increased interest is 'strategic alliances'. Several authors have argued for broad definitions. For example, Borys and Jemison (1989), discussing alliances as 'hybrid organizations', argue for a broad definition to allow research on the multiple purposes that strategic alliances may serve. One could argue that such a broad definition of the concept of strategic alliances would be a way of developing a generic term covering all forms of interorganizational cooperative relationships. However, positioning current literature on the basis of what authors have already defined as strategic alliances would become more confusing and, considering the concept itself, allowing all kinds of interfirm cooperative arrangements to be called strategic alliances does not seem right. The cooperative arrangements we describe represent not strategic alliances in general, but rather non-equity arrangements between firms that either coordinate or share activities on a project-oriented basis. They include cooperation between two or more firms that have joined forces beyond a 'simple' trading relationship.

Developmental Processes

Although many researchers mention the importance of maintaining the relationship over time, very few studies have examined the manner in which cooperative arrangements are actually managed (Bluedorn et al., 1994). Most frameworks also take the perspective of one firm, evaluating different forms of cooperative arrangements and then choosing the most appropriate.[4] The latest conceptual model on the developmental process of interorganizational relationships is offered by Ring and Van de Ven (1994). They criticize the traditional focus on antecedent conditions and structural properties as factors leading to the formation of cooperative arrangements, introducing a process framework that comprises formal, legal, and informal social-psychological processes. Very few researchers take into account the previous history of the involved partners (Axelrod, 1984; Bonoma, 1976; Levinthal and Fichman, 1988). The choice of cooperative arrangement will reflect previous use and results, and the development of a common social context is of vital importance in understanding evolutionary processes (Heide and Miner, 1992). In addition, the fact that most cooperation research has examined relationships between firms (Smith et al., 1995) seems to have important methodological implications, raising the question of whether measuring influencing factors at the firm level is even possible.

Knowledge Transfer Processes

Our theoretical grounding for knowledge transfer processes is based on contributions from both the sociology of knowledge and the strategic management literature. The sociology of knowledge is concerned with the relationship between human thought and the social context within which it arises. Knowledge is developed, transmitted, and maintained in social situations (Berger and Luckmann, 1966; Schutz and Luckmann, 1985). In focusing on knowledge transfer within a cooperative context, our interest is in the process of how actors from different social contexts, in cooperation, develop a common stock of knowledge. More specifically, we are interested in how observable differences in terms of what is known within the boundaries of the collaborative companies can be reduced through the transfer of knowledge.

In dealing with knowledge transfer, the focus of the study will be on task-related knowledge. However, as we base our main arguments on human interpretations and conceptions, we take into account both the person's attributes and the characteristics of the task activities performed. We argue that a person's use of knowledge in accomplishing a task is preceded by and based on his/her interpretations of the task, that is the individual's way of making sense of the task.[5] Thus, task-related knowledge must be seen as an integration of the two. Building on *analogies* from Berger and Luckmann's (1966) analysis of the foundation of knowledge in everyday life, we describe both the processes on which the theoretical model is based, and the link between our study and other research in the field of strategic management.[6]

As people actively engage in making sense of their tasks, they make reference to the interpreted context within which they have developed knowledge that guides their conduct (Schutz, 1970). People accumulate knowledge pertaining to their occupation, knowledge that meaningfully orders the events/tasks they encounter in their work situation (Berger and Luckmann, 1966). Through their educational background and previous work experience, people develop knowledge that makes them more or less fit for performing their current tasks. They also know that other people share at least part of their stock of knowledge, and that those people know that they know so. Their interaction with others in their performance of tasks is therefore constantly affected by their common participation in the available social stock of knowledge.

'Participation' in the social stock of knowledge thus permits the location of individuals in society and the handling of them in the appropriate manner (Berger and Luckmann, 1966). Within a network of cooperating companies, this could be reflected in the sharing of a common task, as in a project-oriented manner. Through distribution of work on an integrated task between the partners, each partner representative contributes his/her knowledge in the performance of the task. Either through the development of a team or through interaction in some other form, the representatives actively take part in the development of a social stock of knowledge (in the sense of both performing the task at hand and the location and handling of the respective partner representatives). Moreover, the companies involved in the cooperative arrangement could shift some persons with specific knowledge around on each project, enabling them not only to gain knowledge through the projects, but also to transfer knowledge to people not involved in the projects – thus increasing the total stock of knowledge among the involved companies.

The social stock of knowledge also differentiates each situation by degrees of familiarity (Berger and Luckmann, 1966). The validity of a person's knowledge in the performance of tasks is taken for granted by the person and by others until a problem arises that cannot be solved in terms of that knowledge. As long as an individual's knowledge works satisfactorily, he/she generally suspends doubts about it. However, an individual cannot know everything there is to know about a task. 'His/her knowledge of everyday life has the quality of an instrument that cuts a path through a forest and, as it does so, it projects a narrow cone of light on what lies just ahead and immediately around; on all sides of the path there continues to be darkness' (Berger and Luckmann, 1966, p. 59). Thus, the social stock of knowledge includes knowledge of a person's situation and its limits.

Finally, a person also encounters knowledge as socially distributed, that is, as possessed differently by different individuals and types of individuals. A person does not share his/her knowledge equally with everyone, and there may be some knowledge that he/she does not share. The social distribution of knowledge can become highly complex and even confusing to the outsider. In such cases, people need not only advice from experts, but also prior advice of experts on experts. Knowledge of how the socially available stock of knowledge is distributed, at least in outline, is an important element of that stock of knowledge. In a cooperative context, a person knows at least roughly what he/she can hide from whom, to whom he/she can turn for information on what he/she does not know, and generally which types of individuals can be expected to have which types of knowledge.

We see, then, that when continuity in the performance of tasks is interrupted by the appearance of a problem, people seek to interpret the task through their 'current frame of reference' (i.e. to interpret the 'stimuli' through their current belief systems and thus reinforce existing beliefs).[7] Because the performance of the task(s) is perceived as problematic, the individual is not directly able to make sense of it with his/her current stock of knowledge. However, even if the problem is something outside his/her experience, it still may be well within the range of problems that his/her knowledge can address.[8] In drawing a parallel to the strategic management literature, one might view such a situation as characterized by lower-level learning (Fiol and Lyles, 1985), in which the learning process is merely reflected in adjustments at a routine level (although different from pure adaptation with no association development). At that level there is a strong emphasis on how to carry out the task in a right way. According to Garvin (1993), knowing how is partial knowledge; it is rooted in existing norms of behavior and standards of practice. At an organizational level, lower-level learning could be reflected as changes in standard operating procedures, programs, short-term goals, and decision rules (Cyert and March, 1963).

However, individuals may be faced with a task that transcends the boundaries of their initial frame of reference. They may not be able to integrate the problematic situation into unproblematic working routines. Consequently, the validity of their stock of knowledge can no longer be taken for granted and they might have to look to others to handle the task. In such situations, the doubts of one's knowledge open the 'current frame of reference' to changes. Again, referring to the strategic management literature, one might view the situation as characterized by higher-level learning (Fiol and Lyles, 1985). In these cases, a person might experience major adjustments in overall beliefs and norms, and changes may be in organizational strategy and structure. There is a strong focus on doing the right things, and capturing the underlying cause-and-effect relationships (Garvin, 1993).

In summary, an organization's pursuit of cooperative strategy might in itself mean a change in beliefs, and individuals might be more exposed to different ways of perceiving a task.[9] We are considering processes in which the organization, through individual partner representatives working across the collaborative membrane,[10] takes an active part in the development of knowledge. Both organizational and contextual factors will influence knowledge transfer processes, which in turn will affect the construction and development of those factors (e.g., knowledge creation in R&D intensive collaboration will, to a varying extent, spur changes in the wider knowledge system of the organizations involved). We are therefore considering knowledge-driven developmental processes.

Determining Factors of Knowledge Transfer

On the basis of our theoretical understanding of the creation of social knowledge, we identify from the literature four determining factors that influence knowledge transfer between two or more cooperative partners: openness, channel of interaction, trust, and prior experience.

Openness

One determining factor of knowledge transfer in a cooperative context is the partners' openness in terms of willingness to share knowledge and partner interaction. Stata (1989) defines openness as the partners' willingness to put all the cards on the table, eliminate hidden agendas, make their motives, feelings, and biases known, and invite other opinions and points of view. Hamel (1991) discusses the concept of 'transparency', the knowability or openness of each partner. He explains that it is a determining factor in the potential for learning, and argues that the openness and accessibility of the partners is due partly to their attitude toward outsiders.

Badaracco (1991: 16) states that 'openness is paramount in knowledge links because much of what the parties are trying to learn from each other, or create together, is so difficult to communicate. It is often embedded in a firm's practices and culture, and it can only be learned through working relationships that are not hampered by constraints.' Hence, a distinction seemingly can be made between the transfer context and the actual attitude of the partners involved. Hamel (1991) found that the number of people from each partner seconded to the other was a determinant of relative transparency position. Elaborating on that point, Crossan and Inkpen (1992) describe how organizational systems can be designed to facilitate the integration of joint venture knowledge, giving as examples the rotation of managers from the joint venture back to the parent, regular meetings between joint venture and parent managers, and joint venture plant visits and tours. However, one can expect partners to limit openness by, for example, restricting the collaborative agreement to a narrow range of products or markets. Harrigan (1985) found that experienced managers of joint ventures wrote strong technological-protection contracts to protect the intellectual property rights of all partners.

Beyond the more manifest indicators, Hamel (1991) found that the penetrability of the social context that surrounded the partners was perceived as being an important factor in determining the degree of openness. It is closely linked to the process of institutionalization (Berger and Luckmann, 1966), which describes how persons within a given social context can inwardly appropriate the others' 'roles'. Through the resulting typifications developed over time (see next section, 'Channel of Interaction'), the partner representatives are actively involved in the process of institutionalization. Their history of interaction achieves the quality of 'objectivity', meaning that the knowledge pertaining to the context of interaction appears to become more transparent.[11] This underscores not only the importance of having the partner representatives working closely together (at least initially), enabling them to connect with each other through more or less complex relationships,[12] but also the importance of knowledge at a pre-theoretical level, knowledge that is learned in the course of socialization and supplies the partner representatives with institutionally appropriate rules of conduct.[13] We see that the concept of openness is related to both the partners' perceived willingness to share knowledge as such, and their previous history of interaction.

In summary, openness can be understood in terms of overall perceived openness of dialogue, the degree to which the partner representatives work closely together on a common task, and the degree to which the partner representatives perceive that the others withhold (shield) their knowledge.

H1 The higher the degree of openness, the more effective the knowledge transfer within a cooperative context.

Channel of Interaction

A second factor influencing knowledge transfer in a cooperative context is the channel of interaction. Partner representatives working on projects share experiences with each other in various ways, such as mail, telephone, computer conferences, and face to face. The cooperative context in which they interact is an important determining factor in the degree to which they develop a common stock of knowledge. Berger and Luckmann (1966) argue that most experiences of others take place in face-to-face situations because there another's subjectivity is available through a 'maximum of symptoms' and the here and now of the persons continuously impinge on each other, both consciously and subconsciously, as long as the face-to-face situation continues.[14] The authors further argue that misinterpretation and/or having the other actor hide his/her intentions is less likely in a face-to-face interaction than in less close forms of social relations. The reason is that even when interacting face to face, the actors apprehend each other by means of typificatory schemes. Both persons' typification schemes are susceptible to each other's interference, and they will enter into an ongoing 'negotiation', being more vulnerable the less remote the forms of interaction. Hence, the interaction channel has important implications for the perceived openness among companies pursuing a cooperative strategy.

Linking this factor to research in the field of strategic management, we can examine it in terms of media richness as a determinant of the extent to which knowledge is successfully transferred. The richness of the media can be analyzed in terms of two underlying dimensions: the variety of cues the medium can convey and the rapidity of feedback the medium can provide (Daft and Huber, 1987). Trevino et al. (1987) propose a link between the selection of media and the ambiguity of the message to be conveyed. In situations characterized by a high degree of ambiguity, no established scripts or symbols are available to guide behavior. 'Meaning must be created and negotiated as individuals look to others for cues and feedback to help interpret the message' (1987: 557). Daft and Lengel (1984) propose that the media have varying capacities for resolving ambiguity, meeting interpretation needs, and transferring knowledge (see also Mohr and Nevin, 1990), and that they can be placed along a five-step continuum: (1) face-to-face, (2) telephone, (3) written personal, (4) written formal, and (5) numeric formal.

Our framework proposes an indirect causal relationship between the richness of the channel of interaction and the effectiveness of knowledge transfer. We argue that face-to-face interaction is the richest medium because of its capacity for immediate feedback (increasing the vulnerability of the partner representatives' typification schemes and their ability to converge on a shared system of meaning relating to their task and non-task interactions) and the availability of multiple cues (including the firm representatives' ability to comment/act on the expressed experiences interactively). It creates the richest, most open social context through which knowledge is transferred.

> H2   The richer the channel of interaction, the more the perceived openness in the social context of interaction.

Trust

The importance of trust within cooperative arrangements has been noted by several authors (e.g. Dogson, 1993; Lorange and Roos, 1992; Ring and Van de Ven, 1994; Smith et al., 1995). In fact, trust has been emphasized as one of the most important elements in long-term cooperative ventures (Beamish, 1988; Harrigan, 1986; Quinn 1992). As Harrigan explicitly points out: 'Managers can be as crafty as they please in writing clauses to protect their firm's technology rights, but the joint venture's success depends on trust' (1986: 148). More specifically, learning within cooperative arrangements has been found to depend on high levels of trust between partners (Buckley and Casson, 1988; Faulkner, 1993; Lundvall, 1988).

Several considerably different operationalizations of trust have been used in the literature. They can be divided into four categories or clusters (Sitkin and Roth, 1993). First, *trust as an individual attribute* is the individual's trust in the motives of others (Rotter, 1967). Second, *trust as a behavior* is based on cooperation and competition as determinants of high and low levels of trust (Axelrod, 1984; Deutsch, 1958; Deutsch and Krauss, 1962). Within this category, some authors have also studied trust in terms of mutual openness and cooperation over time (Gabarro, 1978; Zand, 1972). For example, when he asked what mattered most to successful alliances, Badaracco (1991) found consistency in his managers' replies: they stated that trust and open communications were indispensable. Third, *trust as a situational feature* is trust that is needed only in situations of interdependence and uncertainty. For example, without trust, partners can easily make scapegoats of each other when a cooperative agreement encounters difficulty (Deutsch, 1962; Larzelere and Huston, 1980). Finally, *trust as an institutional arrangement* is the use of contracts and legalistic procedures as formal substitutes for trust based on interpersonal relationship (Shapiro, 1987; Zucker, 1986).

In taking a micro-level perspective of knowledge transfer within a cooperative context, we argue that trust at the firm level will only develop over time as a consequence of individual interaction. We therefore consider ways in which the partner representatives in a cooperative arrangement affect the developmental process of trust building. Rempel et al. (1985) posit that people attempt to understand their partners in terms of acts, dispositions, and motives that would predict positive response. They regard trust as a generalized expectation related to the subjective probability an individual assigns to the occurrence of some set of future events (Rotter, 1980; Scanzoni, 1979). First, trust is seen to evolve from past experiences with partner behavior. Through social learning experiences based on specific behavioral sequences, one forms belief about the *predictability* of a partner's future behavior. Rempel et al. therefore expect beliefs about the partner's predictability to relate to the strength of past experience in the relationship and the degree to which that experience suggests consistency, stability, and control over the pattern of behavior.

Rempel et al. (1985) further argue that as a relationship progresses, the focus inevitably shifts away from assessments involving specific behaviors to an evaluation of the qualities and characteristics attributed to the partner. Thus, trust is placed in a person, not in that person's specific actions. For example, is the partner a reliable person, someone who is honest and can be counted on? This notion of dependability is in line with Rotter's (1980) view of trust as an expectancy held by a representative of one partner that the word, promise, or written statement of the other partner can be relied upon.[15] The dispositional inferences that develop in response to such questions are likely to depend heavily on an accumulation of evidence from a more limited and diagnostic set of experiences involving risk and personal vulnerability. At an early stage of the partnership, initial structures of safeguards are often developed to protect partners and minimize risk. For instance, when two companies join forces, managers usually treat their partner with caution and suspicion, and employees are naturally inclined to be circumspect. By necessity, then, trust that transcends a rudimentary sense of predictability will typically emerge only in later stages of the relationship (Rempel et al., 1985).

Predictability and dependability are both based on past experience and the reliability of previous evidence. In partnerships, however, the future brings novel situations and circumstances for which past or present experience is not necessarily an accurate guide. Over time, the relationship may be faced with new stresses and forces that could not have been anticipated and to which no past encounters reasonably correspond. To capture the essence of trust that is not securely rooted in past experience, Rempel et al. (1985) use the term 'faith'. Given that a successful relationship is not guaranteed, continuing commitment to and belief in the relationship require some degree of faith. Still, a partner's past predictability and dependability would provide an important basis for generalizing to future situations. Predictability and especially dependability therefore should be related to faith, although faith does not fully subsume those factors.

Each component of trust reflects a different perspective or basis from which subjective probability judgments about a partner's future behavior can be made. Predictability, dependability, and faith arise from different levels of cognitive and emotional abstraction. The analysis of trust is based on the notion that people attempt to understand their partners in terms of acts, dispositions, and motives that would predict positive responses. That process is captured in progressively more symbolic terms as relationships develop. As feelings of trust become more firmly established and rooted, they depend more heavily on beliefs about the partners' motivations and less on direct coding at the behavioral level (Rempel et al., 1985). Hence, we propose that trust has an indirect effect on the effectiveness of knowledge transfer through its influence on perceived openness of the partner representatives.

H3 The higher the degree of trust, the higher the degree of perceived openness.

Prior Experience

The last determining factor of knowledge transfer in a cooperative context is the firm's ability to internalize knowledge. Badaracco (1991) argues that knowledge cannot migrate and become useful to a company unless the company itself has the appropriate 'social software' to acquire and exploit it. Similarly, Cohen and Levinthal (1990) introduce the concept of 'absorptive capacity', arguing that a firm's ability to recognize the value of new external knowledge, assimilate it, and apply it to commercial ends is largely a function of the firm's level of prior related knowledge. Dierickx and Cool (1989) also argue that firms that already have an important stock of R&D know-how are often in a better position to make further breakthroughs and add to their stock of knowledge than firms that have low initial levels of know-how. Thus, the relatedness of prior knowledge to the knowledge being sought seems to be an important determining factor in the effectiveness of knowledge transfer between the partners.

There is a crucial difference, however, between acquiring the knowledge and actually exploiting it (Cohen and Levinthal, 1990). Hamel (1991), examining the process of interpartner learning in strategic alliances, underlines the distinction between gaining access to knowledge and the actual internalization or accumulation of a partner's knowledge (e.g. a company might gain access to the partner's files on quality management, but without underlying knowledge of how the practices were developed and how they are actually carried out, they are of no value outside the narrow terms of the agreement) (see also Daft and Huber, 1987; Huber, 1991).

Closely related is the role of the diversity of knowledge. 'A diverse background provides a more robust basis for learning because it increases the prospect that incoming information will relate to what is already known' (Cohen and Levinthal, 1990: 129). That is, learning is dependent on the richness of the existing knowledge structure (Lyles and Schwenk, 1992). Those observations, drawing on studies at the individual level in the cognitive and behavioral sciences, are supported by researchers such as Bower and Hilgard who claim that 'the more objects, patterns and concepts that are stored in memory, the more readily is new information about these constructs acquired' (1981: 424). In addition to the diversity or breadth of knowledge, the depth of the firm's existing knowledge structure positively influences its ability to acquire and exploit new knowledge. Thus, the richness (breadth and depth) of the existing knowledge structure will influence both the assimilation and the exploitation of external knowledge. In the literature on cooperative strategies, Gupta and Singh

Table 3.1 *Latent and manifest variables*

Latent variables	Manifest variables	Selected theoretical support
Openness	Quality of dialogue Common task Shield knowledge	Harrigan, 1985; Stata, 1989; Hamel, 1991; Badaracco, 1991; Crossan and Inkpen, 1992
Channel of interaction	Face to face Telephone	Daft and Lengel, 1984; Daft and Huber, 1987; Trevino et al., 1987
Trust	Predictability Dependability Faith	Rempel et al., 1985; Harrigan, 1986; Quinn, 1992; Dogson, 1993; Ring and Van de Ven, 1994
Prior experience	Cooperative task Cooperative partner Other partners	Westney, 1988; Dierickx and Cool, 1989; Cohen and Levinthal, 1990; Gupta and Singh, 1991; Kogut and Zander, 1992

(1991) have used the term 'asset appropriability', claiming that a firm's skills and capabilities in appropriating the partner's know-how are a function of the firm's prior experience in managing alliances (the more experienced firms are more capable of appropriating the partner's know-how). A similar argument is presented by Westney (1988) and Harrigan (1986), who state that the more managers experience strategic alliances, the better they become at exploiting the benefits. However, it is not only prior alliance experience in general that can contribute to increased internalization, but also prior experience with the specific partner (Inkpen, 1992). A prior relationship between partners suggests that the firms have overcome initial uncertainty, and that the prior knowledge of the partner's operation may stimulate learning efforts associated with the collaborative agreement. (For more discussion on prior experience in the context of cooperations between firms, see Chapter 4).

H4 The higher the degree of prior experience, the more effective the knowledge transfer within a cooperative context.

Summary

The literature on strategic management combined with the sociology of knowledge has provided a basis for suggesting four factors that influence knowledge transfer within a cooperative context: (1) openness, (2) channel of interaction, (3) trust, and (4) prior experience. Table 3.1 summarizes the constructs, including the manifest variables on which they are measured (see also Appendix 1). Our conceptual model (see Figure 3.1) incorporates the hypothesized direct and indirect effects on the effectiveness of knowledge transfer.

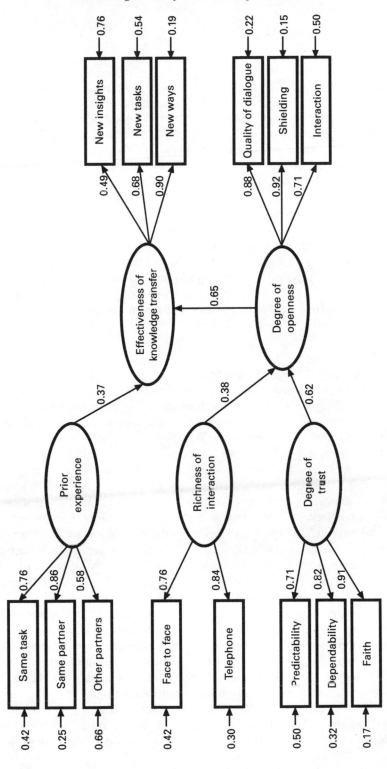

Figure 3.1 *Conceptual model*

Methodology

Sample

The empirical setting for our research was cooperative relationships between Nordic companies. In a cross-sectional field study, we collected data from 62 partner representatives actively involved in project-oriented cooperative arrangements in 45 companies. The unit of analysis was partner representatives and their perceptions of the cooperative setting. Data were collected through structured telephone interviews over a period of four months. The interviews consisted of one part structured questions with a given set of alternatives, one part semi-structured/open questions, and one part general comments related to the cooperative arrangement. Our three criteria for selecting the sample of cooperative partners were that (1) at least two partner representatives were involved, (2) the projects had made knowledge transfer possible in accordance with our theoretical framework, and (3) the projects had gone beyond the initiating phase. In choosing among cooperative arrangements, we asked senior managers within three governmental venture capital groups to suggest which projects to select.[16]

Measures

As shown in Table 3.1, we measured the latent variables by using a variety of items (designed as statements). In constructing the questionnaire, we discussed the statements with representatives for the governmental venture capital groups to ensure the relevance of the constructs and conducted a pilot test to diagnose problems with the scales and response formats. Each partner representative responded on a six-point Likert scale for each item. The scale ranged from 1 'strongly agree' to 6 'strongly disagree'. In total, the *openness* construct was measured by three items ($\alpha = 0.87$), the *richness of interaction* construct by two items ($\alpha = 0.77$), the *trust* construct by three items ($\alpha = 0.86$), and the *prior experience* construct by three items ($\alpha = 0.78$). The perceived effectiveness of knowledge transfer was measured by three items: the degree to which the partner representatives had acquired knowledge that generally caused them to develop new insights, the degree to which they had received knowledge that enabled them to see new ways of performing current tasks within their own company, and the degree to which the cooperative project enabled them to perform new tasks as a result of acquired knowledge ($\alpha = 0.82$).

Examination of the *t*-values associated with the loadings indicates that for every variable they *exceed* the critical value for 0.01 significance. Thus, all variables are related significantly to their specified constructs, verifying the posited relationships among indicators and constructs.

In addition to examining the loading for each indicator, we computed estimates of the reliability and variance extracted measures for each construct to assess whether the specified indicators were sufficient in their representation of the constructs. All constructs exceeded the recommended level for both measures. Computations are shown in Appendix 2.

Analyses

We used structural equation modeling (SEM) to examine the hypothesized relationships.[17] Several estimation methods can be applied to calculate the causal relationships between the different constructs (β_i and γ_j) and their correspondence (λ_i): partial least squares (PLS), maximum likelihood (ML), and general least squares (GLS). The choice of estimation procedure, and thus computer program (e.g. EQS, LISREL, and PLS), depends on the theoretical purpose of the estimation.[18] As our main purpose was empirical testing of our theoretical model, an ML(GLS)-based estimation technique was appropriate.

The model was tested with LISREL VIII (Jöreskog and Sörbom, 1993). Figure 3.1 shows the paths among the latent constructs and between the latent constructs and their measures that emerged from the analysis. The overall fit of the hypotheses to the observed correlations was assessed through five indicators:[19] the chi-square test, the normed chi-square test, the goodness-of-fit index (GFI), the adjusted goodness-of-fit index (AGFI), and the root-mean-square error of approximation (RMSEA). Chi-square indicates the probability that the measurement matrix is of the form implied by a model. It is sensitive to sample size, and a fit with significance greater than 0.05 is generally considered acceptable (Hayduk, 1989). As our study was limited in sample size and as we included a relatively large number of factors and estimated parameters, we also used several goodness-of-fit measures that attempt to eliminate or reduce its dependence on sample size. The goodness-of-fit index (GFI) is a non-statistical measure ranging from 0 (poor fit) to 1 (perfect fit), and indicates the relative amount of variables' covariance accounted for by the model (Jöreskog and Sörbom, 1988; Tanaka and Huba, 1985). A value greater than 0.90 is considered an indication of good fit (Mathieu et al., 1992). The adjusted goodness-of-fit index (AGFI) is an extension of the GFI, adjusted by the ratio of degrees of freedom (d.f.) for the proposed model to degrees of freedom for a null model. Browne and Cudeck (1993) propose several fit measures that take particular account of the error of approximation in the population and the precision of the fit measure itself. They suggest that a value of 0.05 of ϵ indicates a close fit and that values up to 0.08 represent reasonable errors of approximation in the population.

Results

The chi-square value ($\chi^2 = 79.47$, 70 d.f.) has a statistical significance level of 0.21, above the minimum level of 0.05 and also above the more conservative levels of 0.10 and 0.20. The normed chi-square (χ^2/d.f.) value is 1.14, which is within the recommended range of 1.0 to 2.0. The GFI value of 0.85 is acceptable. The AGFI value is 0.77 (below the recommended level of 0.90), and hence is only marginally acceptable. Combined with the chi-square, this result provides conditional support for model parsimony.

Following the guidelines of Browne and Cudeck (1993), we find that the point estimate of root-mean-square error of approximation (RMSEA) is 0.047 and that the 90 per cent confidence interval is from zero to 0.091. As the lower bound is below the recommended value of 0.05, we conclude that the model fits well and represents an acceptably close approximation to the population.

Another class of fit indices measures how much better the model fits than a baseline model, usually the independence model (null model). The null model has a χ^2 value of 595 with 91 degrees of freedom. With this information, we can calculate the Tucker-Lewis measure:

$$TL = \frac{(\chi^2_{null}/d.f._{null}) - (\chi^2_{proposed}/d.f._{proposed})}{(\chi^2_{null}/d.f._{null}) - 1} = \frac{(595/91) - (79/70)}{(595/91) - 1} = 0.98$$

This incremental fit measure exceeds the recommended level of 0.90, further supporting acceptance of the proposed model. Another indication that the model fits well is that the ECVI (Expected Value of Cross-Validation Index) for the model (2.45) is less than the ECVI for the saturated model (3.44). The confidence interval for ECVI is from 2.30 to 2.88.

In summary, the various measures of overall model goodness of fit show the results to be an acceptable representation of the hypothesized constructs. Figure 3.1 includes the LISREL solution coefficients between the measures and the latent constructs and among latent constructs. The results support all four hypotheses.

H1 posits that the higher the degree of perceived openness, the more effective the knowledge transfer within a cooperative context:

knowledge transfer = 0.65 × openness
(2.58)

indicating that openness is associated significantly (critical *t*-value of 1.96) with the effectiveness of knowledge transfer.

H2 holds that the richer the channel of interaction, the more perceived openness in the social context of interaction. The causal relationship of

openness = 0.38 × channel of interaction
(2.23)

is statistically significant.

H3 states that the higher the degree of trust, the higher the degree of perceived openness:

openness = 0.62 × trust
(3.04)

indicating a significant causal relationship. The combined effect of the two latent variables, channel of interaction and trust, on openness has an R^2 value of 0.88; hence they account for 88 per cent of the variance in openness.

H4 posits that the higher the degree of prior knowledge, the more effective the knowledge transfer within a cooperative context:

knowledge transfer = 0.37 × prior experience
                    (2.27)

indicating that prior experience is associated significantly (critical *t*-value of 1.96) with the effectiveness of knowledge transfer.

The combined effect of the perceived openness of partner representatives and prior experience can be shown as:

knowledge transfer = 0.65 × openness + 0.37 × prior experience
    (R^2=0.82)

This relation indicates that one can expect perceived openness (including the richness of the channels of interaction and the level of trust) to have an overall effect that is twice that of prior experience on the effectiveness of knowledge transfer within a cooperative context.

Discussion

We explored the issue of knowledge transfer and learning in cooperative arrangements by studying factors that influence the processes taking place within a cooperative relationship. Our study was different from previous work on partnership formation and general motives for joining forces. In addition to shifting the focus from content to cooperative processes, we treated the knowledge and skills exchanged between the partners as dynamic assets. We based our main arguments on human interpretation and conceptions, looking at how actors from different social contexts, in cooperation, come to develop a common stock of knowledge. In examining the management of cooperative arrangements, we sought to contribute to the understanding of the development processes by considering both the previous history of the partners and relationships at an individual level rather than at a firm level.

Interpretation of Path Results

Much of the literature on cooperative strategies pertains to the motives for establishing interorganizational relationships. It gives very little guidance about the processes necessary to develop and nurture partnerships over time (Bluedorn et al., 1994; Mohr and Spekman, 1994; von Krogh et al., 1994). With the objective of gaining insight into factors influencing an essential managerial issue in those developmental processes, knowledge transfer between cooperative partners, we chose to develop and empirically test a conceptual model containing four selected theoretical constructs. Our findings suggest that the greater the prior experience, richness in the channel of interaction, trust, and perceived openness, the greater the effectiveness of knowledge transfer is likely to be.

The statistical support for prior experience as a predictor of the effectiveness of knowledge transfer is similar to findings from other emerging research in the strategic management literature. Although focusing on the impact of organizational learning on the decision to form new joint ventures, Lyles (1994) stresses the importance of experience as knowledge accumulated through history. She argues that the partner representatives learn from their past experience and can transform their experiences into useful knowledge that will make them competent in making future cooperation-related decisions. Such competence is important not only for forming joint ventures, but also for the success of the development of cooperation as defined by Hamel (1991).[20]

Our findings for trust are also consistent with those from emerging research on cooperative relationships. For example, Ring and Van de Ven (1994) argue that faith in the moral integrity or goodwill of others (i.e. trust) is essential for the development of more open interorganizational relationships. Our findings add support for the emerging notion that the level of perceived openness of the relationship influences the effectiveness of knowledge transfer, as has been expressed for example by Faulkner (1993). In relation to channels of interaction, Mohr and Spekman (1994) stress the importance of accuracy, timeliness, adequacy, and credibility, supporting the notion of honest and open channels of interaction as essential for achieving more frequent and relevant information transfer between cooperative partners.

Overall, the strong, consistent findings for openness as a predictor of effectiveness of knowledge transfer support Hamel's (1991) notion of transparency as determining the potential for learning. Our study also extends the underlying factors of penetrability and attitude toward outsiders, showing the positive relationship to the notion of trust building and making use of rich channels of interaction. In relative numbers, the model shows that the perceived openness of a cooperative relationship has twice as much influence on effectiveness of knowledge transfer as the partner representatives' prior experience. Hence, our research provides managerial guidelines for developing openness in a strategic cooperative relationship.

One of the great advantages of our methodological choice, LISREL, is that it functions within both the context of discovery and the context of justification. In the context of justification, LISREL enables the researcher to formulate a statistical model that corresponds to the initial theoretical model. Additionally, on the basis of the estimated model, LISREL gives the researcher information on what parameters/relationships in the specified model would have to be changed to achieve a better fit (Medsker et al., 1994). The technique thus functions within the context of discovery, helping to broaden the researcher's perspective on 'new' relationships.

Managerial Implications

The managerial implications of our research relate to the way in which partners attempt to manage the development of the cooperative relationship. We found the quality of the cooperative relationship to be an important factor in the partners' assessment of the degree of success in the projects. Although other authors have argued for the importance of trust and cooperative behavior (e.g. Harrigan, 1986; Smith et al., 1995), explicit linkages with performance measures have not been examined. Trust, richness of the channel of interaction, perceived openness, and the partner representatives' prior experience all have a significant effect on the knowledge transfer processes within a cooperative context. The most important and perhaps most difficult challenge, however, seems to be the development of open business relationships, wherein trust and rich channels of interaction are crucial aspects.

Almost 75 per cent of the respondents in our study indicated that the cooperative arrangements had been a success. The main reasons given were the feeling of goal achievement and the fact that the intended areas of cooperation in many cases were extended beyond those originally decided upon (i.e. the success had resulted in a strengthening of the relationships between the companies). When asked what contributed the most to this success, the respondents emphasized open relationships built on trust and common understanding. The respondents who indicated a lack of success in the cooperative arrangements gave such comments as 'we have experienced internal problems with our partner', 'the process is developing too slowly', 'strong commercial interests have made cooperation difficult', 'the knowledge base of the partners differed too much – it resulted in distrust', 'the cooperative environment was not good enough', and 'it took too much time to develop trust'.

As argued from a resource-based perspective, the overall strategic objective of entering a cooperative arrangement is the pooling of resources to create value in a way that neither partner could achieve by acting alone (Borys and Jemison, 1989). Value creation is the process of combining the competence and resources of the partners to perform a joint task that has the potential to create monetary or other benefits for the partners. Although the perceived value need not be the same for both partners, our findings suggest that the partners may place greater emphasis on factors such as trust and openness than has been noted previously in the literature.

Limitations and Directions for Further Research

Our study is one of the few in which cooperative arrangements are modeled from an interorganizational process perspective and therefore lays the groundwork for understanding the causal sequences of partner interactions. Nevertheless, the findings should be interpreted in the light of several limitations.

First, because the model is not comprehensive in terms of systematically investigating a large number of constructs, it runs the well-known risk of reducing theoretically complex phenomena to simple observable indicators. Also, a larger sample size might have enhanced the findings, although our goodness-of-fit measures were constructed to eliminate their dependence on sample size.

Another issue is the extent to which questions could be raised about several of the path directions in the model. Openness is shown as a consequence of trust. One might hold that openness is antecedent to trust because trust is a present state and openness taps past cooperative behavior. Although we argue that trust helps to establish expectations of openness, conclusions about causality derived from a static model must be viewed as tentative. In addition, although we found no significant reciprocal relationships, the question of prior knowledge being influenced interactively by the effectiveness of knowledge transfer is open for further research.

Finally, the question of how the dependent factor, effectiveness of knowledge transfer, should be evaluated remains a complex issue. We encourage further research on both the antecedents and nature of knowledge transfer within a cooperative context. In trying to identify areas for future research on interorganizational cooperation, Smith et al. (1995) question whether past theories can be applied to new organizational forms and realities. Focusing on the link between intra- and interorganizational relations, they emphasize the importance of understanding the dynamics of interpersonal trust, cross-functional boundary spanning, team behavior, and collaborative interorganizational relationships. Referring to the work of Ring and Van de Ven (1994), they stress the importance of understanding the dynamics of cooperation, the processes through which the cooperative relationship is continually shaped and restructured by actions and symbolic interpretations of the parties involved. We hope our study provides a useful foundation for examining such issues.

Appendix 1: Items

Indicators of Trust

Respondents were asked to rate, on a six-point Likert scale, three measures reflecting trust: the partner representatives' perceived predictability, the partner representatives' perceived dependability, and the partner representatives perceived willingness to maintain a good relationship. High scores represent high degree of trust and low scores represent low degree of trust.

Indicators of Openness

Respondents were asked to rate, on a six-point Likert scale, the openness within the cooperative arrangement. The three indicators of openness were overall perceived openness of dialogue, the degree to which the partner representatives were working together on common tasks, and the degree to which each partner representative perceived the other to shield knowledge. Low indicators represent low degree of openness and vice versa.

Indicators of Prior Experience

Research shows that the partner representatives' degree of related knowledge positively influences their receptive capacity. Respondents were asked to rate, on a six-point Likert scale, three measures reflecting prior knowledge: the degree to which they had prior experience within the field in which they cooperated, their degree of prior experience from related projects with the same company/partner representatives, and the partner representatives' prior experience from related projects with other companies. High scores represent high degree of prior knowledge and low scores represent low degree of prior knowledge.

Indicators of Interaction Channel

Multiple measures were used to assess the channel of interaction between the partner representatives. One set of measures examined what could be grouped as rich media and another examined less rich media. On a six-point Likert scale, the lower the score, the lower the degree of richness.

Indicators of Effectiveness of Knowledge Transfer

Respondents were asked to rate, on a six-point Likert scale, three measures reflecting the perceived effectiveness of knowledge transfer: the degree to which they had acquired knowledge that generally caused them to develop new insights, the degree to which they had received knowledge that enabled them to see new ways of performing current tasks within their own company, and the degree to which the cooperative project enabled them to perform new tasks as a result of acquired knowledge. High scores represent higher effectiveness of knowledge transfer.

Appendix 2: Goodness-of-Fit Findings for Measurement Model

Reliability is a measure of the internal consistency of the construct indicators, showing the degree to which they 'indicate' the common latent construct. A commonly used threshold value for acceptable reliability is 0.70 (Fornell and Larker, 1981). That is, values above 0.70 are reliable (although for exploratory studies the values can be lower).

$$\text{construct reliability} = \frac{(\sum \text{std loading}_j)^2}{(\sum \text{std loading}_j)^2 + \sum \epsilon_j}$$

Latent variable	Reliability measure
Effectiveness of knowledge transfer	0.74
Openness	0.88
Prior experience	0.79
Channel of interaction	0.78
Trust	0.86

All constructs exceed the recommended level of 0.70.

Another measure of reliability is the variance extracted measure. It reflects the overall amount of variance in the indicators accounted for by the latent constructs. The variance extracted value for a construct should exceed 0.50.

$$\text{variance extracted} = \frac{(\sum \text{sq.std loading}_j)^2}{(\sum \text{std loading}_j)^2 + \sum c_j}$$

Latent variable	Reliability measure
Effectiveness of knowledge transfer	0.51
Openness	0.71

Prior experience	0.55
Channel of interaction	0.62
Trust	0.66

On the variance extracted measure, all constructs exceed the recommended level of 0.50.

Notes

This chapter is based on the MSc thesis of Kenneth Wathne, Norwegian School of Management.

1   In distinguishing between knowledge that can be clearly and fully articulated, and knowledge that resides primarily in specialized relationships among individuals and groups, Badaracco (1991) claims that the latter type of knowledge forms the main argument for developing knowledge links.

2   Teece et al. (1990) discuss the concept of static routines that embody the capacity to replicate certain previously performed tasks. Dynamic routines, in contrast, are directed at learning and new product–process development.

3   Several authors have stressed the transferability of resources, using terms such as 'invisible assets' (Itami, 1987), 'intangible assets' (Hall, 1992),and non-teachable assets (Winter, 1987).

4   With the exception of population ecologists such as Hannan and Freeman (1989).

5   In contrast to cognitive approaches, this rejects the idea that a person's perceptions of a task are an inner representation of an external 'truth' (see Abercrombie, 1980; Lazenga, 1992; Sandberg, 1987; Spier, 1967).

6   In the terminology of Nagel (1961), analogies are often used as theoretical grounding. They are used to draw on theoretical contributions within several fields of research, where models in one area of interest are used as a 'hermeneutic remedy' to further developments within other areas. The importance of analogies is the way in which they help strengthen the theoretical understanding of the internal logic in the initial theory that is to be developed.

7   As actions are not treated as objective – beyond human perception – beliefs are seen as mental representations of human understanding (Sproull, 1981). They serve as value premises and expressions of normative structures.

8   For example an individual might not have experienced the same task currently faced, but through interaction with others can acquire new knowledge that helps him/her order the task and make the needed 'adjustments' in behavior in accordance with his/her interpretations (still well within the frame of reference).

9   Depending on the organization's history. An organization with extensive experience with cooperative strategies might face limited change.

10   The term 'collaborative membrane' is used by Hamel (1991).

11   It is important to keep in mind that this objectivity, however great it may appear to the representatives, is humanly produced, constructed objectivity. In addition, it is the knowledge developed in the cooperative context that is expected to become most transparent, as knowledge 'brought into' the relationship is institutionalized outside that setting.

12   In the literature on interorganizational relationships, authors have referred to the degree of interaction intensity (Aldrich, 1979; Axelrod, 1984; Johanson and Mattsson, 1988). Intensity has been defined as the amount of investment an organization has in its relations with other organizations (in terms both of resources and the strength of the interactions), and it has been argued that the more intensive the interactions, the more willing partner firms may be to adapt to each other and share knowledge about each other's strategies, needs, and capabilities (Johanson and Mattsson, 1988).

13   Several authors have emphasized the importance of such social structures within organizations, separating the normative (including values, norms, and role expectations) and behavioral dimensions (Davis, 1949; Lawrence and Lorsch, 1967; Scott, 1992).

14   Although the actors interacting may misinterpret some of the symptoms, no other form

of social relations can reproduce the plenitude of symptoms of subjectivity present in the face-to-face situation. That is, all other forms of interacting are in varying degrees remote.

15   In the field of social psychology, trust is also seen to encompass the element of honesty, to stand by one's word (e.g. Anderson and Narus, 1990) and to fulfill promised role obligations (e.g. Dwyer et al., 1987; Kumar et al., 1993). From this perspective, trust can be viewed as a social 'lubricant', increasing people's reliance on other people's word (Arrow, 1974).

16   The governmental venture capital groups are the Swedish-Norwegian Industrial Development Fund (SNI), the Nordic Industrial Fund (NI), and the Norwegian Industrial and Regional Development Fund (SND).

17   A well-known limitation of traditional multivariate techniques such as multiple regression, canonical analysis, and multivariate analysis of variance is that they can examine only a single relationship at a time (i.e. between the dependent and independent variables) – even the techniques allowing for multiple dependent variables. However, we continuously face interrelated problems that these multivariate techniques do not allow us to address with a single comprehensive method. This limitation is one of the main reasons why the technique of *structural equation modeling* has been used in almost every conceivable field of study, including education, marketing, psychology, sociology and management (Schumacker, 1994). Its attractiveness in such diverse areas is also based on the fact that its ability to assess the relationships comprehensively provides a transition from *exploratory* to *confirmatory* analysis. The desire of researchers to develop a systematic and holistic view of problems, requiring the ability to test a series of relationships constituting large-scale models or even entire theories, has made structural equation modeling particularly attractive (e.g. Bagozzi and Yi, 1988; Bentler, 1980; Blalock, 1985; Hagedoorn and Schakenraad, 1994; James et al., 1982; Marcoulides and Heck, 1993).

18   A fundamental distinction can be made between the use of structural equation modeling for theory testing and development and its use in prediction application (Fornell and Bookstein, 1982; Jöreskog and Sörbom, 1988; Wold, 1982). For theory testing and development, the maximum likelihood (ML) or generalized least squares (GLS) approach has several relative strengths, whereas for application and prediction, a partial least squares (PLS) estimation approach has relative strength. These two approaches to structural equation modeling can be thought of as complementary. The choice depends on the purpose of the research (Anderson and Gerbing, 1988).

19   Use of multiple criteria is recommended in evaluating the overall fit of a LISREL model (Bollen, 1989).

20   Success in terms of both financial and learning outcomes.

References

Abercrombie, N. (1980). *Class, Structure and Knowledge: Problems in the Sociology of Knowledge*. Oxford: Blackwell.

Aldrich, H.E. (1979). *Organizations and Environments*. Engelwood Cliffs, NJ: Prentice-Hall.

Alter, C. and Hage, J. (1993). *Organizations Working Together*. Beverly Hills, CA: Sage.

Anderson, J. C. and Gerbing, D. W. (1988). Structural equation modeling in practice: a review and recommended two-step approach. *Psychological Bulletin*, 103(3): 411–23.

Anderson, J. C. and Narus, A. (1990). A model of distributor firm and manufacturing firm working partnerships. *Journal of Marketing*, 54(1): 42–58.

Arrow, K.J. (1974). *The Limits of Organization*. New York: Norton.

Axelrod, R. (1984). *The Evolution of Cooperation*. New York: Basic Books.

Badaracco, J.L. (1991). *The Knowledge Link: How Firms Compete through Strategic Alliances*. Boston, MA: Harvard Business School Press.

Bagozzi, R.P. and Yi, Y. (1988). On the evaluation of structural equation models. *Journal of the Academy of Marketing Science*, 16(1): 74–79.

Barney, J.B. (1986). Strategic factor markets: expectations, luck and business strategy. *Management Science*, 10 (October): 1231–41.

Barney, J.B. (1991). Firm resources and sustained competitive advantage. *Journal of Management*, 17(1): 99–120.

Beamish, P.W. (1988). *Multinational Joint Ventures in Developing Countries*. London: Routledge.

Bentler, P.M. (1980). Multivariate analysis with latent variables: causal modeling. *Annual Review of Psychology*, 31: 419–56.

Berger, P. and Luckmann, T. (1966). *The Social Construction of Reality*. New York: Penguin.

Blalock, H.M. (1985). *Causal Modeling in the Social Sciences*. New York: Academic Press.

Bluedorn, A.C., Johnson, R.A., Cartwright, D.K. and Barringer, B.R. (1994). The interface and convergence of the strategic management and organizational environment domains. *Journal of Management*, 20(2): 201–62.

Bollen, K.A. (1989). *Structural Equations with Latent Variables*. New York: Wiley.

Bonoma, T.V. (1976). Conflict, cooperation and trust in three power systems. *Behavioral Science*, 21: 499–514.

Borys, B. and Jemison, D.B. (1989). Hybrid arrangements as strategic alliances: theoretical issues in organizational combinations. *Academy of Management Review*, 14: 234–49.

Bower, G.H. and Hilgard, E.R. (1981). *Theories of Learning*. Englewood Cliffs, NJ: Prentice-Hall.

Browne, M.W. and Cudeck, R. (1993). Alternative ways of assessing model fit. In K.A. Bollen and J.S. Long (eds), *Testing Structural Equation Models*. Beverly Hills, CA: Sage. pp. 136–62.

Buckley, P. and Casson, M. (1988). A theory of cooperation in international business. In F. Contractor and P. Lorange (eds), *Cooperative Strategies in International Business*. Lexington, MA: Lexington Books. pp. 31–55.

Chi, T. (1994). Trading in strategic resources: necessary conditions, transaction problems, and choice of exchange structure. *Strategic Management Journal*, 15(4): 271–90.

Cohen, M. and Levinthal, D. (1990) Absorptive capacity: a perspective on learning and innovation. *Administrative Science Quarterly*, 35(1): 128–52.

Contractor, F. J. and Lorange, P. (1988). Why should firms cooperate? The strategy and economics basis for cooperative ventures. In F.J. Contractor and P. Lorange (eds), *Cooperative Strategies in International Business*. Lexington, MA: Lexington Books. pp. 3–28.

Crossan, M.M. and Inkpen, A.C. (1992). Believing is seeing: an exploration of the organization learning concept and evidence from the case of joint venture learning. Working paper, Western Business School, University of Western Ontario, Canada.

Cyert, R.M. and March, J.G. (1963). *A Behavioral Theory of the Firm*. Englewood Cliffs, NJ: Prentice-Hall.

Daft, R.L. and Huber, G.P. (1987). How organizations learn: a communication framework. *Research in the Sociology of Organizations*, 5: 1–36

Daft, R.L. and Lengel, R.H. (1984) Information richness: a new approach to managerial behavior and organization design. *Research in Organizational Behavior*, 6: 191–233.

Davis, K. (1949). *Human Society*. New York: Macmillan.

Deutsch, M. (1958). Trust and suspicion. *Journal of Conflict Resolution*, 2(4): 265–79.

Deutsch, M. (1962). Cooperation and trust: some theoretical notes. In M.R. Jones (ed.), *Nebraska Symposium on Motivation*. Lincoln, NE: University of Nebraska Press. pp. 275–320.

Deutsch, M. and Krauss, R. M. (1962). Studies of interpersonal bargaining. *Journal of Conflict Resolution*, 6(1): 52–76.

Dierickx, I. and Cool, K. (1989). Asset stock accumulation and sustainability of competitive advantage. *Management Science*, 35(12): 1504–11.

Dogson, M. (1993). Learning, trust, and technological collaboration. *Human Relations*, 46(1): 77–95.

Dwyer, R.F., Schurr, P.H. and Oh, S. (1987). Developing buyer–seller relationships. *Journal of Marketing*, 15(2): 11–27.

Faulkner, D. (1993). International strategic alliances: key conditions for their effective development. Dissertation, Oxford University.

Fiol, M.C. and Lyles, M.A. (1985). Organizational Learning. *Academy of Management Review*, 10(4): 803–13.

Fornell, C. and Bookstein, F.L. (1982). Two structural equation models: LISREL and PLS applied to consumer exit-voice theory. *Journal of Marketing Research*, 19: 440–52.

Fornell, C. and Larker, D.F. (1981). Evaluating structural equations models with unobservable variables and measurement error. *Journal of Marketing Research*, 18: 39–50.

Gabarro, J.J. (1978). The development of trust, influence and expectations. In A.G. Athos and J.J. Gabarro (eds), *Interpersonal Behavior, Communication and Understanding in Relationships*. Englewood Cliffs, NJ: Prentice-Hall. pp. 290–303.

Garvin, D.A. (1993). Building a learning organization. *Harvard Business Review*, 71 (July–August): 78–91.

Gupta, A.K. and Singh, H. (1991). Exploiting synergies: external alliances vs. inter-SBU coordination. Working paper, University of Maryland.

Hagedoorn, J. and Schakenraad, J. (1994). The effect of strategic technology alliances on company performance. *Strategic Management Journal*, 15(4): 291–309.

Hall, R. (1992). The strategic analysis of intangible resources. *Strategic Management Journal*, 13(2): 135–44.

Hamel, G. (1991). Competition for competence and interpartner learning within international alliances. *Strategic Management Journal*, 12 (Special Issue): 83–103.

Hannan, M.T. and Freeman, J. (1989). *Organizational Ecology*. Cambridge, MA: Harvard University Press.

Harrigan, K.R. (1985). *Strategies for Joint Ventures*. Lexington, MA: Lexington Books.

Harrigan, K.R. (1986). *Managing for Joint Venture Success*. Lexington, MA: Lexington Books.

Hayduk, L. A. (1989). *Structural Equation Modeling with LISREL*. Baltimore: Johns Hopkins University Press.

Heide, J.B. and Miner, A.S. (1992). The shadow of the future: effects of anticipated interaction and frequency of contact on buyer–seller cooperation. *Academy of Management Journal*, 32(2): 265–91.

Huber, G. (1991). Organizational learning: the contributing process and the literatures. *Organization Science*, 2(1): 88–116.

Inkpen, A.C. (1992). Learning and collaboration: an examination of North American–Japanese joint ventures. Dissertation, University of Western Ontario.

Itami, H. (1987). *Mobilizing Invisible Assets*. Cambridge, MA: Harvard University Press.

James, L.R., Muliak, S.A. and Brett, J.M. (1982). *Causal Analysis: Assumptions, Models and Data*. Beverly Hills, CA: Sage.

Johanson, J. and Mattsson, L.G. (1988). Internationalisation in industrial systems – a network approach. In N. Hood and J.E. Vahlne (eds), *Strategies in Global Competition*. London: Croom Helm.

Jöreskog, K.G. and Sörbom, D. (1988). *LISREL VII: Analysis of Linear Structure Relationships by the Method of Maximum Likelihood*. Mooresville, IN: Scientific Software.

Jöreskog, K.G. and Sörbom, D. (1993). *LISREL VIII, User's Reference Guide*. Chicago: Scientific Software.

Kogut, B. (1988). Joint ventures: theoretical and empirical perspectives. *Strategic Management Journal*, 9(4): 319–32.

Kogut, B. and Zander, U. (1992) Knowledge of the firm, combinative capabilities and the replication of technology. *Organization Science*, 3(3): 383–97.

Kumar, N., Scheer, L.K. and Steenkamp S.J. (1993). Powerful suppliers, vulnerable resellers, and the effects on supplier fairness: a cross-national study. Working paper, Smeal College of Business Administration, Pennsylvania State University.

Larzelere, R.E. and Huston, T.L. (1980). The dyadic trust scale: toward understanding interpersonal trust in close relationships. *Journal of Marriage and the Family*, 42: 595–604.

Lawrence, P.R. and Lorsch, J.W. (1967). Differentiation and integration in complex organizations. *Administrative Science Quarterly*, 12 (June): 1–47.

Lazenga, E. (1992). *Micropolitics of Knowledge*. New York: Walter de Gruyter.

Levinthal, D.A. and Fichman, M. (1988). Dynamics of interorganizational attachments: audio-client relationships. *Administrative Science Quarterly*, 33: 345–69.

Lippman, S.A. and Rumelt, R.P. (1982). Uncertain imitability: an analysis of interfirm differences in efficiency under competition. *The Bell Journal of Economics*, 13 (Autumn): 418–38.

Lorange, P. and Roos, J. (1992). *Strategic Alliances: Formation, Implementation, and Evolution*. Cambridge, MA: Blackwell.

Lundvall, B.Å. (1988). Innovation as an interactive process: from user–producer interaction to the national system of innovation. In G. Dosi et al. (eds), *Technical Change and Economic Theory*. London: Pinter. pp. 349–69.

Lyles, M.A. (1994). The impact of organizational learning on joint venture formation. *International Business Review*, 3 (Special Issue): 37–45.

Lyles, M.A. and Schwenk, C.R. (1992). Top management, strategy, and organizational knowledge structures. *Journal of Management Studies*, 29(2): 155–79.

Mahoney, J.T. and Pandian, J.R. (1992). The resource-based view within the conversation of strategic management. *Strategic Management Journal*, 13(5): 363–80.

Marcoulides, G.A. and Heck, R.H. (1993). Organizational culture and performance: proposing and testing a model. *Organization Science*, 4(2): 209–25.

Mathieu, J.E., Tannenbaum, S.I. and Salas, E. (1992). Influences of individual and situational characteristics on measures of training effectiveness. *Academy of Management Journal*, 35(4): 828–47.

Medsker, G.J., Williams, L.J. and Holahan, P.J. (1994). A review of current practices for evaluating causal models in organizational behavior and human resources management research. *Journal of Management*, 20(2): 439–64.

Mohr, J. and Nevin, J.R. (1990). Communication strategies in marketing channels: a theoretical perspective. *Journal of Marketing*, 36(4): 36–49.

Mohr, J. and Spekman, R. (1994). Characteristics of partnership success: partnership attributes, communication behavior, and conflict resolution techniques. *Strategic Management Journal*, 15(2): 135–52.

Nagel, E. (1961). *The Structure of Science*. London: Routledge & Kegan Paul.

Parkhe, A. (1991). Interfirm diversity, organizational learning, and longevity in global strategic alliances. *Journal of International Business Studies*, 22(4): 579–601.

Polanyi, M. (1962). *Personal Knowledge: towards a Post Critical Philosophy*. London: Routledge.

Powell, W.W. (1987). Hybrid organizational arrangements. *California Management Review*, 30(1): 67–87.

Prahalad, C.K. and Hamel, G. (1990). The core competence of the corporation. *Harvard Business Review*, 68 (May–June): 79–91.

Pucik, V. (1988). Strategic alliances, organizational learning, and competitive advantage: the HRM agenda. *Human Resource Management*, 27(1): 77–93.

Quinn, J.B. (1992). *Intelligent Enterprise: a Knowledge and Service Based Paradigm for Industry*. New York: Free Press.

Reed, R. and DeFillippi, R. (1990). Causal ambiguity, barriers to imitation, and sustainable competitive advantage. *Academy of Management Review*, 15(1): 88–102.

Rempel, J.K., Holmes, J.G. and Zanna, M.P. (1985). Trust in close relationships. *Journal of Personality and Social Psychology*, 49(1): 95–112.

Ring, P.S. and Van de Ven, A. (1994). Developmental processes of cooperative interorganizational relationships. *Academy of Management Review*, 19(1): 90–118.

Rotter, J.B. (1967). A new scale for the measurement of interpersonal trust. *Journal of Personality*, 35: 651–65.

Rotter, J.B. (1980). Interpersonal trust, trustworthiness, and gullibility. *American Psychologist*, 35(1): 1–7.

Rumelt, R.P. (1984). Towards a strategic theory of the firm. In R.B. Lamb (ed.), *Competitive Strategic Management*. Englewood Cliffs, NJ: Prentice-Hall.

Sandberg, J. (1987). *Human Competence at Work: an Interpretative Approach*. Dissertation, Handelshøyskolen ved Gøteborgs Universitet.

Scanzoni, J. (1979). Social exchange and behavioral interdependence. In R.L. Burgess and T.L. Huston (eds), *Social Exchange in Developing Relationships*. New York: Academic Press.

Schumacker, R.E. (1994). Editor's note. *Structural Equation Modeling*, 1(1): 1.

Schutz, A. (1970). *On Phenomenology and Social Relations*. Chicago: University of Chicago Press.

Schutz, A. and Luckmann, T. (1985). *The Structure of the Life-World*. Evanston, IL: Northwestern University Press.

Scott, W.R. (1992). *Organizations: Rational, Natural, and Open Systems*. Englewood Cliffs, NJ: Prentice-Hall.

Shapiro, S.P (1987). The social control of impersonal trust. *American Journal of Sociology*, 93(3): 623–58.

Sitkin, S.B. and Roth, N.L. (1993). Explaining the limited effectiveness of legalistic remedies for trust/distrust. *Organization Science*, 4(3): 367–92.

Smith, K.G., Carroll, S.J. and Ashford, S.J. (1995). Intra- and interorganizational cooperation: toward a research agenda. *Academy of Management Journal*, 38(1): 7–23.

Spier, M. (1967). Phenomenology and social theory: discovering actors and social acts. *Berkeley Journal of Sociology*, 12.

Sprull, L.S. (1981). Beliefs in organizations. In P.C. Nyström and W.H. Starbuck (eds), *Handbook of Organizational Design*, vol. 1. Oxford: Oxford University Press. pp. 203–24.

Stata, R. (1989). Organizational learning – the key to management innovation. *Sloan Management Review*, 17 (Spring): 63–74.

Tanaka, J.S. and Huba, G.J. (1985). A fit index for covariance structure models under arbitrary GLS estimation. *British Journal of Mathematical and Statistical Psychology*, 38: 197–201.

Teece, D.J., Pisano, G. and Shuen, A. (1990). Firm capabilities, resources and the concept of strategy. Working paper, University of California at Berkeley.

Trevino, L.K., Lengel, R.H. and Daft, R.L. (1987). Media symbolism, media richness, and media choice in organizations – a symbolic interactionist perspective. *Communication Research*, 14(5): 553–74.

von Krogh, G., Sinatra, A. and Singh, H. (1994). *The Management of Corporate Acquisitions*. London: Macmillan.

Wernerfelt, B. (1984). A resource-based view of the firm. *Strategic Management Journal*, 5(2): 171–80.

Westney, D.E. (1988). Domestic and foreign learning curves in managing international cooperative strategies. In F.J. Contractor and P. Lorange (eds), *Cooperative Strategies in International Business*. Lexington, MA: Lexington Books. pp. 339–47.

Winter, S.G. (1987). Knowledge and competence as strategic assets. In D.J. Teece (ed.), *The Competitive Challenge*. New York: Harper & Row. pp. 159–84.

Wold, H. (1982). Soft modeling: the basic design and some extensions. In K.G. Jöreskog and H. Wold (eds), *Systems under Indirect Observation: Causality, Structure, Prediction. Part II*. Amsterdam: North-Holland. pp. 1–54.

Zand, D.E. (1972). Trust and managerial problem solving. *Administrative Science Quarterly*, 17: 229–39.

Zucker, L.G. (1986). Production of trust: institutional sources of economic structure, 1840–1920. In B.M. and L.L. Cummings (eds), *Research in Organizational Behavior*, vol. 8. Greenwich, CT: JAI Press. pp. 53–111.

4

The Impact of Individual and Organizational Learning on Formation and Management of Organizational Cooperation

Marjorie Lyles, Georg von Krogh, Johan Roos and Dirk Kleine

Managers spend increasingly more time and attention on developing interorganizational cooperation such as alliances and joint ventures. So far, much of the research on formation and evolution of cooperative ventures has focused on 'making the deal': the objectives for cooperation, the options for cooperative ventures, the direction and the management processes involved. However, traditional approaches addressing the formation processes of cooperative ventures, like Lorange and Roos (1992), ignore to a large extent the importance of individual and organizational learning, memories and history as factors that have a significant impact on how and why a firm will enter different kinds of alliances.

Thus, important questions are to what extent firms have learned from previous processes, how learning has taken place and in which way individual and organizational learning influences the future actions taken. These questions become even more critical due to the fact that more and more organizations enter cooperative arrangements and view them as a major option for long-term survival and competitive success (Hamel, 1991).

This chapter aims to develop new insights into the impact of individual and organizational learning on the decision process to form a new cooperative venture (building on some specific issues previously raised in Chapters 1 and 3). We will argue that learning on the individual and organizational level is a critical variable influencing whether and how an organizational cooperation will be formed and how it will be managed. This line of argument builds on models of learning that address the relevant aspects influencing important choices in cooperative strategies.

First, we will provide a brief overview of learning models and their application in management theory. In the section 'From Individual Learning to Organizational Learning' we will argue that individual learning is the fundamental building block of organizational learning. Building on this theoretical framework, the impact of learning at the individual and organizational levels on the formation and management of interorganizational cooperation will be discussed in detail. Finally, we will outline the implications for practice and future research.

From Individual Learning to Organizational Learning

In order to understand how organizations learn, we have to explore the issue of individual learning and then add the complexity of an organizational setting. Crossan and Inkpen (1992) argue that organizational learning theories often ignore that individual learning is the foundation for understanding the process of organizational learning. Thus, a useful starting point for building a bridge between individual and organizational learning is reviewing some aspects of human learning theory with its disciplinary roots in psychology.

What does learning at the individual level mean? Through learning processes individuals develop new understandings, and research in the field of cognitive and behavioral sciences describes this process as involving the acquisition and interpretation of knowledge (Lindsay and Norman, 1977). The process does not need to be conscious or intentional (Bower and Hilgard, 1981), nor does it always increase the learner's effectiveness or result in observable changes in behavior (Friedlander, 1983). Rather, learning occurs through processing of information and changes one's 'cognitive maps or understandings' (Friedlander, 1983) and as a result the range of one's potential behavior changes (Huber, 1991).

Thus, learning has to be linked to a change in an individual's interpretation of events and action. This process of interpretation has been defined by Daft and Weick (1984) as the process through which people give meaning to information. The product of the individual process of interpreting is a change in individual beliefs or schemata and individual behavior. In this sense, an individual learns through developing different interpretations of new or existing information and thereby developing a new understanding of surrounding events (Fiol, 1994).

Learning from past events is a frequently applied way to increase the ability for problem solving. This claim is supported by results from cognitive psychological research. Several studies have given empirical evidence for the dominating role of specific, previously experienced situations in human problem solving (e.g. Ross, 1989). Schank (1982) has developed a theory of learning and reminding based on retaining of experience in a dynamic, evolving memory structure. Anderson (1983) has shown that people use past situations or cases as models when learning to solve problems, particularly in early learning. This can be described as a cyclic and integrated process of solving a problem, learning from this experience and solving a new problem.

Then, what is organizational learning? In the first instance it is important to note that organizational learning is different than the sum of individual learning (Cohen and Levinthal, 1990). Organizations represent patterns of interactions among individuals, especially through communication, and therefore learning in organizations to a large extent depends on the ability to share common understandings so as to exploit it (Daft and Weick, 1984). It has been proposed that organizational learning involves at least four phases: information acquisition, information distribution, information interpretation, and information storage in organizational memory, including knowledge retrieval (Huber, 1991).

Barnett (1994) presents a composite of the most common definitions of organizational learning: 'Organizational learning is an experience-based process through which knowledge about action–outcome relationships develops, is encoded in routines, is embedded in organization memory, and changes collective behavior.' In line with this composite definition most strategic management theorists assume that firms, like individuals, learn from their past experience and can transform these experiences to useful knowledge that will make them more competitive in the future (Chandler, 1962; Hamel, 1991; Lyles and Schwenk, 1992). Learning from past experience is enhanced by the availability and analysis of feedback. As a result, organizational learning refers to the development of insights, knowledge and associations between past actions, the effectiveness of those actions and future actions (Fiol and Lyles, 1985). Hence learning is a change in the state of knowledge within the organization. The product of this process is a change of organizational knowledge structures which deal with goals, cause and effect beliefs and other cognitive elements (Lyles and Schwenk, 1992). It is important to note that organizational knowledge structures differ from individual knowledge structures because they are socially constructed and depend on negotiations and consensus among the organizational members (Daft and Weick, 1984).

Finally, how can individual and organizational learning be linked? In line with Crossan and Inkpen (1992), the concept of individual learning should be embedded in the context of group learning, which in turn should be embedded in a concept of organizational learning.

On the individual level, the process of interpreting results in schemata and scripts whereby the latter contain information about particular, frequently occurring events (Schank and Abelson 1977). Through frequent interaction of individuals in groups within the organization a shared belief structure is developed. At top management levels this shared set of schemata has been defined by Prahalad and Bettis (1986) as the dominant logic. The development of such shared belief structures takes place through language and connection of individuals. Organizational learning refers to a process of institutionalizing individual concepts and schemata resulting in organizational knowledge structures. They are socially constructed and rely on consensus and agreement. Weick and Bougon (1986) suggest three stages that organizational members go through when developing organizational knowledge structures: (1) agreement on which concepts capture and abstract their experience; (2) consensus on relations among these concepts; and (3) similarity of view on how these concepts and schemata affect each party. Finally, it should be mentioned that individuals and groups are also influenced by the organizational knowledge structures and vice versa. This is a process of mutual learning where the individual learns about the organizational knowledge structures through socialization and the organization learns from the individual by adapting to individual beliefs and interpretations (March, 1991).

As a conclusion from the previous discussion about individual and organizational learning, we will use the following model to describe the impacts of different learning levels on formation and management of interorganizational cooperation. It should be noted that we have included the relationships between the individuals of the two firms which aim to collaborate because we consider individual relationships as crucial for the formation process. This relationship is outlined in Figure 4.1 and will be discussed in detail in the following section.

Impacts of Individual Learning

To start with, we propose that the basis for formation of interorganizational cooperation is the relationships between organizational members of two firms willing to cooperate. Interorganizational know-how is a multifaceted construct which involves many individuals and stages in the life of a cooperation. In order to describe the importance of individuals in the formation process we refer to Gray's (1989) model of sequence of events in the creation of a multiparty collaboration. We suggest that individual learning takes place in all three stages. The first stage of this process is described as problem setting which is often considered as a pre-formation activity because there are no formal negotiations between companies. Olk and Earley (1995) argue that the typical formation process starts with the efforts of a 'champion', someone who initiates the contact with potential partners. Through individual discussions, individuals from both sides explore informally the potential for cooperation in terms of the objective and structure. This stage is followed by direction setting where the collaboration is formally defined resulting in a contract. This process has been described by Ring and Van de Ven (1994) as 'congruent sense-making activities' among individuals through combining formal negotiations and informal activities. The final stage involves the implementation of the agreement by committing resources to build the cooperative venture. Olk and Earley (1995) argue that this process occurs primarily at an organizational level; however, the contribution of key individuals in this stage can facilitate implementation. We can conclude from this short discussion that the goals and commitment for an interorganizational cooperation start at an individual level and, as the process develops, the weight of the organizational level increases. Therefore, it seems of major

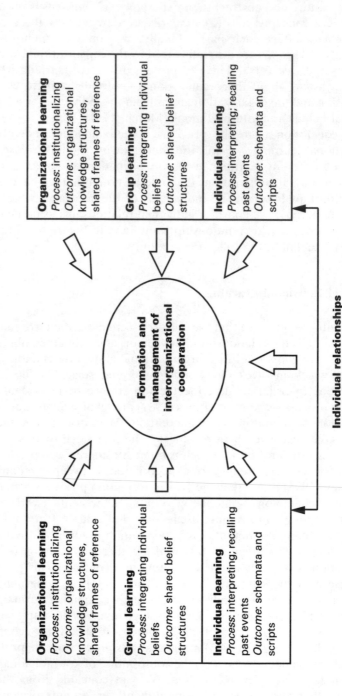

Figure 4.1   *Learning levels influencing formation and management of cooperations*

importance to outline some attributes of individual learning due to the high impact of individual involvement in the formation of collaborations.

Focusing on learning at the individual level we refer back to its characteristics outlined before and propose that experience is one of the most important aspects that impacts the formation and management of collaborations. In the course of engaging and managing a cooperative venture, the individuals involved learn over time how to make these processes more effective and efficient based on their increasing experience. This proposition can be applied to the three-stage model of Gray (1989) outlined above. Individuals learn how to become better at setting problems and directions as well as how to implement new cooperative linkages.

As has been pointed out in the theoretical framework of this chapter, individuals develop cognitive maps and schemata for problem solving. In the case of interorganizational cooperation this would mean that a manager applies a certain logic to enter and manage new cooperative ventures. Confronted with a new problem situation in a cooperative setting, managers will retrieve previous similar cases and then reuse the information and knowledge which can be applied to this specific situation. This will be followed by revising the proposed solution based on reusing previous experiences in cooperative strategies, and retaining the parts of the new experience likely to be useful for future problem solving and decision making. We can conclude that the more prior experience an individual has, the more likely is the existence of schemata for problem solution.

The process of turning individual learning into organizational learning is a major challenge. As we have outlined in Figure 4.1, organizational learning is based on learning at the group level. Crossan and Inkpen (1992) suggest three mechanisms that can promote individual to collective integration. The first is *personal facilitation*, where a leader or influential individual guides the integration of the various schemata to develop a shared understanding. This would mean in a cooperative setting that the key individuals involved in the formation and management would more or less construct a common basis in the organization based on their superior understanding of the situation. The second is *shared facilitation*, where the individuals involved share enough common ground. Through extensive discussions of people involved in collaborations based on trust and respect, a shared understanding is developed on which most organizational members agree. The third is *artifactual faciliation*, where systems and structures of the organizations act as integrating mechanisms. Integration through organizational artifacts can be very effective in cooperative settings. For example, artifactual integration can be achieved through rotation of managers involved in the interorganizational cooperation, regular meetings and discussions of internal teams and partners or senior management involvement in collaborative activities.

From this discussion, we conclude that organizational learning in cooperative settings depends on the extent to which people disseminate their individual learning by discussing, briefing and training others and the extent to which the learning of individuals becomes institutionalized in the organization's rules and routines.

It is important to look back to the previous section where it was argued that organizational learning is not simply the sum of individual learning. This can be due to barriers between individual and organizational learning. One barrier may be that there is a dominance of certain key individuals who 'govern' the learning process in the cooperation. This would result in blocking the process of integrating different individual beliefs and schemata on the organizational level. Therefore, it is important that the views and beliefs of all people involved in the formation and management of the collaboration are considered to develop a shared frame of reference.

Impacts of Organizational Learning

Focusing on organizational learning, we will first outline the activities that are of significance for organizational cooperation. From these activities we can derive several key factors that influence the process of setting up and managing a new cooperation. Finally, we look at the different types of learning and their consequences for this process.

Key Learning Activities

We will now refer to a model of organizational learning adapted from Lyles (1988; 1994) that is partly based on the assumptions on organizational learning discussed in the first section of this chapter. This model helps to address questions like: How do firms learn from collaborations? How does this learning takes place? How does learning affect decisions and actions when entering new interorganizational cooperations?

The model highlights two levels of learning. This conceptual distinction between lower-level learning and higher-level learning is based on the assumption that organizations can learn within a frame of reference, or can develop a new frame of reference. Both levels are closely linked by processes and histories within the organization.

Lower-level learning is the result of repetition and routine. This results in standard operating routines or success programs or in a new management system that handles repetitive, unchanging situations. Higher-level learning refers to an adjustment of overall missions and beliefs and norms. It also involves developing new frames of reference, new skills for problem formulation and solving, new values, unlearning of past success programs as well as enhancing discrimination skills.

From the model shown in Figure 4.2, we can derive four activities in the learning process that are particularly important for the formation and management of interorganizational cooperation. The first is the development of *success programs* which refers to methods and solutions which have been applied in previous situations. Through frequent occurrence of

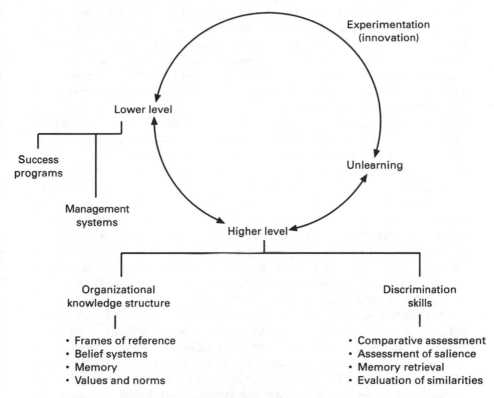

Figure 4.2   *Model of organizational learning*

specific situations, success programs become the standard methods for handling repetitive decisions that result in standard operating procedures. Firms develop success programs over time that define structures, systems, and management processes. For example, standard decisions would refer in general to the type of collaboration chosen or specify the percentage of equity when forming a joint venture. Standard operating procedures can be applied during the whole life-time of a collaboration, including the process of selecting a partner, the process of negotiating, and the process of managing and terminating the cooperation. Success programs can be either formal when they are written down as guidelines or informal when they are commonly understood and followed by managers. We propose that rules and procedures embedded in success programs significantly affect the firm's position and predisposition in going through the structuring and management process of future interorganizational cooperation.

As has been pointed out in the theoretical framework of this chapter, *organizational knowledge* structures include the storage of belief systems, memories of past events, stories, frames of references and values. It is important to note that organizational knowledge structures remain relatively stable over time. They have long-term effects and impact the whole organization, not just in terms of cooperation. Organizational knowledge structures can be considered to be a 'collective system of constructs' based on experiences (Daft and Weick, 1984). Typically, the process for sharing these experiences is through story-telling within the organization, the rules that are developed, and the social construction of meanings of past events (Lyles, 1988). Story-telling about past collaboration and experiences of other firms with cooperative strategies results in a shared belief and value system which influences future actions. For example, one firm tells the story how their partner (a small company with financial problems) went bankrupt, and this resulted in their need either to withdraw or to do business with another partner or to make the partner a wholly-owned subsidiary. The message that was stated was: 'In conclusion the partner should not be too small for us and should be a financially healthy company.' This story conveys rules for the future and also the belief system of the firm. Another example would be that a firm has developed a shared understanding through story-telling in terms of managing a strategic alliance: 'We believe that when forming a strategic alliance we have to specify concrete goals. We all know from our past experience that if we do not have a specific goal the alliance will fail.'

Discrimination skills refer to the ability of an organization to discern differences among situations and to choose different courses of action. A simple example might be how one discriminates between apples and oranges. There are two separate and distinct behaviors for eating each. Both are fruit and both are round. One learns to discriminate based on the difference between them because the colors are different as well as the textures. Over time one learns to discriminate between apples and oranges and to learn the appropriate 'success program' for each. This is a simple example to illustrate that organizations successful at organizational learning may begin to develop discrimination skills that help them to assess the differences among situations in order to identify future actions. Thus, discrimination can be applied to formation and management of interorganizational cooperation when decision rules are used to define the attributes of one cooperative strategy versus another. One firm stated: 'We know that we have to manage cooperations with Asian partners in a different way compared to European. Negotiations and business culture are extremely different there as we have experienced. Therefore, we have to apply a very different management style in Asia.' Experience has given the firm a frame of reference for direction setting about how to form and manage interorganizational cooperations in different countries.

While there has been a focus so far on learning, we propose that *unlearning* is also of major importance . There is a great deal of literature in the field of organizational learning but unlearning is a relatively unexplored concept (Bettis and Prahalad, 1995). When we talk about unlearning we mean that past success programs have to be reframed to fit changing environmental and situational conditions. The process of unlearning is frequently triggered by mistakes, failures, or poor performance. Unlearning results in innovative problem solutions which mean starting with a 'clean sheet of paper'. Under any circumstances unlearning is not an easy thing and, as Bettis and Prahalad (1995) state, some organizations may find it impossible to unlearn at all and may fail. Forgetting the past is especially difficult in the formation and management of interorganizational cooperation. Managers often ignore the fact that past success programs do not always bring the desired 'success' due to specific problem situations. Very often failures of cooperative strategies lead to rethinking the standard methods and procedures when entering a new cooperation. One manager argued in the following way: 'We have formed this joint venture as we have always done. We tried to say that joint ventures have to be structured this way . . . that was the first mistake because things were just different. We also tried to manage it in the way we are used to . . . but the partner was somehow different and did not accept it. It is obvious that we have to rethink our way of handling cooperation now.' This statement clearly underlines that unlearning is a very important issue.

Key Learning Factors

We will now outline some of the key learning factors determining how cooperations are formed and managed based on the previous discussions.

Organization Memory   'Organization memory is stored information from the organization's history that can be brought to bear on present decisions' (Walsh and Ungson, 1991: 61). As has been pointed out in the first section of this chapter the storage of information in organization memory is highly influenced by the social construction of meanings and pattern of retention. It is obvious that the stored information highly influences forming and managing collaborations. It is important to note that organization memory does not always replicate past events in an exact manner. The histories remembered may only be the impression of a specific event. Especially in situations of superstitious learning, firms do not accurately reflect the events.

Commitment to Past Success Programs   We propose that the stronger the reliance on past success programs based on successful cooperations, the more we would expect firms and managers to rely on them for the future. This can be observed when firms and managers search for similar situations/environments for setting up collaborations and structure/manage them in a similar way.

Number of People Involved   Due to the process of social construction of meanings and histories we would argue that the more people are involved in cooperative processes the more this will have impacts on organization memory, past success programs and unlearning. A broad agreement within an organization about past success programs will lead to difficulties in unlearning them and bringing in innovative aspects. On the other hand people bring in new perspectives, and this can be viewed as positive.

Performance of Past Cooperations Performance of past cooperations influences the learning that impacts future formations and management processes significantly. Failures or mistakes are frequent triggers for the evaluation of past success programs and a process of unlearning/innovation may take place. On the other hand, successful performance will lead to an increasing development of standard methods and routines.

Salience The more the interorganizational cooperation is of strategic importance to the core business of the firm, the more the firm will attempt to analyze its past learning and utilize it in the formation and management process. Furthermore, salience can also refer to the risk involved and we propose that the more risk is involved, the more past experiences will be analyzed and then influence future decisions.

Key Concepts of Learning

Focusing on the concept of learning there seem to be three key types that influence the formation and management of organizational cooperation significantly. All rely on sense-making capabilities of the firm which depend on the growing experience and perceptions in cooperative strategies. Firms create meanings by combining experience and new situations. The result is devising rules and stories that guide their decision making in the future.

Learning from Experience This is the process that is most common in which firms rely upon their own collaborative experiences for determining to what extent they will enter interorganizational cooperations and how they will be managed. We suggest a distinction between *recalling* and *remembering* past events in the concept of learning from experience. Recalling should be understood as referring back to a previous event in an active manner while remembering is done in a more passive and unconscious way. Recalling a previous similar situation in an active way and reusing this knowledge and information is frequently applied to new problems in the context of collaboration. This process will increase the collaborative know-how in terms of searching for, negotiating, managing and terminating interorganizational cooperation and will result in more appropriate decisions and formation processes as well as setting more realistic and achievable targets for future collaboration (Simonin and Helleloid, 1993). As has been stated above, remembering past events is a more passive and unconscious process. It refers to the inner set of biases, assumptions, and presuppositions in the organization memory about past collaborations which are applied to future decisions. These deeply encoded lessons from the past may pose a significant danger for organizations. Over time, organizations and individuals may forget why they believe what they believe.

In the context of learning from experience it is also important to refer to the concept of *superstitious learning*. Superstitious learning refers to statements that make broad judgments based on past experience and create new rules of thumb for future strategic decisions (Van de Ven and Lin, 1989). Usually superstitious learning involves a one-time experience that becomes a rule for the future. The concept of superstitious learning also suggests that organizations have processes in which they may not learn *per se* from past experience (March et al., 1991). Hence, one-time experiences may not lead to improved performance but may lead to some changed behavior. For example, the following expression of belief shows how a firm interpreted a one-time experience and this affected future decisions: 'during our first try to form an alliance with a Japanese partner we noticed very fast that we cannot cooperate with Japanese firms. We would rather form fully-owned subsidiaries in Japan.' Another firm said: 'There were two partners in the JV and we changed the JV into a public company on a voluntary basis. We will avoid doing that as much as we can for the future.'

Learning from Imitation   Learning from imitation incorporates aspects of learning from instruction of others, copying of other firms or simply vicarious learning. The concept and importance of 'imitation' has been discussed in depth in Chapter 2 of this volume. It is common that organizations attempt to learn about the strategies, administrative practices and technologies of other organizations. Possible channels for acquiring such information are consultants, conferences, publications and professional networks. However, it has to be considered that each interorganizational cooperation is set within a context of particular organizations, each with its own values, beliefs, systems and routines which govern the way in which the organizations act. Therefore, knowledge about cooperative ventures obtained from external sources may be of no significant value for a specific firm when it cannot be internalized and applied to a specific situation. Simonin and Helleloid (1993) argue that firms with greater experience in interorganizational cooperation are in a better position to recognize differences between their own situations and those of other firms. As a result, they state that firms with greater collaborative experience are able to make better use of vicarious learning modes and imitating other firms' cooperative strategies. However, this does not mean that inexperienced firms are not able to learn from instruction and imitation of others. There is a definite need to hear the stories of more experienced firms and to use these stories and information to form a knowledge basis for making future decisions within their own firm.

Learning from Experimentation   Improvisation, innovation and experimentation are also ways of learning in organizational settings but it is very difficult to find examples of a truly new and experimental attitude being taken when forming or managing new interorganizational cooperations. In general, one can say that firms would generalize from the past to the future and they would make these past experiences 'fit' the future. Nevertheless, it should be pointed out that there is a trend towards considering especially strategic alliances as experiments. This development is also discussed in Chapter 9 in this book.

Having outlined these various processes or approaches to learning, we can now conclude the following that may help to understand the terms of forming and managing a cooperation in the context of organizational learning:

1 Organizational learning requires individual learning by single members involved in cooperative arrangements.
2 Past experiences of firms and managers have significant impacts on management and formation of cooperative linkages and are used as learning events.
3 Memories are not necessarily grounded in realities (superstitious learning) and there may be more than one memory about a single learning event.
4 Organizations show strong tendencies towards generalizations in co-operative arrangements.
5 Following past success programs may be very 'unsuccessful' in certain cooperative situations and therefore it is important that organizations develop skills to unlearn these standard methods.
6 Developing discrimination skills is a key success factor for organizations involved in cooperations.
7 Learning by improvisation, experimentation and innovation is rare because there are strong pressures that keep pushing back directions to 'what is known'.

Implications for Practice

We have shown that individual and organizational learning provide viable evolution models for forming and managing cooperation between firms. Based on the previous discussions we want to highlight several implications for practice. The central issue to be addressed is how organizations can learn to learn, or alternatively stated, how firms can learn to become better 'cooperators' in terms of forming and managing cooperative linkages.

First, it is essential that firms and individuals develop an intent or desire to learn. This is the crucial factor for the learning process. The more awareness exists in the organization and among individuals for learning, the more effectively past experience will be analyzed and utilized. It is also important to provide time for continuous discussions among individuals involved in the formation and management process to develop a shared frame of reference. The more people are involved in the discussions, the more collaborative know-how will be developed. These discussions should also take place in all stages of the cooperation between the partner firms. Even when the cooperation is terminated both parties should reflect and review the problems and successful events in order to enhance their learning process for future cooperations.

The situational context of a new cooperative linkage needs a very careful and reflective assessment. This is of major importance because it will determine whether firms can use past success programs or whether they have to respond in an innovative way. The critical question to be addressed is: what parts of our past experience can we use for future cooperations and what parts of this experience represent excess baggage? Therefore, the new situations should be assessed by using factors such as objectives of the cooperation (market entry and development, learning, sharing of resources), type of the cooperation (joint venture, strategic alliances), characteristics of partner (size, turnover, employees), cultural differences (national and international cooperation, corporate culture). Reflecting on the new cooperation by using these factors will give insights into how the firm should approach and manage the new cooperative linkage. It is essential to point out that firms should never solely rely on past success programs. Every cooperation is different from past cases and due to this fact organizations should rethink their past success programs in order to succeed in a new cooperative linkage.

It is also important that organizations are not trapped by success. If a firm has been very successful in cooperating with other firms it should always be aware that every new cooperation is distinct and that things may go extremely wrong when applying the standard methods and procedures without questioning their applicability.

Finally, we can summarize the thoughts above and develop a framework that might enable firms to learn more effectively from collaborations.

1 In the first instance, firms should introduce learning visions for cooperative arrangements. These learning visions could be specified for every single cooperative linkage. The purpose of such learning visions is to guide and motivate individuals in the organization to active learning processes.

2 Secondly, it is important to identify collaborative champions in the organizations who are willing to learn. These collaborative champions should set their own learning targets in terms of managing and forming a new strategic alliance or joint venture. Learning targets could be: what are the key success factors in managing this specific cooperation? How can the firm generalize this experience and apply it to new cooperative arrangements? What are the things that we could have done better? Why did the formation and management process of this cooperative linkage turn out to be successful or unsuccessful? In all stages of the cooperation the collaborative champions should reflect on

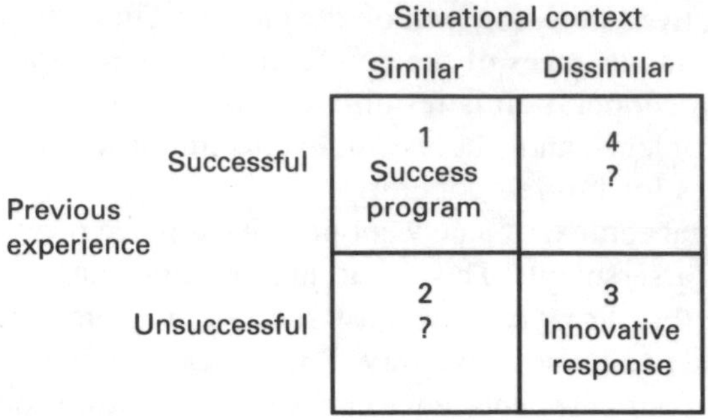

Situational context

		Similar	Dissimilar
Previous experience	Successful	1 Success program	4 ?
	Unsuccessful	2 ?	3 Innovative response

Figure 4.3   *Research issues*

their learning targets in order to develop new insights for effective cooperations in the future.

3 The collaborative champions should bring their experiences and new insights into what we would call a learning arena where they discuss and exchange stories with other members involved in forming and managing interorganizational cooperations. This will enhance the development of discrimination skills.

4 This pool of collaborative experts should be used to undertake new cooperative arrangements. However, before entering a new strategic alliance or joint venture the team of collaborative experts should set its own learning goals and align these with the corporate strategy.

Using this simple four-step approach, effective organizational learning will occur.

Implications for Future Research

The empirical work on organizational learning in interorganizational cooperation mainly focuses on how firms can learn to develop skills through cooperation with other firms that can be used to enhance the competitive advantage of both firms. This chapter has focused on the impact of individual and organizational learning in the formation process and the management of cooperative linkages. The learning concepts which have been discussed provide an interpretative framework within which future decisions can be tied to the past. Still there are several research issues focusing on factors that affect learning skills and the decision process. Figure 4.3 outlines the situational context and its predictability in terms of future decisions.

If the new cooperative setting is similar to past situations and the previous experience was successful, it is most likely that the firm will apply past success programs. If it is dissimilar and the past experience was unsuccessful, then the firm has to respond in an innovative/experimental way. Yet it is cells 2 and 4 that appear to be most interesting for future research. It should be very interesting to study whether firms follow past success programs or innovative responses in these cases. Firms may think that they recognize similarities and force situations into being defined as similar in order to utilize proven success programs. We propose that it will depend on the managers' perception of which aspects of the situation are most important and the degree of sameness or similarity. Bowman and Hurry (1993) suggest that learning from past events does not make its way to future action. The use of the figure may be helpful to explore in which areas they are correct.

Furthermore, there are several future research questions that can be addressed. What are the learning biases cross-culturally at the individual and organizational levels and how do these impact what is learned from interorganizational cooperations? Or alternatively, does experience in managing cooperative ventures in a firm's home country provide advantages when entering a collaboration with a foreign partner organization? Does learning from experience with specific types of organizations (universities, research institutes, government agencies) enhance the cooperation with other organizations? If there exists experience in a certain area of interorganizational cooperation (e.g. research and development or marketing and distribution), does this experience help in managing cooperative linkages in other business functions (e.g. production)? When does the organization need to develop new discrimination skills? At what point and how does the firm develop the skill of knowing that past success programs and previous discrimination rules are no longer relevant? How can learning on the individual level be best transferred to the organizational level? What are the methods for firms to unlearn? How can firms manage stories to enhance their learning from past cooperative arrangements? How can managers and groups be trained to effectively learn from collaboration?

References

Anderson, J.R. (1983). *The Architecture of Cognition*. Cambridge, MA: Harvard University Press.

Barnett, C.K. (1994). Organizational learning theories: a review and synthesis of the literature. *Academy of Management*, manuscript submitted for publication.

Bettis, R.A. and Prahalad, C.K. (1995). The dominant logic: retrospective and extension. *Strategic Management Journal*, 16: 5–14.

Bower, G.H. and Hilgard, E.R. (1981). *Theories of Learning*. Englewood Cliffs, NJ: Prentice-Hall.

Bowman, E.H. and Hurry, D. (1993). Strategy through the option lens: an integrated view of resource investments and the incremental-choice process. *Academy of Management Review*, 18(4): 760–82.

Chandler, A. (1962). *Strategy and Structure*. Cambridge, MA: MIT Press.

Cohen, W.M. and Levinthal, D.A. (1990). Absorptive capacity: a new perspective on learning and innovation. *Administrative Science Quarterly*, 35(1): 128–52.

Crossan, M. and Inkpen, A. (1992). Believing is seeing: an exploration of the organization learning concept and evidence from the case of joint venture learning. Working Paper, Western Business School, University of Western Ontario.

Daft, R.L. and Weick, K.E. (1984). Towards a model of organizations as interpretative systems. *Academy of Management Review*, 9(2): 284–95.

Fiol, C.M. (1994). Consensus, diversity, and learning in organizations. *Organization Science*, 5(3): 403–20.

Fiol, C.M. and Lyles, M.A. (1985). Organizational learning. *Academy of Management Review*, 10: 803–13.

Friedlander, F. (1983). Patterns of individual and organizational learning. In S. Shrivastava and Associates (eds), *Structure of Decision*. Princeton, NJ: Princeton University Press.

Gray, B. (1989). *Collaborating: Finding Common Ground for Multiparty Problems*. San Francisco: Jossey-Bass.

Hamel, G. (1991). Competition for competence and inter-partner learning within international strategic alliances. *Strategic Management Journal*, 12 (Special Issue): 83–104.

Huber, G.P. (1991). Organizational learning: the contributing processes and the literatures. *Organization Science*, 2(1): 88–115.

Lindsay, P.H. and Norman, D.A. (1977). *Human Information Processing*. Orlando, FL: Academic Press.

Lorange, P. and Roos, J. (1992). *Strategic Alliances: Formation, Implementation and Evolution*. Cambridge, MA: Blackwell.

Lyles, M.A. (1988). Learning among joint venture sophisticated firms. *Management International Review*, Special Issue: 85–96.

Lyles, M.A. (1991). Parental desire for control of joint ventures: a case study of an international joint venture. *Advances in Strategic Management*, 7: 185–208.

Lyles, M.A (1994). The impact of organizational learning on joint venture formations. *International Business Review*, 3(4): 459–67.

Lyles, M.A. and Schwenk C.R. (1992). Top management, strategy and organizational knowledge structures. *Journal of Management Studies*, 29(2): 155–74.

March, J.G. (1991). Exploration and exploitation in organizational learning. *Organization Science*, 2(1): 71–85.

March, J.G. Sproull, C.S. and Tamuz, M. (1991). Learning from samples of one or fewer. *Organization Science*, 2(1): 1–13.

Olk, P. and Earley P.C. (1995). Individual-level influences in the design of international joint ventures. Working Paper, University of California at Irvine.

Prahalad, C.K. and Bettis, R.H. (1986). The dominant logic: a new linkage between diversity and performance. *Strategic Management Journal*, 7: 485–501.

Ring, P. and Van de Ven, A. (1994). Developmental processes of cooperative interorganizational relationships. *Academy of Management Review*, 19: 90–118.

Ross, B.H. (1989). Some psychological results on case-based reasoning. Paper presented at Case-Based Reasoning Workshop, DAPRA 1989, Pensacola Beach, Morgan Kaufmann.

Schank, R.C. (1982). *Dynamic Memory: a Theory of Reminding and Learning in Computers and People*. Cambridge: Cambridge University Press.

Schank, R.C. and Abelson, R.P. (1977). *Scripts, Plans, Goals, and Understanding: an Inquiry into Human Knowledge Systems*. Hillsdale, NJ: Erlbaum.

Simonin, B.L. and Helleloid, D. (1993). Do organizations learn? An empirical test of organizational learning in international strategic alliances. Paper prepared for the Academy of Management Best Papers Proceedings, 53rd Annual Meeting, Atlanta, Georgia, 8–11 August.

Van de Ven, A.H. and Lin, T. (1989). Rational and superstitious learning in the temporal development of innovation. Paper prepared for the Conference on Organizational Learning, Carnegie-Mellon University, Pittsburgh, PA, 18–20 May.

Walsh, J.P. and Ungson, G.R. (1991). Organization memory. *Academy of Management Review*, 16(1): 57–91.

Weick, K.E. and Bougon, M.G. (1986). Organizations as cognitive maps: charting ways to success and failure. In H. Sims Jr and D. Gioia (eds), *The Thinking Organization*, San Francisco: Jossey-Bass.

5

Arguments on Knowledge and Competence

Georg von Krogh and Johan Roos

In a recent article the prominent author Peter Drucker elaborated on the enormous social transformations taking place during this century. One manifestation surfaced as particularly important: an economic and social order in which knowledge, not labor, raw material or capital, is the most important resource for individuals, business, governments, nations, and society at large (Drucker, 1994). Therefore, it is not surprising that many authors within the realms of management, as well as practicing managers, have addressed the relative importance of knowledge in business. Some have argued that knowledge-based business enjoys increasing returns, not decreasing returns, which is the lens through which conventional economics views the world (Arthur, 1990). Some even predict a bifurcation point where traditional economic and social thoughts and actions break down into, hopefully, new economic ('bionomic') and social thoughts and actions (Henderson, 1990). On the business scale, it has been argued by Stinchcombe (1986) that the 'crude power' of the classical source of competitive advantage, low cost, needs to make room for knowledge as the key source of such advantages. The point is that firms increasingly compete on a differentiated, difficult to imitate knowledge, which allows them to conceive of and implement strategies not simultaneously conceived of and implemented by other firms in an industry. Thus, it is not surprising that the three domains of knowledge, competence and competitive advantage have aroused much interest both in academia and in practice (see, for instance, Nonaka, 1991; Hamel and Prahalad, 1990; 1994; Barney, 1991, and von Krogh and Roos, 1995). This is also the background to our study.

Despite the recent resurgence of attention to these factors, stemming from the revival of the 'resource-based perspective' of the firm, the conceptualization and the relationship among these concepts still remains rather unclear. In fact, the whole area of 'competence-based competition' can be characterized as a melting-pot of ideas, disagreements, concepts, buzzwords and suggested causal relationships. *Unique resources* are particular types of resources that are often referred to in the strategic management literature. Such resources are discussed under a variety of names, including 'distinctive competencies', 'invisible assets', 'core competencies', 'core capabilities', 'internal capabilities', 'skill and capability accumulation', 'embedded knowledge', 'absorptive capacity', 'underlying capabilities', 'unique combinations of business experience', 'corporate culture', 'valuable heuristics and processes', and 'unique managerial talent'. In a recent debate in the *Harvard Business Review* (1992), involving practicing managers, consultants, and academic scholars, regarding the meaning of the terms 'core competence' and 'capabilities', one letter suggested that there were no real differences, only a question of semantics, whereas others argued the opposite.

Although much importance has been placed on competencies in the literature, the concept of competencies seems, even in the academic literature, to be *used similarly to the way it is used in our daily speech*: to code a broad range of our experiences related to craftsmanship, specialization, intelligence, and problem solving. Thus, the starting point of this chapter is that competence remains an experience-near concept (see Geertz, 1973) that needs further conceptual clarification if it is to serve the purpose of either theory building or managerial practice.

Given this conceptual uncertainty, *the primary purpose of this chapter is to investigate what are some of the underlying dimensions of competence*. Seeing the world as being socially constructed (Berger and Luckmann, 1967), we believe that there is no single conception of one set of underlying dimensions of competence. The ambition of this chapter is to uncover an underlying logic of espoused concepts and theories pertaining to competence, held by some practicing experts.

Our approach is an empirical one. We have chosen to study competence from a human resource managers' perspective, as we believe that this group of managers has had an especially important role in formal competency development in corporations. Because we have been using a relatively unusual method in our quest to uncover the way these managers reason, we begin by explaining how we actually arrived at our findings. After presenting our findings we discuss their implications.

What We Did

Please remember that this study set out to uncover the underlying logic of espoused concepts and theories held by some practicing experts pertaining to competence. We do *not* aim to discover any form of omnipotent truth about the subject matter.

We chose to study an informal group of Scandinavian human resource managers (HRMs), called Group-10. This is a group formed by the HRMs for the purpose of discussing and refining ideas about managing human resources. After observing some of these group discussions, it was noticed that these managers held and actively applied their individual concepts of competitive advantage, company knowledge, individual competence, critical competence, and core competence. The use of these concepts seemed often internally inconsistent, in the sense that a coherent framework for their application did not seem to exist. The words seem to change meaning, and different words, which at one point seemed to complement each other, were at other times used as synonyms. Nevertheless, the managers' examples, drawn from everyday situations, indicated that these concepts somehow informed their interpretation of various organizational events. We assumed that the managers held their own (partly espoused, partly embedded) theories, and that these theories, if uncovered, could serve the purpose of further theorizing.

Thus, we decided to interview each of these HRMs individually. All the respondents of this study are classified as practicing experts (see Chi et al., 1988) in the sense that they: (1) currently perform human resource management functions at the formal level of vice-president, a position they have acquired as a result of outstanding performance; (2) have acquired more than 10 years of experience in human resource management, which qualifies them as experts at least in their own organizations; (3) are involved in strategic planning activities in their respective companies, pertaining to the training and recruitment of personnel; and (4) at a general level have demonstrated knowledge of the subject matter of this study.

During the interviews, the concept of competence naturally appeared as messy and the word seemed to take on varying meanings from context to context. The mixed use often resulted in what may seem to be a paradoxical phenomenon. For example, one executive suggested that competencies always are unique, while in another passage he claimed that the value of competencies depends on how common they are in a market.

In everyday speech competence seems to be used as an attribute of other phenomena such as knowledge or skills. It may be used to describe how good people are at doing their jobs, or how an organization solves a problem with quality costs. Moreover, the competence concept is often linked to business functions, for example, financial competence, technology competence, insurance competence, or construction competence. Although competence appears as a blurred and holistic concept, it is both populist and fashionable.

The competence concept also serves an analytical function. For example, the second executive had formally identified the competencies of his organization and gathered information about them: where they were located, their availability, and their current use. In this context, competence acquires a precise and formal definition, sometimes even quoted from books. Formally defining competencies involves different levels of detail and reflection in order to operationalize them. The analytical usage of the competence concept also has its place in the strategy definitions of firms. For example, the firm of one of the executives had gone through a process of operationalizing the competence concept in order to make it a basis for decisions about the firm's strategy.

A problem with effective discovery of theories held by practicing experts, however, lies in experts' inability, and/or lack of will, to directly describe their knowledge and how they use it.[1] As seen later, this problem suggests that particular care must be exercised in data collection and analysis, and that the method of analysis must be designed in such a way as to allow for the discovery of embedded knowledge.

In the attempt to uncover the HRMs' local theories the *number of cases* was not as important as the *relevance of the data* for the emerging concepts and their properties.[2] We managed to interview seven of the ten HRMs. These managers were similar with respect to their functions, yet they differ on many other variables: their experiences are gained from various industries and within firms of various sizes and performance levels, their education varies, etc. On the one hand, the similarities mentioned made it easier to discover concepts and the relationships relevant to the substantive area under study. On the other hand, the lack of differences created a limitation as to the generalizability of the concepts and relationships discovered.[3]

Data were collected in three stages. The first stage was observing group discussions where the relevance of some general concepts was established. The concepts of knowledge, competence, and competitive advantage were frequent themes brought up by participants in the group discussions. The second stage was a semi-structured questionnaire in which the practicing experts were asked to present a written argument for or against viewing knowledge as part of competence, and moreover, for or against competence as being a factor in creating competitive advantage. This part confirmed that the practicing experts found the three general concepts meaningful, but the arguments presented did not uncover much of their theories. The third stage of data collection consisted of a two to four hour semi-structured interview with the seven practicing experts in their natural environments.

The data collection and analysis from the third phase of the research raised the following question: how does a non-expert make sense of expert knowledge?[4] This problem pertains to the lack of understanding of the content of the experts' speech. It has been documented that experts often define fuzzy boundaries between concepts (Chi et al., 1988). The interviewer often needed additional clarifying questions to control for this effect.

Another problem of accessing expert knowledge resides in the lack of distinctions and concepts that respondents can use to communicate their experiences. Researchers have observed that the use of metaphors may substitute for the lack of a precise language and still communicate complex meanings effectively. The expert's extensive use of metaphors *could* indicate the lack of a conceptual scheme for describing a phenomenon, and, yet, it *could* be a conscious strategy for describing a complex phenomenon to someone not familiar with it.

A third problem of accessing expert knowledge pertains to the novice's lack of familiarity with the expert's form of speech. Expert knowledge is often associated with a particular form of speech that is distinct from more daily forms of speech rooted in everyday knowledge.[5] For example, words and sentences acquire multiple meanings; there are unspoken rules about which questions to ask, when to ask them, and by whom; a process of argument may be organized according to certain rules (for instance those of logic). The form of speech may also convey meaning in a silent, but highly effective, way.

The data collection in the third phase was designed to overcome the first and the third problems of knowledge access. The experts were asked to elaborate on their understanding of knowledge, competence, and competitive advantage, and the possible relationships between these concepts. Moreover, the semi-structured interview was designed on the format of a standard argument composed of claims, warrants, and grounds (Toulmin, 1958). By asking the experts to state the grounds for their claims[6] the study attempted to avoid the form-of-speech problem.

The data analysis phase consisted of two steps, *argument mapping* and *comparative analysis*. The mapping process involved the interviewer together with a second person, who did not attend the interview but served the role of an interpreter. Argument mapping is a way to capture and represent various chunks of knowledge which are conveyed in writing or speech.[7] Holding that the domain of argument, which is that of the credible, plausible and probable, is the domain on which decision makers ground their decisions, we tie argument mapping to *interviews*. Applied in this way argument mapping becomes a method to understand the interview object's underlying mental dimensions pertaining to the theme in focus – competence.

The technique uncovers the logical structures in what may instantly seem to be complex and messy speech. Usually, mapped arguments are of a monological kind, i.e. letters to shareholders, reports from the CEO and president, annual reports, etc. Interviews are different from monologues. The form of speech may change; the feelings will be more spontaneous and may influence the claims and their grounds. Moreover, in the dialogue, arguments are subject to consent as well as to counter-arguments. This 'living nature' of interviews raised certain methodological concerns. For example, it was imperative to the validity of the data collection that the interviewer never counter-argued. Instead he was constrained to just ask for elaborations and clarification of the arguments presented.

In applying the argument mapping technique this study used the following analytical categories: key claims, grounds, subclaims, warrants, qualifiers, disqualifiers, rebuttals, reiterations, elaborations, and metaphors.[8] The logic of the method is that an argument can be broken down into four major components:[9]

- the key claim, or conclusion of an argument
- the data or ground offered to support the claim
- the warrants, which show in what way the data support the claim
- the qualifiers, which refer to possible limitations of claims.

The analytical process involved the following specific steps. First of all, the interview was analyzed with regard to content and sorted into topic blocks. This analysis was facilitated by the interview guide. Then the argument's *key claims* were identified. The most important data for theory building are the claims and the subclaims because this is where the theories of the interviewed executives appear. For instance, one executive suggested that: 'Competence is how you use knowledge to reach a solution to a specific problem.'

This is a claim, and it defines the executive's concept of competence. The key claim is different from the other claims that may be present in an argument, in the way that the key claim represents the main conclusion of the argument. Often the key claim was identified along with a series of *subclaims*, that dampened, complemented or amplified the key claims. Some claims were *definitive*, in the sense of defining the characteristics of a concept; some were *evaluative*, in the sense of assigning value to the concept; others were *designative*, in the sense of establishing the existence of a concept; and others were *advocative*, in the sense of advocating a course of action. Designative and definitive claims contributed to identify concepts and their interrelationships. Advocative and evaluative claims were especially helpful in understanding how the human resource managers viewed the importance of the concepts and which actions they saw as appropriate.

Next, the *grounds*, if any, for the key claims and subclaims were identified, in a sense as giving substance to the argument. The grounds of the argument may be considered the evidence for a theory in claim. Most of the claims were grounded, often by examples, common knowledge, or data. For example, one executive suggested that: 'For competitive advantage, competence is the most important factor.'

As a ground for this claim, the executive gave the example of how battles for a contract in the Scandinavian construction market are decided on the relative competence exhibited by competitors in the market.

Still, many of the arguments concealed a third category, namely *warrants*, which linked the claim with the grounds. A warrant may be considered the method whereby the executive links the theory with the grounds. For example, in one case an executive suggested that: 'Competitive advantage stems from staying close to the customer with important knowledge.' The ground, described in the last paragraph, is an example using the small Norwegian market, while the warrant is expressed as: 'You must not lose a customer in [a small market, as a result of lack of knowledge] . . . because all customers would get to know [of your failure, due to very few players]'. The Norwegian situation is in this respect a bit particular. The last sentence serves as a rebuttal.

The study also identified passages of the speech that were called qualifiers and disqualifiers, which serve the purpose of modifying our, as well as the respondent's, belief in the claim. A disqualified theory in claim was not included in the further theory building, as a general rule. A qualifier, however, strengthened the position of the theory in claim.

In addition to these four analytical tools the following additional categories were applied in the analysis of the arguments. *Rebuttals* often accompanied the claims in an argument. This analytical category was assigned to statements specifying the conditions under which the claim might or might not be valid. *Reiterations* captured recurring claims and subclaims in the argument, while elaboration was used to identify the respondent's clarification, i.e. by way of examples of parts of the argument. The identification of *metaphors* was introduced in order to capture the fact that the experts may extensively use metaphors to convey their messages. Metaphors occurring in the transcripts of the speech were coded and treated as indications of additional explanation and/or lack of concepts. When the theories were based on metaphors, they did not immediately provide the concepts and their relationships. They were treated as elaborations, as illustrations of a particular phenomenon, or as an indication of uncertain knowledge – a stumbling search for meaning.

The comparative analysis was constantly done, simultaneously with the mapping process. When the argument maps were internally compared, concepts were formed on a case-by-case basis. In this process the concepts were enriched, discarded, or changed as new data were connected to the identified concept. The result of this work was a list of concepts and their relationships. Concepts were grouped together into more comprehensive concepts (labeled by us) so as to form a consistent whole. At this stage the managers' local theories began to emerge from the data.[10]

What We Found

The comparative analysis generated a number of concepts and theories which are grouped under the following labels: the competence concept; the competence interplay; and effectiveness of competence application.

The Competence Concept

Based on the concepts and theories in the claims presented, it appeared that this group of managers conceptualized competence as composed of (1) knowledge, (2) experience, (3) attitudes, and (4) the exhibited personal characteristics of an individual. This is depicted in Figure 5.1.

All seven executives argued that knowledge was a part of competence, but that competence, unlike knowledge, implies *enactment*. While knowledge is about specific insights regarding a particular topic, competence is about the skill to carry out work.

As a part of their competence, a person has a particular attitude towards the task to be solved. This attitude, positive or negative, affects the end result of the work. A person is said to be incompetent if she does not show the right attitude. Finally, personal characteristics (i.e. a winning smile)

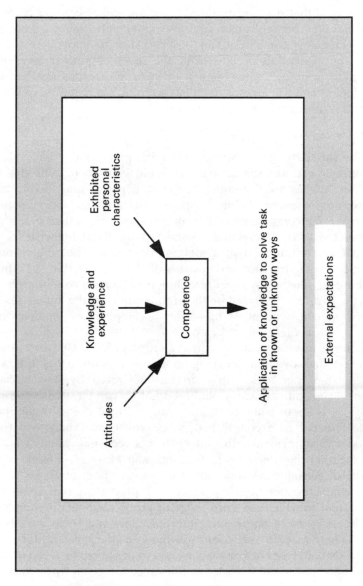

Figure 5.1 *The competence concept*

and skills must also fit the task in question. For instance, one of the executives stated: 'There are tasks where the personal characteristics are of a particular importance, for example in service and sales work, that is, tasks where you have to have interest in relationships with customers to perform well.'

We observed that one constraint to the competence concept seemed to be the social environment's expectations to task performance. In order to judge a person as competent, an observer has to appreciate the task solution, the resolution process, and the level of performance of the implemented solution. Thus 'What actually is competence?' remains context dependent. The questions 'What is the task at hand?' and 'Who are the potential observers?' need answers.

Competence Interplay

A question raised by the executives in the first phase of the data collection was whether there was something that could be named 'collective competence' or 'higher-level' competence (i.e. departmental, divisional, or corporate competence). While mapping the managers arguments, it became clear that competence, if not further specified, in their perspective, was connected to the individual. When talking about higher-level competence, it was often used in a metaphorical sense, i.e. organizational competence *is* the structure and systems of the organization.[11] If there is such a thing as collective competence, however, certain conditions have to be met (see Figure 5.2). Based on the argument maps, the human resource managers' mental concept of higher-level competence[12] emerges *as an interplay of individual competencies.*[13]

Competence interplay can be seen as a group process, characterized by a set of fixed and dynamic working modes and patterns of interaction between group members. This can be illustrated by one manager's statement: 'The ability to carry out and organize complicated construction projects . . . is about connecting a myriad of single events in an optimal fashion. [This is best accomplished] when you have experiences from a couple of similar incidents, the interplay between individuals who have worked together on similar projects earlier and who have a mode of work and a way of getting work done that functions without obstacles.'

Other characteristics of competence interplay are group composition and the extent to which the knowledge of group members is complementary or overlapping. Competence interplay does not seem unrestricted, however. There may be restrictions to what knowledge is relevant to share in a group. Not all types of knowledge need to be shared between members of a group and criteria of knowledge relevance are given by the task to be performed.

Organizational structure makes the identification, formation, and implementation of groups possible. From the data we may also induce that too much hierarchy may be detrimental to the emergence of collective competence. Further speculation leads us to suggest that self-organized

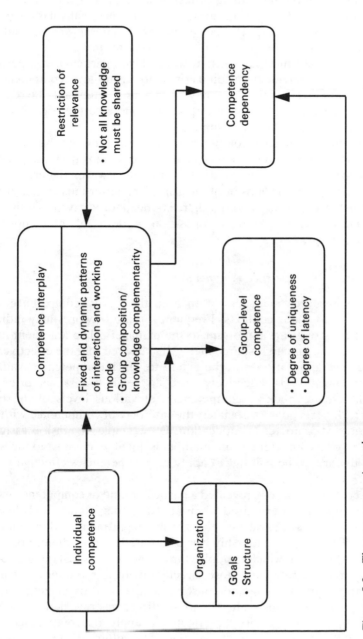

Figure 5.2   *The competence interplay*

groups may positively influence the emergence of collective competence. Such groups are autonomous with respect to job design, the distribution of roles, and parts of the scheduling of task resolution. Organizational goals give a criterion to judge if the group-level competence really has emerged. This is analogous to the expectations of the external observer when judging whether a person is competent or not at solving his tasks.

Since competence interplay is characterized by a particular composition of competencies, individuals become critical for group-level competence to emerge. Group-level competence may be seen as a potential to be realized to solve the task at hand. This interplay may increase the organization's dependency on key individual competencies.

The concept of collective competence that finally emerges has a certain degree of uniqueness and latency. The uniqueness stems from the patterns of interaction and work modes and relates to groups within the firm and, in some instances, other groups in other firms. The latter means that group-level competence may be evoked if there is a need for it, given that the task at hand permits earlier group composition, patterns of interaction and work modes to prevail.

Effectiveness of Competence Application

The human resource managers often used the words 'competence' and 'application' in various contexts. Frequency in use of words may indicate that these constructs are important to the managers. The argument maps indicates that the human resource managers believed that the effectiveness of competence application, i.e. the extent to which competence available in the organization is effectively used to solve a task, is primarily dependent on the stock of competencies at various levels of the firm. Moreover, the executives associated the interplay of competence with the effectiveness of competence application. For example, if a task is assigned to a group, but a competent group member is not able to adjust to the work mode of the group, he will fail to apply his competencies effectively (see Figure 5.3).

The executives indirectly revealed a particular kind of competence which referred to leadership exercised when applying competence. This leadership is found at various levels: the group, departmental, divisional, or corporate. This kind of leadership was elaborated in three dimensions: the delegation of tasks on which to apply competencies, personal integrity, and the ability to cooperate with those directly involved in the task at hand.

From argument mapping and constant comparison, organizational culture, composed of norms, values, and practices, was revealed as grounds for an organization's ability to effectively apply its competence. For example one of the executives stated that: 'The culture in our firm implies that . . . [our organizational members] . . . can do things that are not possible in other firms.' Thus, it appeared that these managers held that organizational culture allows competencies to be applied effectively if an

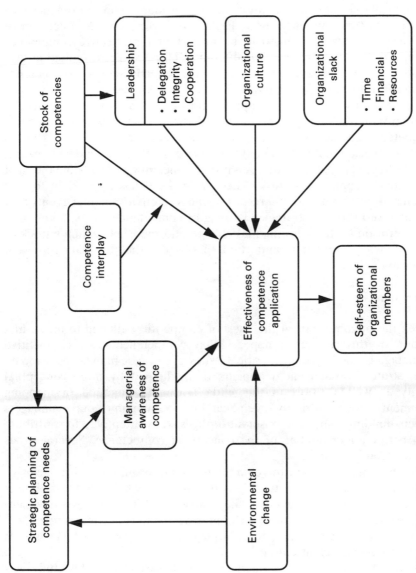

Figure 5.3   *Effectiveness of competence application*

individual's values, norms and practices are in accordance with those of the organization.

The managers' arguments reflected a truism that some people work better as the time available becomes increasingly scarce, while others tend to increase their stress level and perform worse, as illustrated by this quote: 'Time available for task resolution varies considerably in our organization and in turn time influences how the task is performed.' Another sort of organizational slack assumed to be important for effective competence application is finances. The available financial resources exploited in task resolution were believed to influence the effectiveness of competence application for the task at hand. For example, an investment in laboratory equipment may considerably improve the work of a group of scientists.

Environmental changes are believed to strongly influence effective competence application. In particular, the executives here referred to the market situation and tasks linked with it (i.e. sales, product development, etc.). Effectiveness thus acquires a broader meaning of just being the right competence applied to a task. The task in itself has to be right for the organization. Organizational responsiveness to environmental events may be enhanced through strategic planning of competence needs, taking into consideration both environmental change and the organization's stock of competencies. Here it is important to observe that the data represent advocative claims.

Discussion

Given the ongoing shift in the basis of competition alluded to in the first section of this chapter it appears that competence-based competitive advantage is one of the most critical issues in strategic management today. Still, strategic management appears to be helped by more conceptual clarity as well as tools to this end. Through a method of mapping arguments brought forth by seven Scandinavian human resource managers in personal interviews and observations this study attempted to contribute to a better understanding of the concept of competence. Several issues surface from this study.

The findings show that the competence concept may be more inclusive than seen in previous literature: in addition to knowledge and tasks it may include attitudes and personal characteristics. Moreover, we have uncovered what might be a process from individual to collective competence, i.e. what we labeled competence interplay. This is an issue we feel deserves much more research attention.[14]

A major concern among managers which surfaced in this study was the issue of *effectiveness* in competence application, which seems to be influenced by a multitude of rational, political, cognitive and behavioral dimensions. To study the effectiveness of competence application means studying how value for the company is created. In turn, this means studying how resources, competencies and environmental influences interact over time. To understand a firm's value creating process, potentially resulting in competitive advantages, one might need to begin with understanding the competencies of the firm and then the application of these competencies to various tasks.

To reiterate, please note that we have *not* attempted to map any generic truth about competencies. Rather, we have attempted to map the truth of these experts espoused in conversations, reiterating McCloskey's (1985) statement that 'good science is good conversation.' To approach any formal theory, many more data extending beyond the substantive area are needed. Thus, a next research effort might be to study a large group, addressing the issues surfacing in this as in other studies.

Perhaps a first step to a further investigation of the competence concept could be a processual analysis of how performance varies over time. At this point, time series seem to be a promising alternative. Perhaps methods of participant observation also will reveal (real time) how competencies evolve and how they shape performance. The advantage of studying competencies by participant observation is that the observation does not have to rely on an incomplete organizational memory. A disadvantage, however, is the common weakness of qualitative methods: problems of external validity.

All in all, the present study has shown both that *competence* is a multidimensional concept and that the relationship between knowledge, competence and competitive advantage is a complex one. More precisely, we have uncovered theories of experts that may form the building blocks of their own 'competence-based perspective' of their firms, that is distinct from both their environment-based and their resource-based perspectives.

Notes

1 Stubbart and Ramaprasad (1990). The knowledge of the practicing expert is often embedded and hidden from empirical investigation, in the sense that it has not been thematized in language (Schutz and Luckmann, 1973). See also Nonaka (1991) for a review of two forms of knowledge: tacit and explicit. The notion of tacit knowledge has its roots in the philosophy of Michael Polanyi (1962). The difference between his work and that of Schutz to a great extent resides in the problem of making embedded knowledge articulated or thematized.

2 This is excellently illustrated by Mintzberg's (1973) observations of five managers at work.

3 It was important to provide simultaneous maximization or minimization of both the differences and the similarities of data that bear on the categories being studied. See Glaser and Strauss (1967: 55).

4 Although strategy researchers have a fair knowledge of strategic management, in discovering grounded theory we should as much as possible avoid applying our own preconceived concepts and theories. This could lead to a forcing of data in a way that would hinder the emerging new and different concepts and hypotheses.

5 See Foucault (1972). This is confirmed by Walker (1991) who studied 190 hours of video taped therapy sessions. Although the basic categories of Freudian philosophy were not surfacing in the therapy sessions, both therapist and patients formed their speech in a way that

neatly fitted into the patterns of Freudian therapy sessions. The form of speech may convey meaning in a silent, but highly effective, way.

6   To someone familiar with experts, this is immediately recognized as a challenge. 'Experts are often overconfident' (Stubbart and Ramaprasad, 1990: 282) and will not tolerate a request for elaboration. A patient hardly has the 'right' to inquire into the reasons for a diagnosis made by a physician.

7   See Fletcher and Huff (1990), present a method to analyze the underlying reasoning of the decision maker. Tying this method to cognitive psychology, Weick (1990) argues that map making is a way to understand mental maps and thereby the actions of the decision maker.

8   This conceptual scheme was adapted and extended from Fletcher and Huff (1990) by the introduction of the category 'metaphors'.

9   This section builds on Fletcher and Huff's (1990) article 'Argument mapping'. For a more detailed outline of this methodology please refer to this article.

10   The analytical process is not linear as it appears here. To form concepts and to identify their relationships require an extensive amount of iteration, and very often a concept that at first glance seems to hold for a partial set of the data may be refuted at a later stage.

11   As a metaphor and catalyst for creativity, the statement 'organizational competence is the structure' works well. As a denotative statement, however, it does not tell us much. Do we establish the existence of competence or structure?

12   Not to be confused with the notion that a group has a competence.

13   Although interrelations implying that the arrows should point in both directions did not surface from the data, such interrelations seem reasonable to assume.

14   The interplay between individualized organizational knowledge and socialized organizational knowledge has been addressed by von Krogh and Roos (1995), but from a different conceptual domain, namely autopoiesis.

References

Arthur, W.B. (1990). Positive feedbacks in the economy. *Scientific American*, February: 92–9.

Barney, J.B. (1991). Firm resources and sustained competitive advantages. *Journal of Management*, 17: 99–120.

Berger, P. and Luckmann, T. (1967). *The Social Construction of Reality*. New York: Penguin.

Chi, M.T.H., Glaser, R. and Farr, M.J. (1988). *The Nature of Expertise*. Hillsdale, NJ: Erlbaum.

Dierickx, L. and Cool, K. (1990). Asset stock accumulation and sustainability of competitive advantage. *Management Science*, 35: 1514–30.

Drucker, P. (1994). The age of social transformation. *The Atlantic Monthly*: 53-80.

Fletcher, K.E. and Huff, A. (1990). Argument mapping. In A. Huff (ed.), *Mapping Strategic Thought*. Chichester: Wiley.

Foucault, M. (1972). *The Archeology of Knowledge*. London: Tavistock.

Geertz, C. (1973). *The Interpretation of Cultures*. New York: Harper Row.

Glaser, B.G. and Strauss, A.L. (1967). *The Discovery of Grounded Theory: Strategies for Qualitative Research*. New York: de Gruyter.

Hamel, G. and Prahalad, C.K. (1990). The core competence of the corporation. *Harvard Business Review*, May–June: 79–91.

Hamel, G. and Pralahad, C. K. (1994). *Competing for the Future*. Boston, MA: Harvard Business School Press.

Harvard Business Review (1992). Letters to the Editor. June–July.

Henderson, R.M. and Clark, K.B. (1990). Architectural innovation: the reconfiguration of existing product technologies and the failure of established firms. *Administrative Science Quarterly*, 35: 9–30.

McCloskey, D.N. (1985). *The Rhetoric of Economics*. Madison, WI: University of Wisconsin Press.

Mintzberg, H. (1973). *The Nature of Managerial Work*. New York: Harper Row.

Nonaka, I. (1991). The knowledge creating company. *Harvard Business Review*, November–December: 96–105.

Polanyi, M. (1962). *Personal Knowledge: towards a Post Critical Philosophy*. London: Routledge.

Prahalad, C.K. and Bettis, R. (1986). The dominant logic: a new linkage between diversity and performance. *Strategic Management Journal*, 7: 485–501.

Schutz, A. and Luckmann, T. (1973). *The Structures of the Lifeworlds*. Evanston, IL: Northwestern University Press.

Stinchcombe, A. (1986). *Stratification and Organization*. Oslo: Norwegian University Press.

Stubbart, C. and Ramaprasad, A. (1990). Comments on empirical articles and recommendations for future research. In A.S. Huff (ed.), *Mapping Strategic Thoughts*. Chichester: Wiley.

Toulmin, S. (1958). *The Uses of Argument*. Cambridge: Cambridge University Press.

von Krogh, G and Roos, J. (1995). *Organizational Epistemology*. London and New York: Macmillan and St. Martins Press.

Walker. T. (1991). Whose discourse? In S. Woolgar (ed.), *Knowledge and Reflexivity: New Frontiers in the Sociology of Knowledge*. London: Sage.

Weick, K.E. (1990). Introduction: cartographic myths in organizations. In A.S. Huff (ed.), *Mapping Strategic Thoughts*. Chichester: Wiley. pp. 1–13.

Wernerfelt, B. (1984). A resource-based view of the firm. *Strategic Management Journal*, 5: 171–80.

6

Knowledge-Based Strategic Change

Thorvald Hærem, Georg von Krogh and Johan Roos

'Managing strategic changes means designing intentions and implementing them' (Argyris, 1988: 349). One problem managers face is that implemented strategies do not always work as intended. Organizational realities in which managers operate are complex, dynamic and difficult to predict. This often makes the outcome of the strategic change different from that intended. To keep their intentions alive, managers may most of their time rely on 'keeping well informed, manipulating their ideas through streams of often unidentifiable resistance' (Wrapp, 1988). To manage the intended, an increased understanding of the knowledge in the organization may be helpful: 'Organization members, including the CEO, need to understand any intended change in a way that 'makes sense' or fits into some revised interpretative scheme or system of meaning' (Gioia and Chittipeddi, 1991: 434).

In organizations information streams can be analyzed as feedback loops. Stacey argues that: 'The patterns of change a system displays over time depend entirely on the nature of the feedback interaction of that system' (1993: 153–4). In this chapter such feedback loops refer to the knowledge transfer processes. Thus, it appears that one of the most important determinants of the outcomes of the strategic change process are the streams of often contradicting information and knowledge in the organization.[1] Based on a six-month ethnography, this chapter argues that understanding the knowledge transfer process is a key to understanding the change processes in an organization. Thus, the objective of this chapter is to shed more light on the knowledge and information transfer during strategic change processes.

After a methodological declaration, a brief description of the situation of the company is provided. Then a definition and a conceptualization of the knowledge transfer process is presented. Subsequently we hold that a 'knowledge gap' is a critical stage in the strategic change process. Arguing that the relation between the knowledge gap and the knowledge transfer process determines the future strategic change direction of the organization, we present a model for understanding this change. With these two models as background, examples are provided to demonstrate how managers in the organization influenced the knowledge transfer process to implement their new local strategies. Through analysis of these attempts, barriers to strategic change are discovered.

Methodology

Because the way that information is transferred, interpreted, and influenced is typically a subtle and continuously evolving process, traditional survey methods like questionnaires and interviews did not suffice. In organizations and societies the reality may be seen as socially constructed (Berger and Luckmann, 1967; Weick 1979). An understanding of the subjectivity of the reality is therefore important to understand what happens in the organization, including strategic change processes (Gioia and Chittipeddi, 1991). One way to gain this understanding is to learn to understand the culture, by studying the interaction of the members of the culture. 'The data of cultural anthropology derive ultimately from direct observation of customary behavior in particular social societies. Making, reporting and evaluating such observations are the task of ethnography' (*Encyclopedia of Social Sciences*, 1967). Thus, the method we chose was an ethnographic study (Van Maanen, 1983; 1988; Denzin, 1989; Geertz, 1983).

The observations concentrated on interpersonal contacts, conversations and sharing of printed information. The data on which this chapter is grounded stem mainly from the observer's diary, which contained the content of and reflections upon the everyday interaction in the company. In addition, bid documents, studies of the corporate electronic information systems, and company publications, including newspapers, annual reports, and product and service brochures, formed the background for the subsequent interpretations.

The immersion in the social context of the company allowed a set of first order findings to develop, which represented 'the facts' of an ethnographic investigation (Van Maanen, 1983). The first order concepts were developed after the first half of the study. The building of the second order concepts began when the report about the first order findings was finished. However, due to the nature of the methodology and the constant comparison analysis (Glaser and Strauss, 1967) we made minor adjustments of the concepts as we gained new information which changed the logic of our previous interpretations. 'When generation of theory is the aim, however, one is constantly alert to emergent perspectives that will change and develop [this] theory . . . so the published word is not the final one, but only a pause in the never ending process of generating theory' (Glaser and Strauss, 1967: 40).

The second order concepts were developed during the second half of the study and thus gave the opportunity to compare the second order concepts to the reality. A clear distinction between the first and second order concepts does not exist, since the second order concepts build on the first order concepts. The difference is that the second order concepts are not so closely knitted to the data as the first order concepts. The second order concepts (Van Maanen, 1983) contain inspirations from related theories and analogies that we have experienced ourselves. The second order concepts are a result of an interpretative process[2] (Denzin, 1989) and a second order analysis (Van Maanen, 1979). This chapter is a *presentation of this model*, illustrating its potential for shedding new light on strategic change processes.

The focus of the observations was on a local sales department. Of particular interest was the interaction between the sales managers, sales people and engineers. There was a contrast in information complexity, between the picture that we were served from top management and what we got from observing and interviewing sales and service personnel. This chapter attempts to comprehend the point of view of both the managers on the one hand and the sales and service people on the other. During the six-month ethnographic study, an understanding of how the intended changes were implemented and brought about in the everyday life of the organization emerged. Not only did management's perception of everyday life often seem to differ from the grass-roots perception, but the perception across the different 'grass-roots professions' also seemed to differ. However, certain characteristics were common. These differences seemed to cause contradictions in understanding. Therefore understanding the knowledge transfer processes may contribute to explaining why so many strategic change processes fail or have unintended effects.

The Company

The company studied is in the computer industry, an industry which has gone through rapid development, not least manifested by the recent problems in IBM, Apple, Digital, Sun and Hewlett-Packard. Several of the actors in the computer industry have initiated major change programs to cope with the changing world.

By talking to sales people and engineers it was difficult to access the history of the company, as they seldom talked about it. It was possible to pick up fragments, but in order to get an overview it was best to talk with the managers. An illustrative example of the history provided by managers was provided by a director who was acting as country manager during the company's summer holiday:

> We put the customer in focus, and our task was to provide our products. We were very technically focused, we produced the fastest, biggest and best products. But after a while it became important to provide complementary products. Then we engineered the best software. Our competence included now both software applications and hardware tools. But we were arrogant; as customers asked for platforms from which they could use all kinds of applications – we just stated that they did not need anything else than proprietarian brands. But the world moved on. After a while the standards become open and we had to change. The customer did not want anymore our proprietary systems, locking everybody else out.

The corporate strategy tuned its focus to 'system integration'. It was not enough to know our own products anymore, we had to know everybody else's hardware and software too. Therefore, the demand for knowledge and information increased. Now, the customers did not only ask for machines or software packages. Customers asked for particular services. They wanted the equipment to perform specific tasks, and they did not care what kind of hardware and software that was put in, as long as it did the work it was supposed to. Due to the open standards, we had to be able to integrate other vendors' equipment and applications to our products. We had to develop advanced consulting competence. We had to be able to go into a company and identify the opportunities for IT solutions, select the best solution and prescribe its configuration.

This story reflects major events in the computer industry in the period from the early 80s until today: the environment changed, and the products of the company had to meet new requirements which not were met in time. This was the main reason for the initiation of the change in strategy. Main events from the change process are illustrated in Figure 6.1.

Towards a Model of Knowledge Transfer

Although faced with the diversity, individuality and complexity of knowledge, researchers have often attempted to make broad divisions between different types of knowledge. Two major distinctions have been made in cognitive science between *semantic* and *episodic memory* and between *declarative* and *procedural* knowledge (Eysenck and Kean, 1992).[3] In management literature the focus has been on other dimensions of knowledge. For example, one may discuss articulated or non-articulated knowledge (Itami, 1987), thematized or non-thematized knowledge (von Krogh and Roos, 1993), degree of embeddedness (Badaracco, 1991), tacitness (Polanyi, 1962; 1967), 'transferable' knowledge (Winter, 1987) and migratory knowledge (Badaracco, 1991). Common to the resulting typologies of knowledge is that mutually exclusive and clear-cut categories do not exist. For example, some knowledge is quite articulatable and some is not: some is only partly articulatable.

Definitions of information transfer are found in cognitive psychology. We may say that information has been transmitted when the state of one system, 'B, is somehow contingent on the state of another, A, so that in principle an observer could discover something about A by examining B' (Neisser, 1976: 40). Knowledge may be defined as the way this information is stored in the brain, that is as 'knowledge schemata' (Neisser, 1976; Eysenck and Kean, 1992). We say that knowledge of a matter is transferred, when the receiver of information has gained a principally similar understanding of the matter as the transmitter.[4]

The Knowledge Transfer Model

During the initial analysis of the knowledge transfer in the organization the universe of knowledge fell into four categories, which subsequently were

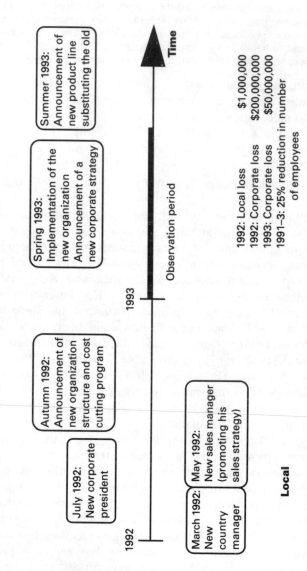

Figure 6.1 *Situation of the company*

developed into a theoretical model.[5] This section presents the model, the four main concepts and their interrelations.

The first knowledge concept is called 'scarce knowledge'. Individuals have *scarce knowledge* about a thing when they know that they lack knowledge about a thing. The alternatives to deal with this scarce knowledge are several. They may ignore the scarcity, or try to decrease it by searching for knowledge in secondary sources. Knowledge may also be obtained by speaking with others. The knowledge searched for may not be accessed if it is asked for in a wrong fashion. However, if behavior is in accordance with what the opposite party's behavior knowledge finds acceptable, the opposite party may diffuse information that reduces the first party's scarce knowledge, provided that the first party understands the other party's behavioral knowledge. These relationships are illustrated in Figure 6.2.

Scarce Knowledge

Scarce knowledge is knowledge about lack of knowledge. The existence of a lack of knowledge is often a sudden insight, but the insight might also be subconscious. The consciousness about a lack of knowledge led to a particular condition. This condition was, during the study, often observed and was correlated with an externalization of uncertainty. The insight gained when scarce knowledge came into existence was reflected by one of the employees as he stated: 'most of the necessary knowledge to solve this problem is not in my brain.' Similarly, a sales manager gradually realized that his deliberate strategy did not work out as he had supposed it to. This manager gradually become conscious of his scarce knowledge, that is, he understood that he did not know how sales people really behaved and why they really behaved as they did. He gained an understanding that he did not know why the sales decreased.

According to the typology presented here the manager may lack knowledge in three dimensions: he may lack knowledge about others' *knowledge*, about *how to behave* and about *how to perform a task*.[6] The main characteristics of these concepts of knowledge are presented in the next sections.

During the product development project, the presence of scarce knowledge led to a condition, often characterized by externalization of discomfort and uncertainty, in which there was a more or less manifest need to obtain the missing information. This condition seemed to have one of three outcomes: (1) the condition could be latent or manifestly ignored, (2) it could lead to a limited search (e.g. passive listening to the diffusion of information),[7] or (3) it could lead to an extensive search (e.g. asking questions). Scarce knowledge was typically evoked when facing a new problem or a problem that was not solved by previous occasions/experiences with the problem. The example of lack of knowledge about the cause for the limited success of the sales strategy is an example of a problem that has been faced earlier. Now the problem is perceived as so

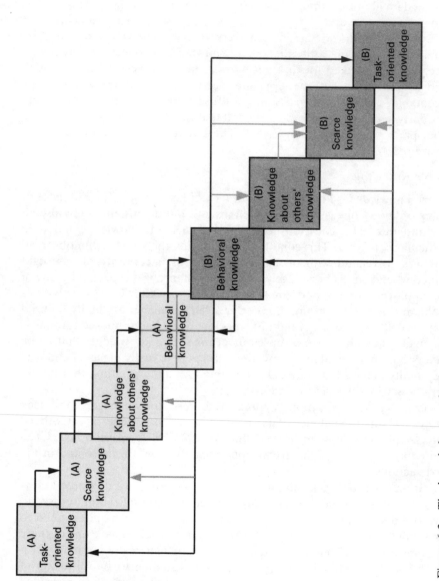

Figure 6.2 *The knowledge transfer process*

important that a search is initiated. The next question is, 'how can the scarce knowledge be obtained?'

Knowledge about Others' Knowledge

Knowledge about others' knowledge was frequently demanded and it was a prerequisite in getting help to solve tasks.[8] This category helped the person with scarce knowledge to ask the right person for help and to formulate the question so that the other party could easily answer. The organization depended on this kind of knowledge since the tasks were complex and no single person was able to solve all aspects of a task. For example, the sales manager knew that several of the sales people had tried out his strategy concept and therefore had knowledge about the results from 'these experiments'. This was valuable knowledge for the manager and in order to access this knowledge the sales manager decided to ask one of the salesmen. But it was often difficult for the manager to obtain this information. According to the knowledge transfer model we are developing here, the answer the sales manager will receive depends on the match between his behavioral knowledge and that of the respondent.

Behavioral Knowledge

Behavioral knowledge is knowledge about how to behave and how not to behave. In the knowledge transfer process, behavioral choices are determined by behavioral knowledge. As one engineer put it, 'You learn what you have to learn.' The engineer's statement implies that there are certain things 'he has to do'. In the model 'what the engineer has to do' is an implication of his behavioral knowledge. When faced with scarce knowledge, knowledge search could be triggered, provided that the perceived importance of the problem is strong enough. This perceived importance of the problem seems mainly to be determined by behavioral knowledge. 'What actually happens in an organization . . . depends on behavioral factors: belief systems, social interactions, cultures, group behavior and individual psychology' (Stacey, 1993).

Behavioral knowledge is knowledge that includes and determines the interplay of these behavioral factors. The behavioral knowledge concept has several dimensions. First, it has a formality dimension. This dimension includes formal knowledge (knowledge about incentive systems, organizational structure, strategy, company vision, ethical rules, etc.) and informal knowledge (knowledge about how to behave with peers, customers, partners, vendors, etc.). The formal knowledge is well articulated and is often easily learned by knowledge transfer. Informal behavioral knowledge can be more difficult to learn by knowledge transfer. For example, when two new account managers were hired, one engineer stopped by their office and joked with them. The engineer told the two new employees a story about one boss who, while he was fresh in his position, had tried to get the communication into formal patterns:

This boss, in another department, got a letter from a sales person in our department. The new boss, who enjoyed his new powerful position, sent the mail back, with this inscription: 'The mail shall go through the formal channels. If you want to send mail to me, you are supposed to go through your boss, who may take it further to me – if he finds it appropriate.' Then he called the sales person's boss about the irregular communication. This boss burst out in laughter, such a silly complaint he had not heard in a long time. The story went to the other bosses in the company, who all had a good laugh. The new boss never tried to get the information into formal channels after this incident.

The story was concluded by making the moral of the story explicit: 'In this company we are very informal and we may tease each other.' In this way the two newcomers were introduced to informal behavioral knowledge in the organization.

The other dimension of behavioral knowledge is the *social–individual dimension*. Some behavioral knowledge is shared among many, and some behavioral knowledge is individual. Individual behavioral knowledge includes a category that may be called personal traits: this category explains the subjective reason of why we select one action rather than another. Our embedded knowledge usually includes some anticipation of our own future situation (Neisser, 1976). Our initial knowledge structures also influence how the search process will be performed (Neisser, 1976). Through the process the schemata will be refined, so that next time the process is performed the process will be adjusted accordingly. Common characteristics of knowledge structures (organizational schemata) contribute to the opportunity to identify a pattern in information search and outcomes.

Thus, behavioral knowledge includes not only commonly held conventions, but also individual traits. Examples of such individual traits are individual risk attitudes, utility functions, need for social status and self-image. These kinds of traits are factors that contribute to individual differences in behavioral knowledge, and therefore lead to individuality in behavior.

Some of these traits are attempted thematized through a recognition of common characteristics in the needs of the employees. Performance metrics and job plans, which are developed for each individual, may be seen as attempts to recognize these individual traits.

Task-Oriented Knowledge

Task-oriented knowledge may concern a technical problem, may be of a strategic character, or may be related to the reasons why an implemented strategy does not work. The task may also be to develop knowledge within each of the other categories of knowledge. The task-oriented knowledge is the knowledge specifically needed to solve the tasks – the 'how to do it' knowledge. It is in many ways the 'inverse' of the scarce knowledge, since it is the answers to the questions that arise when scarce knowledge is present. The task can vary in kinds. In 'knowledge terms' it may be to develop scarce knowledge, it may be to access knowledge about others' knowledge, it may be to find the appropriate behavior or it may be to find the knowledge necessary to solve a particular task.

However, it should be emphasized that the typologies presented here are not totally clear-cut categories: knowledge that may seem clearly task oriented may also contain information about behavioral knowledge, knowledge about others' knowledge, scarce knowledge and vice versa. Some people may perceive only the task-oriented information while others may perceive both the task-oriented and the behavioral knowledge. During the observations the conversations could repeatedly be categorized in terms of these four categories of knowledge. Therefore, it seems useful to analyze the knowledge transfer process in terms of these four knowledge concepts. This usefulness may only be proven if the model can function as a practical analytical tool to improve the efficiency of learning by knowledge transfer. To get knowledge transferred the challenge is (1) to know what you do not know but need to know, (2) to know where the task-oriented knowledge exists, (3) to know how to access it.

Contextual Variables

The four concepts of knowledge discussed so far determine the internal interrelations in the knowledge transfer process. However, during the study it was obvious that the knowledge transfer was influenced by external factors too. Contextual variables are variables which influence the knowledge transfer process and are exogenous to the model, i.e. they are not directly influenced by the process. For example, time constraints and stress imply that the set of working behavioral knowledge is changed. A 'stress portfolio' which reflects a subset of the total behavioral knowledge is applied. Characteristics of this 'stress portfolio' of the behavioral knowledge are that reflective knowledge transfer was reduced, social talk and post-experience reviews were reduced to a minimum[9] and new problems were, if not solved immediately, given another priority or solved preliminarily. Thus, the scarce knowledge to be evoked and the task-oriented knowledge to be diffused differed according to the stress level and stress subject. The whole atmosphere became changed, a feeling of strain and pressure kept people from disturbing the process. The appropriate behavioral knowledge to be applied was not necessarily easily learned by those who did not know it in advance. Important contextual variables are:

- *the stress level in the organization*, and the cause of stress (the stress subject), for example a critical stage of the sales cycle or of the corporate planning cycle
- *the physical environment*
- *the status of the participator*, e.g. customers, peers, suppliers or partners.

The example of the sales manager's knowledge transfer with his organization can be summarized as in Figure 6.3. The interrelations are explained in the sequence 1–6.

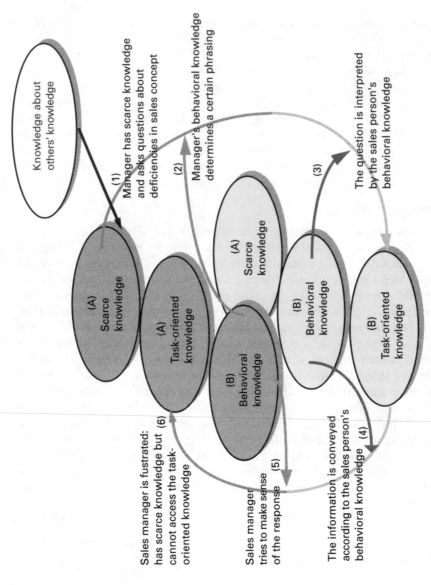

Figure 6.3   *An example of the knowledge transfer process*

Knowledge Transfer and Strategic Change

As a result of the changes in customers' behavior, and the lack of corresponding change in the company's behavior, a major recession struck the company in 1990. After a couple of years of serious losses, a major turn round was initiated. A new corporate president was hired, major downsizing and strategic change were initiated, and every fourth employee had to leave. A new organization was introduced, and the formal reporting structures were changed from the account manager upwards. The compensation system for the sales staff was changed. Key aspects of this change were increased incentives for sales, decreased base salaries and changes in performance measures. The product–market focus was changed. The former organization, which had evolved as a result of an emerging strategy, with incremental adjustments to the market, was restructured and formalized.

However, the changes in 'what to do' and 'how to do it', with regard to the sales organization, were implemented by the local sales managers. And sales managers all had personal opinions of how the implementation could best be done. Being highly educated people with strong personalities, their individual interpretations and visions were promoted. An array of 'sales strategies', within the limits of the corporate strategy, emerged across the various local sales departments.

These differences were reflected in several aspects, for example by the requirements that the sales managers developed for their subordinates and in what they communicated as important for success. The *success and failure* of the various departments were assumed, by the sales people, to be caused by the sales departments' strategies. As a result of employees' interaction a pattern of information diffusion was recognized. Thus, knowledge about the success and failure of other sales departments became a determinant of the propensity to adopt a sales manager's sales strategy.[10]

A main point, which emerged from the observations, is that this knowledge often became fragmented: people had different access to the information and even the same information was interpreted differently among employees. This phenomenon seemed to inspire the differences in 'theories in use' among both individual sales people and sales departments. Typical sources of such inspiration were information about the success or failures of sales departments and country subsidiaries. Differences in knowledge about competitors and customers strategies are other examples of knowledge often leading to different conclusions among the sales people.

The complexity of knowledge may partly explain why the information seemed fragmented and individual knowledge differed. A firm's knowledge system consists of several levels of knowledge: individual, group, department, division, as well as corporate. Individuals have unique knowledge that allows them to make sense of and do their job (von Krogh and Roos, 1992a). A part of this knowledge may be shared by other individuals, and may be 'tacit' in the sense that it is impossible to convey by language (Berger and Luckmann, 1967). The complexity of these information flows and the knowledge systems makes the cause and effect relationship difficult to comprehend in an organization. For example, it might be difficult to understand what the real reason for success of one sales manager's strategy really was. In the next section the knowledge transfer model developed in the previous section will be used to analyze the knowledge transfer as a strategic change process.

Knowledge Gap

The present *stock of knowledge* in the organization determines the way that the environmental changes are interpreted and the way that the internal changes are made. A main task of managers is often to design intentions and implement them, i.e. create deliberate strategies. Such deliberate strategies will inevitably differ from the organization's present stock of knowledge, since not the whole organization will share the manager's knowledge. Therefore, implementation of an intended strategy will be a change in strategy. *A change in strategy* implies a new way to think about the organization's reality (Gioia and Chittipedi, 1991), since the stream of information will be changed in the sense-making process. Thus, the strategic change leads to a *corresponding change in the company's stock of knowledge*.

Often, a *knowledge gap* occurs, between what the organization knows and what the manager 'intends it to know'. Due to this knowledge gap the organization will continuously search for new information to close the gap and 'the corporate memory is constantly updated as a consequence of knowledge transfer' (von Krogh and Roos, 1992b; see also Walsh and Ungson, 1991). This continuous knowledge transfer contributes to shape the feedback loops, which determine the future change direction of the organization. The realized strategy is the output of this process. The realized strategy will tend to be an emergent one, somewhat different from the pure intentions of the manager. The manager's *ability to influence the knowledge transfer process* will determine how 'successful' the implementation of his intentions will be. Consequently, what seems to be the real issue is how to manage the information and knowledge transfer process that shapes the information feedback loops. This is illustrated in Figure 6.4.

An example may illustrate this relation between an intended strategy, a knowledge gap, the corresponding knowledge transfer process and the consequences thereof. The sales manager in the sales department observed has a very deliberate sales strategy, and is frustrated about his account managers and sales people who do not seem fully committed to and capable of implementing the sales manager's strategy. The manager's strategy has been explained to the employees and has even been tried, but success has been limited. The vision is developed and clear. But the

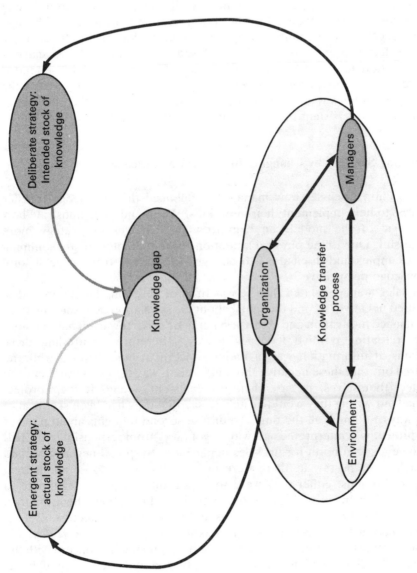

Figure 6.4 *The strategy formation process*

organization's task-oriented knowledge, about how to go about the concrete details, is not as clear and developed. The organization's present stock of knowledge does not include the knowledge needed to implement the strategy of the sales manager; thus the knowledge gap exists. The sales force has gained several experiences with the concept, and has met problems that have made them hesitate to commit themselves. Through experiences with the concept and corresponding knowledge transfer the knowledge gap has not yet been closed. Now, the sales manager's organization has found ways around the difficult parts of the intended strategy. This way becomes a new emergent strategy, different from the manager's intended strategy. Thus a gap still exists, and the manager is perceived as persistent in trying to implement the strategy.

Changing Strategy by Changing Behavioral Knowledge

This section discusses how managers influenced the knowledge transfer process to help implement their intentions. We intend to demonstrate how the logic of the model can help to make changes in strategy more successful. Due to the physical limitations of this chapter we are confining the examples and discussions to changes in strategy from a 'behavioral knowledge perspective'.

A sales manager stated that he was tired of observing his subordinates' diffused negative 'second thoughts' about his sales approach, since he tried to enhance motivation and create a synergistic drive towards creating more sales (creating positive feedback loops). Therefore, controlling these streams of information was of major concern to him. After a while he figured out that these negative thoughts were a way for his subordinates to protect themselves, in case their project went wrong. If their project turned out wrong they would be able to say that they had been skeptical of this way of doing it all the time. To diffuse second thoughts about parts of the project was interpreted as a way to get away from responsibility. It had become a social norm for his sales department to spread negative second thoughts. As he saw it, there were two sensible ways to go about such second thoughts: either they were so important that it was legitimate to talk about them, in which case he wanted to know about them; or they were just creating negative vibrations and hurting the project.

By making this interpretation he was *able to create a new reality*. He wrote a letter to every subordinate where he expressed his concern with the negative feedback, and he stated that he interpreted the second thoughts as an attempt to get rid of responsibility. But, he said, 'I do not accept them as a legitimate way to recede from responsibility.' However, the manager recognized that there was a need for a way to recede from responsibility – if the problem were real. In order to provide the subordinates with a channel to fulfill this need, he stated that: 'if there were a part of the project that they could not accept responsibility for, the only way that he accepted such

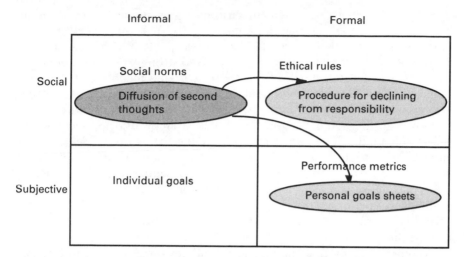

Figure 6.5   *A redefinition of behavioral knowledge I*

a rejection was that the subordinate explicitly made an agreement with him.'

By this action the manager created a new reality. To diffuse negative second thoughts was now implicitly the same as trying to free oneself from responsibility – in an illicit manner. If serious second thoughts had any significance they should be stated directly to the manager. In terms of the typology of behavioral knowledge a social norm had been pin-pointed, and formalized with consequences pertaining to the individual concerned. The change in behavioral knowledge is illustrated in Figure 6.5. By changing the behavioral knowledge in the organization the manager influenced and changed the knowledge transfer process as illustrated in Figure 6.3, so that he could better implement his intended strategy as illustrated in Figure 6.4.

Crowding Out Confusing Feedback Loops

In the example in Figure 6.3, the sales manager did not get the answer he wanted because the sales person had a different behavioral knowledge than the sales manager. The sales person had success with the traditional way of selling – the old strategy. 'Besides,' the sales person said, 'the bureaucratic procedure one has to go through, using the new sales strategy, is best to avoid – it takes so much time.'

In term of the sales person's 'behavioral knowledge', the informal dimension was dominant. He had got so much feedback about other sales concepts that he had justified sticking to another concept. Thus, the knowledge gap existed and the realized strategy was very different from the manager's intended strategy. The way that the sales manager handled this and corresponding problems with other sales people was to increase the promotion of his sales concept. He had arranged to have all the walls of a meeting room decorated with the sales process that reflected his sales concept. This room was used for customer presentations, and the illustrations were used in the presentations, so that they worked as an implementation and diffusion of his sales concept all over the organization. In this way his sales concept was promoted so strongly that the feedback it created crowded out much of the contra working feedback of the other sales concepts. He even institutionalized his sales concept by implementing the visions of his concept in the work instructions of his subordinates.

However, it should be noted that this strategy did not seem totally successful in the long run, since some deficiencies of the sale concept created new negative feedback loops, which again influenced the behavioral knowledge of the sales people. The consequence was that parts of the concept were widely adopted – but some crucial parts which were difficult to operationalize were suppressed. In the typology of the behavioral knowledge the sales manager's effort and the consequences thereof can be illustrated as shown in Figure 6.6.

Another strategy that the manager took advantage of was to hire two new account managers. When these two people were hired they were specifically briefed in the manager's sales concept. So when interacting with the others, they were promoting the sales manager's concept. But the deficiencies of the concept still lurked in the background. These deficiencies were difficult for the sales manager to identify, as he did not use the sales and delivery concept in his everyday work and as it was not usual for his subordinates to tell him about them. In addition it seemed difficult to pin-point exactly what did not work.

Conclusions

This chapter has taken the knowledge perspective as a point of view on the strategic change process. Taking this starting point, a model for analyzing and understanding the knowledge transfer process was presented. We argued that it is the knowledge transfer processes which determines the change direction of a company. More specifically we showed that a knowledge gap will occur in a strategic change process. The resulting knowledge transfer processes determine how the gap between the manager's intended knowledge and the emergent organizational knowledge will evolve – and consequently also how the gap between the intended and emergent strategy will evolve.

By focusing on interpersonal knowledge transfer and knowledge development we discussed how one important variable of the knowledge transfer process, behavioral knowledge, influenced the process. From the discussions it may be concluded that one barrier to knowledge transfer is differences in behavioral knowledge.

In a world which is becoming more and more knowledge intensive and in which the information streams are getting increasingly complex, managing knowledge and information processes is becoming critical. This chapter is an attempt to contribute to an understanding of these processes in a

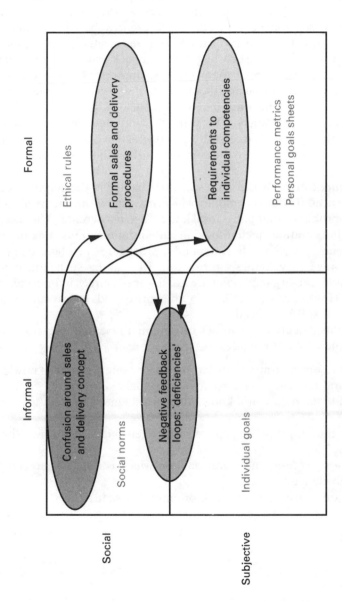

Figure 6.6 *A redefinition of behavioral knowledge II*

strategic change context. In the following chapter, we will discuss the impact of knowledge on corporate restructuring.

In managing the strategic change process in a knowledge perspective, the differences in knowledge stocks between managers and employees represent a barrier to implement the intended strategy. In particular, negative feedback loops contribute to differences between managers' intended strategies and the organization's realized strategies. It seems that a successful way to handle such negative feedback loops is to thematize them, and eventually channel them into the appropriate adjustments of their source. By managing such a thematization process, deficiencies in the strategy and in the organization may be fed back to those empowered to adjust the strategy accordingly. This will be a continuous process, and only by managing this process successfully can one achieve a strong stream of positive feedback that can take the company further in the strategic change process.

Another implication that emerges in this chapter is the importance of identifying procedures or techniques which may allow the organization to escape some problems that behavioral knowledge may create. The increasing use of information technology in organizations may enable new solutions to such problems. For, example, procedures can be created for electronic storage of valuable information. By making such information easily accessible, the organization may use fewer resources in interpersonal interaction. However, the ability to thematize and adjust the reality accordingly will still be crucial.

Based on this research, a number of potential research questions have surfaced. Some of these include:

- What is the optimal mix between the use of interpersonal knowledge transfer and the use of electronic or secondary sources?
- How should the behavioral knowledge be influenced to facilitate such a diffusion?
- What is the appropriate balance between individual and shared knowledge?
- How can one access crucial information which is not yet perceived as scarce knowledge?
- How can one ease access to task-oriented knowledge?

Notes

This chapter is based on the Msc thesis of Thorvald Hærem. The work is part of a larger research project at the Norwegian School of Management, within the realm of knowledge transfer and cooperation.

1   The different flows of information in the company can be seen as feedback loops. Some are negative feedback loops, adjusting the system just like a heat regulator. If a sales strategy does not work the sales manager may receive negative feedback, making him adjust his strategy. Some are positive feedback loops, strengthening the effects of the last feedback and – working in an opposite way from the heat regulator – moving the system further away from its initial state.

2 Denzin describes the interpretative process as including six phases: (1) framing the research question, (2) deconstruction and critical analysis of prior conceptions of the phenomenon, (3) capturing, (4) bracketing, (5) construction and (6) contextualization. This process is quite similar to a phenomenological approach. However, we chose to postpone the deconstruction phase to the end, since we wanted to avoid any prejudgment and instead let the theory be as grounded as possible (Glaser and Strauss, 1967).

3 Semantic knowledge refers to our decontextualized memory for facts about the entities and relations between entities. Episodic memory refers to knowledge about episodes and events. Simply stated, declarative knowledge is to know what, and procedural knowledge is to know how.

4 Another definition of the relation between information and knowledge is as follows. First, data are combined to create information. Second, information is transformed into knowledge of an individual or a group. Third, competence comes into existence when knowledge and skills are applied to solve a task (von Krogh et al., 1993)

5 A detailed discussion of the findings and the development of the categories can be obtained from the authors.

6 It is also possible to search for knowledge about knowledge about lack of knowledge, but we will not elaborate on this issue here.

7 People who noticed that somebody had scarce knowledge often tried to diffuse this information to the one with the scarce knowledge.

8 We thank Øystein Fjeldstad for helpful comments about this category, from his work on managing cross-functional teams.

9 Post-experience reviews are sessions which were initiated by a person who had experienced what it felt like to diffuse to the others in the organization. These sessions were often spontaneous, and took place in the middle of the office landscape. The subject of the experience might speak loudly and inspirationally about some events. The sessions could concern experiences with customers, partners, colleges or superiors. They could also be more reflective, asking for advice on how to interpret some new information.

10 Parallel word-of-mouth effects, in connection with adoption of new ideas, is well researched in the literature about diffusion of innovations (see, for instance, Robertson, 1967; Rogers, 1983).

References

Argyris, C. (1988). Crafting a theory of practice: the case of organizational paradoxes. In R.E. Quinn and K.S. Cameron (eds), *Paradox and Transformation: toward a Theory of Change in Organization and Management*. Beverly Hills, CA: Sage. pp. 255–79.

Badaracco, J.L. (1991). *The Knowledge Link: How Firms Compete through Strategic Alliances*. Boston, MA: Harvard Business School Press.

Berger, P. and Luckmann, T. (1967). *The Social Construction of Reality*. New York: Penguin.

Denzin, N.K. (1989). *Interpretive Interactionism*. Newbury Park, CA: Sage.

Encyclopedia of Social Sciences (1967). New York: Macmillan.

Eysenck, M.W. and Kean, M.T. (1992). *A Cognitive Psychology*. UK: Lawrence Erlbaum.

Geertz, C. (1983). *Local Knowledge*. New York: Basic Books.

Gioia, D.A. and Chittipeddi, K. (1991). Sensemaking and sensegiving in strategic change initiation. *Strategic Management Journal*, 12(6): 433–48.

Glaser, B.G. and Strauss, A.L. (1967). *The Discovery of Grounded Theory*. Chicago: Aldine.

Itami, H. (1987). *Mobilizing Invisible Assets*. Cambridge, MA: Harvard University Press.

Neisser, U. (1976). *Cognition and Reality: Principles and Implications of Cognitive Psychology*. San Francisco: W.H. Freeman.

Polanyi, M. (1962). *Personal Knowledge: towards a Post Critical Philosophy*. London: Routledge.

Polanyi, M. (1967). *The Tacit Dimension*. Garden City, NY: Anchor.

Robertson, T.S. (1967). The process of innovation, and the diffusion of innovation. *Journal of Marketing*, 31 (January).

Rogers, E.M. (1983). *Diffusion of Innovations* (3rd edn). New York: Free Press.

Stacey, R.D. (1993). *Strategic Management and Organizational Dynamics*. London: Pitman.

Van Maanen, J. (1979). The fact of fiction in organizational ethnography. *Administrative Science Quarterly*, 24: 539–50.

Van Maanen, J. (1983). *Qualitative Methodology*. Beverly Hills, CA: Sage.

Van Maanen, J. (1988). *Tales of the Field*. Chicago: University of Chicago Press.

von Krogh, G. and Roos, J. (1992a). Towards a competence-based perspective of the firm. Working Paper, Norwegian School of Management.

von Krogh, G. and Roos, J. (1992b). Figuring out your competence configuration. *European Management Journal*, 10(4): 422–7.

von Krogh, G. and Roos, J. (1993). Imitation: a short-cut to knowledge acquisition? Paper presented at the conference on Tacit Knowledge and Core Competence in the Innovation Process, Rome, Italy, 5 April.

von Krogh, G., Roos, J. and Slocum, K. (1993). An essay on corporate epistemology. Paper presented at the SMS Conference, Chicago.

Walsh, J.P. and Ungson, G.R. (1991). Organizational memory. *Academy of Management Review*, 16: 57–91.

Weick, K.E. (1979). *The Social Psychology of Organizing*. New York: Random House.

Winter, S.G. (1987). Knowledge and competence as strategic assets. In D.J. Teece (ed.), *The Competitive Challenge*. Cambridge, MA: Ballinger. pp. 159–85.

Wrapp, E. (1988). Good managers don't make policy decisions. In J.B. Quinn, H. Mintzberg and R.D. James (eds), *The Strategy Process*. Englewood Cliffs, NJ: Prentice-Hall.

7

Restructuring: Avoiding the Phantom Limb Effect

Georg von Krogh, Johan Roos and Thorvald Hærem

This chapter concerns corporate restructuring, one of the most published areas within the realm of strategy. Corporate restructuring occurs through a variety of transactions, for instance, mergers, acquisitions, leveraged management buyouts, internal venturing and divestitures. This chapter focuses on the latter kind of corporate restructuring. Corporate divestitures are defined as the selling-off of one or several of a corporation's total portfolio of strategic business units (SBUs) to a third party.

Researchers have given much attention to divestiture's effects on corporate performance, mainly from a financial perspective. From a financial perspective most of the literature seems to reflect the view that the divestiture of SBUs means mainly reallocating assets to managers who think they can make the assets more productive, away from those who cannot. By focusing on cash flows, and estimating the net present value (NPV) of projects and investments, researchers have attempted to find the 'true' price of the divested company. However, some outcomes of divestitures are known: Divestitures are often preceded by poor performance (Duhaime and Baird, 1987; Duhaime and Grant, 1984) and thus often motivated by a need for improvements in performance. It is empirically supported that divestitures increase the divesting firms' performance (Alexander et al., 1984; Jain, 1985; Klein, 1986; Montgomery et al., 1984; Rosenfeld, 1984), particularly for highly diversified firms (Markides, 1992; 1995; Johnson et al., 1993).

Also evidence of substantial negative effects of divestitures has now been identified. In a recent paper Bergh (1995) found that divestitures of related business were associated negatively with post-divestiture performance. It was concluded that the underlying consequences of sell-offs for the organizations' resource portfolios and the corresponding effects on performance are not yet understood. This supports our suggestion that after a divestiture companies may suffer from a phenomenon that we have called 'the phantom limb effect' (von Krogh and Roos, 1994). This chapter applies a connectionistic perspective to analyze consequences of divestitures (von Krogh and Roos, 1995).

To explore the phenomenon of divestitures, we used the example of a global materials corporation, with a turnover in excess of US$1.6 billion.

The company is forced to reduce its capital employment, which will involve the sale of business units. One of the company's senior vice-presidents urges a careful strategic evaluation of the effects of divestitures. His concern is that: 'Similar knowledge is used in several divisions. Process knowledge from one division is often used to develop production processes in another. Knowledge transfer takes place through contacts between people in the units, and through specific, *ad hoc* efforts by specialists from different units helping one another to improve production processes.' According to this executive: 'A careful evaluation of the knowledge synergies at our company is needed – how each unit mutually contributes today and how they could contribute tomorrow.' This statement indicates that SBUs are involved in an ongoing transfer of knowledge: inter-SBU and intra-SBU, and between SBUs and corporate management. Despite extensive research based on the traditional theories of human resource management (Belohlav and LaVan, 1989; Wallum, 1980; Murray, 1987), the consequences of divestitures on knowledge transfer have not previously been discussed.

This chapter takes a novel approach to the phenomenon of divestitures. First we briefly discuss the competence-based perspective on the firm. Then, we suggest how a divestiture may influence knowledge transfer between SBUs as well as between SBUs and corporate management. As a result of this discussion we propose implications for corporate management to avoid the potential negative effects of divestitures.

A Competence-Based Perspective

This perspective builds on the resource-based hypothesis that expansion by firms into activities in which they have comparative advantages is most likely to yield rents (Penrose, 1959). A competence-based perspective of the firm should be seen as a subset of the resource-based perspective. Whereas the latter views the firm as a bundle of physical, organizational and human resources (see also Barney, 1991; Daft, 1983; Itami, 1987), the former sees the firm as a bundle of tasks and knowledge (von Krogh and Roos, 1992; 1995).

Application of a resource-based perspective to analyze the phenomenon of divestitures and acquisitions has been called for (Mahoney and Pandian, 1992) and a few studies with such a perspective have already emerged (e.g. Markides and Williamson, 1994; Bergh, 1995). These studies argue that the definition of relatedness hypotheses has to be rethought, since the present definition of relatedness does not distinguish between contestable synergy and idiosyncratic bilateral synergies (Mahoney and Pandian, 1992). Only with idiosyncratic bilateral synergies is the achievement of abnormal returns possible (Barney, 1986). The present definition of relatedness, where the contestable relatedness is included, will therefore tend to conclude that relatedness matters less than it possibly does.

In order to explore the nature of idiosyncratic bilateral synergy we have chosen to focus on one of the most important sources of idiosyncrasies, namely competence development (von Krogh and Roos, 1995). Competence-intensive industries, such as semiconductor, pharmaceutical, ceramic, aerospace, automotive, and telecommunication industries, require large initial investments in R&D and manufacturing. However, once sales begin, incremental production is relatively cheap. Moreover, increased production means learning more about the specific and related product and production processes, further reducing the costs. In addition, the benefit of using the competence-based products increases with the number of produced units. When one product or brand, for instance a certain version of a PC or an optical cable, gains a strong market share, customers have strong incentives to buy more of the same product so as to exchange information with those already using it.

Science-intensive products are also harder to substitute than other products as they become increasingly embedded with 'product wisdom'. A typical example of a product where knowledge is actually built in is a drug. The time period between the initial research activities and the actual approval and registration is *de facto* a knowledge accumulation process. During the development phase a multitude of experiments are made so that when the drug gets approved there may be thousands of pages of documentation regarding virtually all aspects of the product and its applications.

Most managers are aware of this trend. In the May 1993 edition of a large Scandinavian business magazine, one of the division heads of Norsk Hydro, a multinational company listed on Wall Street, made the point that: ' today we build in more and more knowledge into our products.' Or, as a senior executive of the world's largest classification company, Veritas, recently stated: 'It is really knowledge we are selling!' Because most firms already are, or soon will be competing on knowledge, possession of relevant knowledge is clearly the key to success. The problem is that both economic theory as well as managerial behavior 'keep on trucking' with old mental models based on more 'energy-based' products and industry traditions.

But what does the notion of 'competence' really mean? As has been discussed in our study of arguments on competence in Chapter 5, each of us probably has our own definition of competence. For instance, a senior executive, head of the personnel function in a large Scandinavian firm, defined competence as: 'the potential to solve tasks that need to be solved. In addition to knowledge, experience, and potential, competence encompasses the collective resources built into technologies, routines, planning and problem solving mechanisms, organizational structure, products and services.' Like most people this executive had a relatively vague and broad definition of competence. Another director of personnel, in a different

Scandinavian firm, defined competence as: 'the ability to get the job done. To be competent in a certain area, you need knowledge and the ability to turn knowledge into work.' This executive pin-pointed that competencies denote some ability of the firm to act in a given environment. Still, what is clear is that the picture is not totally clear. In our opinion the competence concept is simply the synthesis of a firm's particular task and knowledge systems (Latin *competentia*, agreement between task and knowledge). Following this definition, a firm's competencies must be analyzed in terms of its task system and its knowledge system. The two dimensions are in themselves necessary but not sufficient conditions for the creation of sustainable competitive advantages. Only when knowledge and tasks are synthesized into particular competencies will they represent a basis for value creation. Thus, the foundation of competitive advantages lies in understanding and managing the firm's knowledge and task systems, and their intersection.

Knowledge System in a Connectionistic Perspective

Different theories have depicted organizations as functioning like information-processing systems (Galbraith, 1977; Tushman and Nadler, 1978). In these systems, it is individuals that acquire information and develop knowledge. Individuals' cognitive activities and transfer of knowledge are the central mechanisms by which organizations are enabled to build future action on acquired wisdom. It is through the process of sharing that the interpretation system transcends the individual level. This is why organizations may preserve knowledge of the past even when key organizational members leave (Weick and Gilfillan, 1971).

This system may be seen as a neural system. Each part of the organizational body contributes, by signals sent through individual links, to the corporate memory (Walsh and Ungson, 1991), and thereby influences the firm's actions and responses. Each individual or work unit functions as a connecting node in a complex network. Every firm's neural system is dynamic in the sense that knowledge is exchanged continuously between individuals, groups, SBUs, and corporate management (von Krogh and Roos, 1994) while their interrelations continuously transform in an evolutionary process. The basic activity of these entities is seen as information processing and knowledge creation. Information is taken from the environment through the organization's sensory surface and it will activate various components in the network that comprises the organization. The information processing depends on stimuli from the environment but also on the stimuli generated by the connections in the neural network which the organization comprises (von Krogh and Roos, 1995).

Likewise, groups, departments, divisions or corporations share a social knowledge (Berger and Luckmann, 1967). These entities function as decentralized storage systems and the shared social knowledge functions as the code that enables connections and transfer of knowledge between the different systems. Research has shown that this type of knowledge comes into being when individuals share their experiences verbally (e.g. Sims and Gioia, 1986). Thereby, they engage in the formation of a group, department or corporate language (Fiol, 1991) and knowledge structures (Lyles and Schwenk, 1992; Prahalad and Bettis, 1986). This gives a shared interpretation of events and allows for a shared agreement of the strategic direction and legitimization of the firm. Also, social knowledge may be tacit in the sense that it is embedded in complex social relationships.

Task System

A firm's task system consists of tasks of various degrees of complexity. Campbell (1988), in a review of task-related literature, suggests that there are four complexity drivers for a given task: the presence of (1) multiple desired solutions to a task, (2) multiple paths to reach these solutions, (3) conflicting interdependencies between the solutions of a task, and (4) uncertainty in linking resolution paths to task solutions.

Simple tasks, such as putting a stamp on an envelope, have only one solution, and few possible paths of task resolution. Complex tasks on the other hand, like deciding on a new business venture, have multiple desired solutions, many possible resolution paths that are uncertain with respect to outcome, and many conflicting interdependencies between task solutions. Complex tasks also have another characteristic in common with other complex phenomena, namely the difficulty of being observed, understood or communicated.

In addition to complexity as defined above, three other variables – task variability, work-flow interdependence, and problem analyzability – are major determinants for the knowledge need and the corresponding uncertainty in the organization (Perrow, 1967; Thompson, 1967; Van de Ven et al., 1976). SBUs and corporate management constitute a range of dynamic task systems utilizing the knowledge system of the organization. If the knowledge system is unable to meet the task system's requirements for knowledge, the organization's task resolution will be impeded. Thus, it is critical to the functioning of the organization that the neural knowledge network runs smoothly and is able to exploit earlier experiences from problem resolutions.

Environmental Claim System

The organization responds to changes and variations in the environment (Lawrence and Lorsch, 1967). These changes and variations can be seen as contingent claims on the organization: if the organization wants to maintain its position the organization has to adjust its task system to the new environmental claims. If the organization want to change its strategic position it means that it has to fulfill a new set of claims and accordingly

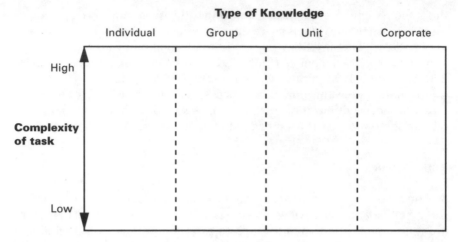

Figure 7.1   *Competence configuration*

solve a new set of tasks. These claims arise from different sources in the environment, e.g. customers' changing preferences, governmental regulations, competitors' moves and new substitutes and entrants (Porter, 1980). The degree of variation and change in environmental claims varies across different strategic positions in different markets: some are quite stable, while others are dynamic.

The changes in the tasks to be solved as consequences of changing environmental claims and/or changing goals of the organization lead to corresponding need for change in the knowledge system. Thus, there are strong interrelations between the three systems which lead to a need for coordination between the systems.

Competence Configuration

To simplify the analysis we now keep the environmental claim system constant. When coupling the knowledge system and the task system of the firm, assuming the knowledge matches the task, the firm's 'competence configuration' appears, as shown in Figure 7.1 (von Krogh and Roos, 1992). A firm may have several tasks of various degrees of complexity and many different sources and types of knowledge, but a *competence* represents only the intersection between a particular task and a particular knowledge at a given point in time.

Superior firm performance in a given industry stems from the firm's sustainable competitive advantages. The competence-based perspective suggests that sustainable competitive advantages, in turn, stem from the firm's development and exploitation of unique and valuable competencies. It should also be noted that the competence configuration represents a snapshot of the organization because it is not related to organizational processes and other implementational issues.

The Corporate Perspective

A central theme in the theories of corporate strategy is diversification and the degree of relatedness in the corporate portfolio of businesses (Ansoff, 1965; Salter and Weinhold, 1979; Rumelt, 1974; Montgomery and Singh, 1984). The relatedness of businesses has typically been expressed in terms of product and market commonality, asset commonality, and industry commonality.

Several authors have also suggested that degree of relatedness among businesses implies commonality in distinctive competencies, industry-specific competencies, know-how, skills, and knowledge (Drucker, 1981; Barney, 1988; Lubatkin, 1987). Rumelt described the Harvard view of strategy as 'the relation between competence and opportunity' (1974: 11). In the same vein Porter (1987) prescribed that a diversification strategy should be based on the possibilities of knowledge transfer among businesses that may improve the competitive advantage in target industries.

As in the case of the SBU, corporate management can also be seen as a specific task and knowledge system, forming specific competencies. It is the task and knowledge system of each SBU and corporate management that forms the *corporate competence configuration*. The competence configuration of the corporation should be understood as the accumulated tasks and knowledge throughout the corporation. As previously mentioned, it is useful to make the distinction between the different types of knowledge pertaining to the individual, team, unit, and corporate levels. The competence-based view of the corporation in two related SBUs and an unrelated SBU is illustrated in Figure 7.2.

As depicted in the figure, the corporation is analyzed in terms of connections of interdependencies between three systems, the *environmental claim system*, the *task system* and the *knowledge system*. In order to meet the requirements from the environment the organization has to solve various tasks, which needs different kinds of knowledge to be solved. The figure demonstrates that relatedness in a competence perspective comes in many forms. These interdependencies are best analyzed at the interface between the systems. There are two interfaces: the *environment–task interface* and the *task–knowledge* interface.

First there are interdependencies at the environment–task interface. Claims from the environment may require that the organization combine tasks performed by different SBUs, while other challenges can be met by tasks performed only by a single SBU. But, the SBU which seems independent at this interface may be dependent on other SBUs at the task–knowledge interface. For example, the SBU that is able to meet the environmental claim with respect to task resolution may be dependent on knowledge from other SBUs. The figure illustrates a situation where the organization that meets environmental claims by cooperation on the task level also needs to cooperate in order to utilize knowledge from other SBUs to solve the task.

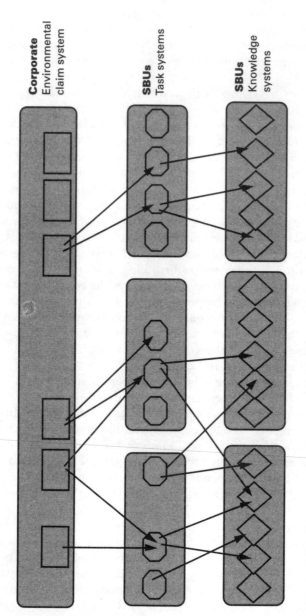

Figure 7.2   *Competence configuration in a related and an unrelated context*

The enviroment–task interface and the task–knowledge interface illuminate types of relatedness that are grounded in the development of idiosyncratic bilateral synergies in terms of competence utilization. Relatedness in this context is the degree that the SBU meets an environmental claim in cooperation with other organizations, either in the environment–task interface or in the task–knowledge interface or in both.

It is easy to see that these kinds of relatedness may exist fairly independent of the traditional measures of relatedness in terms of standard industrial classification (SIC) codes and more subjective measures (Markides and Williamson, 1994). In the concept of relatedness advocated here a firm may serve the same market measured by SIC codes (and therefore, in terms of the traditional measures of relatedness, be related) and still be defined as unrelated. This is because the SBU (e.g. to the right in the figure) serves its environmental claims by solving all tasks itself, utilizing merely its own knowledge base.

This model depicts our initial example of the organization which experienced a situation where similar knowledge was utilized in several divisions. Process knowledge from one division was often used to develop production processes in another. Knowledge transfer between people in the units led to innovations in the production processes across the units, so that more efficient task resolutions resulted in better ways to meet the environmental claims; it even provided opportunities to meet new environmental claims.

The Neural System

By viewing the firm in a connectionistic perspective, as a bundle of connections within and between the environmental claim, task and knowledge systems, management of these connections becomes crucial. Each part of the organizational body contributes, by signals sent through individual links, to the corporate memory, and thereby influences the firm's actions and responses to the environmental claims by developing and solving different tasks (Hærem, 1993; Hærem et al., 1993). We see this system of connections and individual links in which signals are transferred as analogous to the human neural system. Every firm's knowledge system is dynamic in the sense that knowledge is exchanged continuously between individuals, groups, SBUs, and corporate management.

Knowledge is also transmitted through the history of a firm (Berger and Luckmann, 1967). This transmittal is the purpose of organizational memory (Douglas, 1986; Kantrow, 1987; Walsh and Ungson, 1991) where knowledge is stored, for example, as meaning-based representations (Anderson, 1985).The SBU, as well as the corporation, can be seen as drawing on and maintaining its own organizational memory.

The notion of organizational memory implies that knowledge is acquired, stored, and retrieved through five types of organizational 'storage bins': (1) knowledge tied to key individuals, (2) physical archives, (3) the corporate culture of learning and transmitting knowledge, (4) knowledge embedded in organizational processes, and (5) organizational structure (Walsh and Ungson, 1991). Moreover, organizational memory is distributed throughout the organization: it 'is both an individual- and an organizational-level construct' (1991: 61), which corresponds with our notion of a multi-level knowledge system.

The knowledge transfer processes involve both storage and retrieval of several types of knowledge: individual, group, business unit, or corporate. Each SBU and corporate management stores and retrieves knowledge from the other units to solve specific SBU tasks or corporate management tasks. This synthesis of knowledge and tasks forms organizational competencies, which rely on the utilization of knowledge from one part of the organization to solve a task in another part of the organization. We call this process *direct* knowledge transfer.

In the resources-based perspective, centralization of activities and resources allows the firm to apply its scarce resources to multiple purposes. Similarly, centralization of corporate knowledge allows the firm to apply its corporate knowledge to multiple tasks and thereby form a portfolio of organizational competencies.

Because the tasks, in principle, are given for each SBU, the most common knowledge linkage between SBUs and the corporate level is the shared corporate-wide knowledge. *All* business units of a corporation contribute to, and retrieve knowledge from, this part of the corporate memory. The interrelationships between SBU and corporate knowledge imply that: (1) corporate knowledge is highly dynamic (stored and retrieved from corporate memory), and (2) corporate memory is constantly updated as a consequence of knowledge transfer. We call the knowledge transfer via a corporate memory *indirect* knowledge transfer: that is, knowledge that is transferred from the SBU through the corporate center to another SBU. Clearly the magnitude of direct and indirect knowledge transfer differs across corporations.

The principles of direct and indirect knowledge transfer, in both the related and conglomerate settings, are depicted in Figures 7.3 and 7.4.

It should be noted that the intensity of the knowledge transfer between SBUs and between SBUs and corporate management differs. In particular, the intensity of the knowledge transfer depends on the relatedness of the SBUs as well as on the degree of centralization. This is illustrated in Figure 7.5.

The intensity of the knowledge transfer processes within the corporation influences the total amount of corporate knowledge. In a portfolio of related businesses the amount of corporate-wide knowledge (memory) is larger than in the conglomerate, as illustrated in Figure 7.6. This phenomenon is due to two factors. As direct knowledge transfer occurs, a business unit gradually builds up its local knowledge. Commonalties will remain between the transferring business unit's local knowledge and the target's

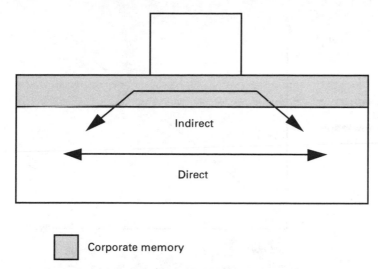

Corporate memory

Figure 7.3 *Direct and indirect knowledge transfer in a related context*

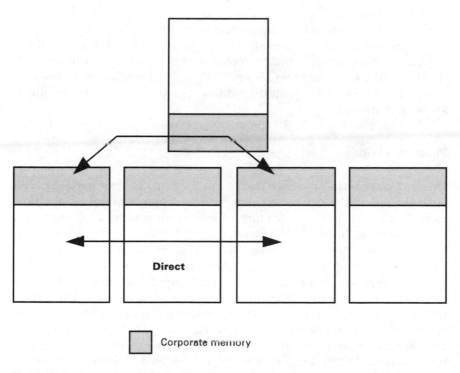

Corporate memory

Figure 7.4 *Direct and indirect knowledge transfer in a conglomerate context*

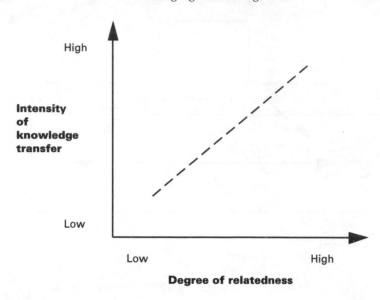

Figure 7.5   *Theoretical relationship between knowledge transfer intensity and degree of relatedness*

local knowledge. Also, as the degree of relatedness among businesses increases, the degree of centralization of activities increases. Traditionally, it is suggested that the implementation of synergies in a related portfolio requires centralization. Some examples are the centralization of research (Bettis, 1981), core resources (Rumelt, 1974), and production technology (Kitching, 1973). This centralization leads to the increase of direct knowledge transfer.

Phantom Limbs

Ongoing corporate knowledge transfer in the firm can, in a sense, be seen as analogous to the nervous system with a corporate brain and multiple individual neural linkages. Victims of amputations suffer a phenomenon called 'phantom limb'. Although the person knows that the limb is gone, the brain acts as though the limb is still there, and a person can feel pain, itching or other discomfort. The phantom limb varies in strength and longevity depending on both the body part amputated and how the nerve system heals. Corporate divestiture can be seen as analogous to amputation of a 'corporate body' part or limb because it means selling off one or several of a corporation's total portfolio of SBUs. Medical analogies have also earlier been made to improve the understanding of corporate restructuring. Duffy, for instance, in arguing that the best kind of re-structuring is no restructuring at all, suggests that 'restructuring is rather like surgery. It is something you undergo, preferably under anesthetic,

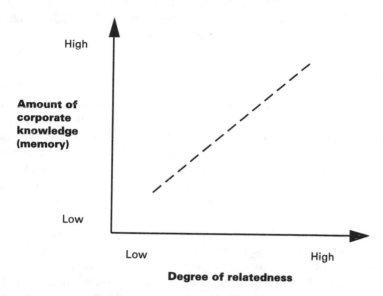

Figure 7.6 *Theoretical relationship between degree of relatedness and amount of corporate knowledge (memory)*

only after you have become seriously ill' (1990: 116). But sometimes surgery, and even an amputation, may be the best solution.

We have previously discussed how the corporation continuously maintains and improves its organizational memory through knowledge transfer with SBUs and thereby improves its competitive edge. From the discussion in this chapter two types of negative phantom limb effects may occur: reduced direct and indirect knowledge transfer. The magnitude of these effects is influenced by the type and degree of relatedness of the divested limb.

First, reduced *direct* knowledge transfer is caused by the missed opportunity for knowledge transfer with the divested unit to resolve specific tasks. SBU tasks which have previously been resolved by using knowledge from the divested part of the organization now have to find paths to solutions.

Second, the *indirect* negative effect results from a weakened corporate memory. Since the corporate memory of the firm is no longer continuously updated with knowledge from the divested unit, corporate and SBU tasks depending on this knowledge can no longer be resolved by utilizing the corporate-wide knowledge of the firm.

The phantom limb effect is the sum of both these negative effects. Since the knowledge necessary for solving particular tasks is lost in the divestiture, the phantom limb effect can be seen as lost competencies in the *corporate* competence configuration. In a worst case scenario, a divestiture may result in deprivation of each SBU's strategic competence, i.e. the SBU's basis for sustainable competitive advantage. On the other hand, if the divested SBU is totally unrelated to the remaining SBUs, the phantom limb effect is avoided and the negative causal chain is broken.

Conclusions

Coupled with the financially constrained situations of many corporations, many divestitures are bound to cause problems. Add to this the embedded negative phantom limb effects discussed in this chapter and the consequences may be really serious. In our opinion it is necessary to begin any divestiture attempt with an *inter-SBU focus*, not a corporate one as is the case in the majority of divestitures. The traditional view of a portfolio of SBUs is not sufficient, perhaps not even adequate, in this respect. From a competence-based perspective of the firm, divestiture is not simply a matter of selling off SBUs; it is a matter of altering the *raison d'être* of the firm, namely the corporate competence configuration. The implication is that a bottom-up, not a top-down approach to divestiture is required.

In addition, divestitures may impact the remaining units' basis for developing competitive advantages through the phantom limb effect. In turn, this will hurt subsequent corporate performance. The phantom limb effect represents costs stemming from deprived competence configurations. In turn, the phantom limb may accelerate the direct impact of losing a part of the corporate competence. Thus, an implication is that it is necessary for corporate management on an ongoing basis to proactively reflect over how to reduce potential phantom limb effects in the case of future divestitures. To avoid the potential negative effects of the phantom limb effects, managers involved in divestitures need to carefully address at least the following questions:

- What *intra*-SBU knowledge is used for building *inter*-SBU competence?
- What expertise from one SBU is critical for the task performance of the other SBUs?
- What are the contributions of the 'divested' experts to the corporate competency configuration?
- What tasks cannot be performed after the divestiture?
- What information transferred to the *corporate memory* (e.g. standard operating procedures, data bases, archives) is lost after the divestiture?
- What is the difference between a management buyout (Seth and Easterwood, 1993) and divestiture – from a phantom limb perspective?
- What are the implications of a divestiture, given the answers to the above questions, for (1) corporate effectiveness and (2) SBU competitiveness?
- What is the unlearning from divestitures (Hedberg, 1981)?
- How can corporate managers, who are often isolated from everyday knowledge transfer (Hærem et al., 1993), understand the consequences of divestitures with regard to the direct knowledge transfer?

- How can a divestiture be scheduled so that the knowledge potential of the divestiture candidate is utilized fully, i.e. through knowledge transfer to the remaining parts of the corporation?
- How can the phantom limb effect be dampened through cooperative strategies?
- How can HRMs reallocate 'experts' preemptively?
- How does the phantom limb effect differ in international, multinational and global settings (Yip, 1994)?
- Who is responsible for understanding the consequences of the divestiture on the corporate competence configuration?

Finally, how can we reduce the effects of a phantom limb? As in medical sciences, healing can take time. The best case scenario is that only time is lost: the knowledge lost can perhaps be recovered. The worst case scenario is that the remaining 'scar' in the corporate competence configuration cannot heal at all because there is neither a task nor a knowledge system readily available to replace the divested 'limb'. The implication is that corporate management need to assess the magnitude of the negative phantom limb effect prior to the divestiture. The impact might depend on the strategic importance of the particular competence and on managerial processes and other leadership issues. Management also needs to proactively establish a program for retaining knowledge from the unit to be divested. Such a program should consider:

1 identifying the competence of the divestment target (knowledge system, task systems of the unit)
2 making explicit the knowledge transfer within the corporation, between the divestment target and other SBUs, and identifying key personnel that have played a central role in knowledge transfer
3 keeping and motivating key personnel that have been central to the knowledge transfer, and other experts that are important for the corporation
4 letting key personnel from other SBUs do a 'knowledge audit': search for and document critical knowledge in the investment target, and suggest training programs to develop this knowledge elsewhere in the corporation
5 identifying and retaining the divestment target's technology, manuals, procedures, information systems that are central to the competitive advantage of other SBUs in the corporation
6 letting the possible phantom limb effect be reflected in the price asked for the target.

As a final consideration, perhaps the 'spin-off mode' could replace divestments as a more experimental way of focusing the corporation. While divestments imply no retention of control by the parent company, spin-offs involve flexible control based on strategic intent, financial participation, and human resource sharing. This is a preferred mode by

Japanese firms and seems to be a viable instrument for realizing corporate growth objectives (Ito, 1995; Ito and Rose, 1994).

The purpose of this chapter was to point to some of the negative effects of corporate divestiture on corporate performance from a competence-based perspective of the firm. As such, this chapter represents a new approach to understanding the reasons for the negative effects of divestitures.

Notes

The chapter is based on the article 'Corporate Divestiture and the Phantom-Limb Effect', *European Management Journal*, 1992, 12(4): 171–8.

References

Alexander, G.J., Benson P.G. and Kampmeyer, J.M. (1984). Investing the valuation effects of announcements of voluntary corporate selloffs. *Journal of Finance*, 39 (June): 503–17.

Anderson, J.R. (1985). *Cognitive Psychology and its Implications*. New York: Freeman.

Ansoff, H.I. (1965). *Corporate Strategy*. New York: McGraw-Hil.

Barney, J.B. (1986). Types of competition and the theory of strategy: toward an integrative framework. *Academy of Management Review*, 11: 791–800.

Barney, J.B. (1988). Returns to bidding firms in mergers and acquisitions: reconsidering the relatedness hypothesis. *Strategic Management Journal*, 9: 791–800.

Barney, J.B. (1991). Firm resources and sustained competitive advantages. *Journal of Management*, 17(1): 99–120.

Belohlav, J. and LaVan, H. (1989). The impact of corporate restructuring on human resource management functions. *International Journal of Management*, 10(3): 24–7.

Berger, P. and Luckmann, T. (1967). *The Social Construction of Reality*. New York: Penguin.

Bergh, D. D. (1995). Size and relatedness of units sold: an agency theory and resource-based perspective. *Strategic Management Journal*, 16: 221–39.

Bettis, R.A. (1981). Performance differences in related and unrelated diversified firms. *Strategic Management Journal*, 2: 379–93.

Campbell, D.J. (1988). Task complexity: a review and analysis. *Academy of Management Review*, 13: 40–52.

Daft, R. (1983). *Organization Theory and Design*. New York: West.

Douglas, M. (1986). *How Institutions Think*. Syracuse, NY: Syracuse University Press.

Drucker, P. (1981). The five rules for successful acquisition. *The Wall Street Journal*, 15 October.

Duffy, S. (1990). Brief case: corporate restructuring – causes and categories. *Journal of Long Range Planning*, 23(4): 114–16.

Duhaime, M.I. and Baird, S. I. (1987). Divestment decision-making: the role of business unit size. *Journal of Management*, 13(3): 483–98.

Duhaime, M.I. and Grant, J. H. (1984). Factors influencing divestment decision-making: evidence from a field study. *Strategic Management Journal*, 5(4): 301–18.

Fiol, C. M. (1991). Managing culture as a competitive resource: an identity-based view of sustainable competitive advantage. *Journal of Management*, 17(1): 191–211.

Galbraith, J.R. (1977). *Organization Design*. Boston, MA: Addison-Wesley.

Hærem, T., Krogh, G. and Roos, J. (1993). Knowledge based strategic change. Paper presented at the SMS Conference, September 1993.

Hærem, T. (1993). Knowledge transfer – the key to change, Unpublished Master of Science Thesis.

Hedberg, B. (1981). How organizations learn and unlearn. In P. Nystrom and W. Starbuck (eds), *Handbook of Organizational Design*. Oxford: Oxford University Press.

Itami, H. (1987). *Mobilizing Invisible Assets*. Cambridge, MA: Harvard University Press.

Ito, K (1995). Japanese spin-offs: unexplored survival strategies. *Strategic Management Journal*, 16: 431–46

Ito, K. and Rose, E.L. (1994). The genealogical structure of Japanese firms: parent–subsidiary relations. *Strategic Management Journal*, Summer Special Issue, 15: 35–52.

Jain, P.C. (1985). The effect of voluntary selloff announcements on shareholder wealth. *Journal of Finance*, 44 (March): 209–24.

Johnson R.A., Hoskisson, R.E. and Hitt, M.A. (1993). Board of director involvement in restructuring: the effects of board versus managerial controls and characteristics. *Strategic Management Journal*, 14: 33–50.

Kantrow, A.M. (1987). *The Constraints of Corporate Tradition*. New York: Harper & Row.

Kitching, J. (1973). Acquisitions in Europe – causes of corporate success and failures. *Business International European Research Report*, Geneva.

Klein, A. (1986). The timing and substance of divestiture announcements: individual, simultaneous and cumulative effects. *Journal of Finance*, 41 (July): 685–97.

Lawrence, P.R. and Lorsch, J.W. (1967). *Organization and Environment*. Cambridge, MA: Harvard University Press.

Lubatkin, M. (1987). Mergers strategies and stockholder value. *Strategic Mangement Journal*, 8: 39–53.

Lyles, A.M. and Schwenk, R.C. (1992). Top management strategy and organizational knowledge structures. *Journal of Management Studies*, 29(2): 155–74.

Mahoney T.J. and Pandian, J. (1992). The resource-based view within the conversation of strategic management. *Strategic Management Journal*, 13: 363–80.

Markides, C.C. and Williamson, J.P. (1994). Related diversification and corporate performance. *Strategic Management Journal*, 15: 149–65.

Markides, C.C. (1992). The consequences of corporate refocusing: ex-ante evidence. *Academy of Management Journal*, 35(2): 398–412.

Markides, C.C. (1995). Diversification, restructuring and economic performance. *Strategic Management Journal*, 16: 101–18.

Montgomery C.A. and Singh, H. (1984). Diversification strategy and systematic risk. *Strategic Management Journal*, 5(2): 181–91.

Montgomery, C.A. and Singh, H. (1987). Corporate acquisition strategies and economic performance. *Strategic Management Journal*, 8: 377–86.

Montgomery, C.A., Thomas, A.R. and Kamath, R. (1984). Divestiture, market valuation, and strategy. *Academy of Management Journal*, 27(4): 830–40.

Murray, T.J. (1987). Bitter survivors. *Business Month*, 129(5): 28–31.

Penrose, T.E. (1959). *The Theory of the Growth of the Firm*. New York: Basil Blackwell.

Perrow, C. (1967). A framework for the comparative analysis of organizations. *American Sociological Review*: 194–208.

Porter, M.E. (1980). *Competitive Strategy*. New York: Free Press.

Porter, M.E. (1987). Diversifikation – Konzerne ohne Konzept. *Harvard Manager*, 4: 30–49.

Prahalad, C.K. and Bettis, A.R. (1986). The dominant logic: a new linkage between diversity and performance. *Strategic Management Journal*, 7: 485–501.

Rosenfeld, J.D. (1984). Additional evidence on the relation between divestiture announcements and shareholder wealth. *Journal of Finance*, 39 (December): 1437–48.

Rumelt, R. (1974). *Strategy, Structure and Economic Performance*. Boston, MA: Harvard Business School.

Salter, M.S. and Weinhold, W.A. (1979). *Diversification through Acquisitions*. New York: Free Press.

Seth, A. and Easterwood, J. (1993). Strategic redirection in large management buyouts: the evidence from post buyout restructuring activity. *Strategic Management Journal*, 14(4): 251–73.

Sims, P.H. and Gioia, A.D. (1986). *The Thinking Organization*. San Francisco, CA: Jossey-Bass.

Thompson, D.J. (1967). *Organizations in Action*. New York: McGraw-Hill.

Tushman, L.M. and Nadler, A.D. (1978). Information processing as an integrating concept in organizational design. *Academy of Management Review*, 3(3): 613–24.

Van deVen, A.H., Delbecq, L.A. and Koenig, J.R. (1976). Determinants of coordination modes within organizations. *American Sociological Review*, 41: 322–38.

von Krogh, G., and Roos, J. (1992). Figuring out your competence configuration. *European Management Journal*, 10(4): 422–27.

von Krogh, G. and Roos, J. (1994). Corporate divestiture and the phantom limb effect. *European Management Journal*, 12(2): 171–8.

von Krogh, G. and Roos, J. (1995). A perspective on knowledge, competence and strategy. *Personnel Review*, 24(3): 56–76.

Wallum, P. (1980). Personnel's role in company mergers. *Personnel Management*, 12: 58–61.

Walsh, J.P., and Ungson, G.R. (1991). Organisational memory. *Academy of Management Review*, 16(1): 57–91.

Weick, K.E. and Gilfillan, D.P. (1971). Fate of arbitrary traditions in a laboratory microculture. *Journal of Personality and Social Psychology*, 17: 179–91.

Yip, G. (1994). *Total Global Strategy: Managing for World-Wide Competitive Advantage*. Englewood Cliffs, NJ: Prentice-Hall.

Part II

Anti-Representationism: New Perspectives on Knowledge and Knowledge Transfer in Organizational Cooperation

The aim of this part is to present an alternative to the perspective on knowledge illustrated in the seven chapters of Part I of this book. Many valuable insights arise from the representationistic perspective used in Part I – but, as has been already argued in Chapter 1, many issues remain to conceptualize and study. We offer the alternative perspective – the anti-representationistic one – to shed more light on those issues and bring forward some innovative implications into the realm of strategic management. We have used a distinction tree, as in Part I, to structure the topics discussed in the four chapters of Part II (see Figure C).

Chapter 8 serves as an introduction to the anti-representationistic perspective. The properties of the anti-representationistic perspective are followed through in the following chapters, in terms of both external and internal knowledge development.

Focusing on knowledge development and transfer *between* firms, Chapter 9 introduces the concept of *cooperative experimentation*. Chapters 10 and 11

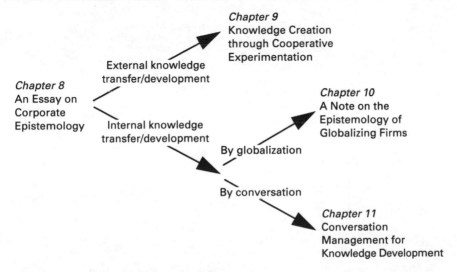

Figure C   *Structure of Part II 'Anti-Representationism'*

take a closer look at internal managerial issues by exploring the impacts of *globalization* and *conversation* on knowledge development respectively.

The anti-representationistic perspective is still in its infancy within the realm of strategic management and organization studies. Therefore, it should not be surprising that the number of chapters (read: the amount of research completed) is smaller in Part II than in Part I. If you return to Figure A in the Introduction – the overall distinction tree – you will see that we have tried to advance by 'stepping back' and take a new 'knowledge road' (read: making new distinctions based on different assumptions). Wherever this road may lead us, we intend to continue to be road constructors rather than passive travellers. Of course, the further advancement of this knowledge road is now up for grabs. You are welcome to join the team!

8

An Essay on Corporate Epistemology

Georg von Krogh, Johan Roos and Ken Slocum

Dear reader, please try to forget the reality you have previously constructed and let yourself be open to the signals this chapter carries. These
signals are truly distinct from those in previous articles and books within
the strategic management field. The starting point is how managers
understand and ensure knowledge development in organizations, and the
theoretical lens is autopoiesis theory.

In our opinion, rethinking the strategy paradigm implies rethinking how
we view the organization. In this chapter, rethinking the organization
means developing a new theory of organizational knowledge, that is, a
corporate epistemology. Epistemology is a branch of one of the grand
divisions of philosophy, namely methodology, and deals with the ways of
interpreting knowledge, i.e. the ways of knowing (Montague, 1962).[1] With
'corporate epistemology' we can construct a theory on how and why
organizations know. But corporate epistemology must deal with some core
questions: what is knowledge, how does it develop, and what are the
conditions for knowledge to develop? The objective of this chapter is,
therefore, to develop a new corporate epistemology which can subsequently contribute to a new perspective of strategic management.

Chakravarthy and Doz (1992) underscored that research within our field
must become more relevant to practice. They called for research that
involves multi-disciplinary team work, that has a focus on corporate
strategy processes, and that is action research oriented (1992: 9–10). The
research presented in this chapter not only fulfills these criteria, but adds to
the authors' line of thinking. It has been conceptualized and thematized by
one practitioner and two strategy professors, and, in addition to addressing
an important managerial issue and drawing on theoretical lenses perhaps
unknown to many people, it is built on a new methodological approach.[2]

Our theme is inspired by the tremendous transformations in contemporary society and economics and in the phenomenon we call the organization. Indicators of these transformations are many. In education,
knowledge has become increasingly differentiated as a result of increasing
efforts in research and development: there is no longer a 'right knowledge',
but many coexisting conflicting pieces of knowledge. In turn, the contest
between different elements of knowledge continually increases the complexity of total knowledge conveyed through education (Lyotard, 1984;

Lawson and Appignanesi, 1989; Hage and Powers, 1992). Further indicators may be discovered in the arts, which, according to Sakaiya, 'is a field of human endeavor that tends to be in the forefront of any imminent social transformation' (1992: 148). Contemporary art presents itself in a way that is different from historical art; it combines elements from many epochs in new ways (Lyotard, 1984). In philosophy, the coming of a postmodern age and its implications for individuals and societies at large are being surveyed and debated (Habermas, 1992). Another indicator is the general shift in the economy from diminishing to increasing returns on resources in many industries (Arthur, 1990).

The most important signals for the strategic management field include: the advent of information technology and new organizational forms (Sproull and Kiesler, 1991); corporate programs to fuse various types of technologies (Kodoma, 1991); the emergence of new forms of manufacturing (Drucker, 1990); the implementation of competitive alliances, i.e. collaboration among competitors (Hamel et al., 1988); the coming of new activity-based accounting systems (Johnson and Kaplan, 1987; Johnson, 1992); and the availability of lifelong learning programs as a partnership between the individual and the educational institution (Lorange, 1992; Goshal et al., 1992). Some consequences of these signals have been addressed by various authors (Davidow and Malone, 1992; Badaracco, 1991; Fombrun, 1992; Hamel and Prahalad, 1989; 1993; Prahalad and Hamel, 1990; Hamel, 1991).

An important conclusion to be drawn from this work is that we need to develop a better understanding of the organization as a knowledge system. We suggest that the organization can be seen as a *stream of knowledge*. This means that the organization, as we have come to know it during the past century, is an inaccurate concept. Likewise, our management practices and theories need to be discarded, altered, or reinvented in order to give adequate descriptions and provide accessible heuristics that can guide managers in this new knowledge-intensive era. That is exactly what this chapter will address.

The essay consists of three main sections. First, our methodological approach is discussed. Second, our speculation on a new corporate epistemology is presented. Building on this epistemology, in the third section we discuss the further advancement of the realm of strategic management.

Methodology: a Process of Matching

Not surprisingly, theorists in the field to an increasing extent seem to acknowledge that the process of strategic management research and the results of research are closely connected (Chakravarthy and Doz, 1992; Lorange et al., 1993). This is in accordance with the well-known principle of indeterminism discovered by Werner Heisenberg in the mid 1920s.[3] In short, this principle acknowledges that observation influences what is seen and vice versa. Thus, any attempt to truly rethink the boundaries of strategic management must acknowledge this effect and, therefore, simultaneously cause a rethinking of the research approach. When we wonder about something, we not only need to look for answers to questions never asked before, we need to become inventive about ways of finding out things. Otherwise, methodology may become a severe constraint on the degree of novelty in the knowledge produced.

Because the process of finding new meaning in the ideas of strategic management essentially is a creative process, the theories and perspectives developed still require sufficient grounding in practical relevance. Our research approach tries to accomplish precisely this balance: while making use of both a new theoretical perspective and a new methodology, we have simultaneously put creative *and* practical relevance weight into this chapter.

Our approach *synthesizes* grounded and grand theories, as opposed to the traditional approach of discussing implications of the one for the other (see Glaser and Strauss, 1967). The approach assumes a joint effort by proponents of grounded and grand theories, and the synthesis is accomplished through numerous iterations and dialogues. Our distinction between grounded and grand theories is analogous to 'empirical' and 'theoretical' aspects of social scientific knowledge as defined by Wold (1969).

The process of matching the two aspects leads to theory construction. This is different from matching as model validation, as discussed by logical empiricists (e.g. Wold, 1969; Chronbach and Meehl, 1955). Rather, 'matching' means unifying languages, theoretical concepts and their interrelationships. The matching that resulted in this chapter involved a two-step process: (1) theoretical discourse, and (2) inscription of theory.

Unification of grand and grounded theory ideally happens through a phase of 'theoretical discourse' in which conflicting theoretical claims, including concepts and their interrelationships, are put forth (Habermas, 1984: 19). Through frequent dialogue between the participants (two strategy professors and one senior executive of a US-based corporation), we unified our theories on knowledge and knowledge development. It follows from this that the academic language was *not* 'victorious', in the sense of being the only legitimate language (Bourdieu, 1991: 5). *In this research, the only legitimate language was the one that results from the matching process.*

The matching process necessary to prepare this chapter took more than one year. During this period we were able to focus on concepts and relationships of common interest, and discard those concepts and relationships that did not create a basis for common understanding. The theoretical discourse included numerous activities, such as discussions of ideas and concepts in personal meetings inside and outside each other's organizations (both in Europe and in the US), and developing a joint frame of reference by ordering and reading each other's reference literature.

The inscription process was the most critical phase in the research project. Inscription implies capturing and making an object (for further study) out of the knowledge that has been co-constructed by the practitioner and academics. The current chapter is a product of a period where every word is tested for the meaning it conveys to both the practitioners and the researchers.

It follows that our research is different from both traditional positivistic and anti-positivistic research approaches. It is different from case study research (Yin, 1984) in which the practitioner is solely conveying a set of data for research, and it is different from grounded theory building (Glaser and Strauss, 1967; Eisenhardt, 1989) due to its focus on participation in theory construction.

This research is also distinct from other participant-oriented research processes, such as participatory action research (e.g. Reason, 1988; Whyte, 1991) or action science (e.g. Argyris et al., 1985).[4] In such processes the researcher assumes that there is some 'kind of questions that concern the researcher more than the participant. These are questions relating to the theorizing and knowledge accumulation process itself' (Karlsen, 1991: 149; see also Elden and Levin, 1991). When epistemology is the focus of study and the interest of the practitioner, this assumption (as we discovered) does not hold. Like any theorist, the practitioner is eager to see if 'local theory' also holds outside his/her immediate action context, i.e. in another organization. The heart of the difference between our matching approach and other research processes lies in the phase of inscription. This is the phase where the knowledge is made presentable such that it may inform other theory-building attempts and the knowledge development of another context.

Towards Autopoietic Epistemology

This section outlines our theoretical lens. Beginning with the roots and applications of the theory, we proceed to discuss the cognitivist and strategic management notion of knowledge. Further, we present a notion of knowledge from the new perspective, the notion of social knowledge and, finally, the conditions for autopoiesis and knowledge development.

Autopoiesis Theory, its Roots and Applications

Originally developed in the field of neurobiology to characterize 'living systems', autopoiesis theory suggests the composition and structure of individual cognitive systems (Maturana and Varela, 1980; 1987). Through its application in the social sciences, autopoiesis theory also emerges as a new theory of knowledge of a social system (von Krogh and Vicari, 1993; Luhmann, 1986).

Since its introduction, autopoisesis theory has gradually evolved into a general theory of systems (Varela, 1979; Luhmann, 1986; van Twist and

Schaap, 1991). The theory's main thesis is that the components of an autopoietic system are used to produce new components and their relations so as to recreate the system.[5] This production of components does not depend on an input–output relation with the system's environment. Everything that the system needs for its reproduction is already in the system. Certain systems, then, and in particular cognitive systems, are created and re-created in a recursive, self-generating, closed, and autonomous manner: hence the term 'autopoiesis' (Greek *auto* self plus *poiein* to make, produce, remake, conceptualize).[6]

Autopoiesis theory is interesting to many scientists in different fields. However, only in some instances can the label 'autopoiesis' be meaningfully applied to processes under observation. The main requirement is that one must be able to give a precise connotation to component production processes (what is the component, and how do you guarantee its reproduction?) and systems (e.g. Varela, 1979). Despite these restrictions and its relatively short history, autopoiesis theory has had an impressive impact in many fields. For instance, in legal theory and the sociology of law, the basic concept of autopoiesis has created awareness as to the legal system's lack of renewal and resistance to adapt to problems in the economy (Luhmann, 1982; 1988; Teubner, 1988; 1991; Deggau, 1988). In the debate on ecological consciousness and corporate responsiveness to environmental issues, autopoiesis theory has helped increase the awareness of communications problems (i.e. between environmentalists and corporate decision makers) and advanced possible ways to overcome these problems (Luhmann, 1992). Autopoiesis theory has also increased our understanding of how computers and their function are related to the evolution of human language, thought, and action (Winograd and Flores, 1987). In the philosophy of science, autopoiesis theory has been used to point out the constitution of 'everyday knowledge' as opposed to 'scientific knowledge' (Maturana, 1991, Becker, 1991). In the field of management, the concept of autopoiesis is used to address the evolution of organization knowledge (Vicari, 1991; von Krogh and Vicari, 1993). It has also formed a reference point for understanding (more in a metaphorical sense), evolutionary organization change (Morgan, 1986; Smith, 1982; Weathly, 1992).

In this chapter, autopoiesis theory is used to articulate a perspective of organization epistemology for strategic management. That is, we develop further the notion of knowledge and the conditions for autopoiesis.

*The Cognitivist Notion of Knowledge and the Heritage of
Strategic Management Research*

One of the basic questions of epistemology concerns the *notion* of knowledge. Our primary concern is organizational knowledge, that is, knowledge shared by organizational members. However, because autopoiesis theory has deep roots in what are known as the cognitive sciences, and since we will later claim that knowledge development at the individual level resembles knowledge development at the social level, this investigation starts by briefly contrasting the notion of knowledge from autopoiesis theory with the more traditional notions of knowledge. This section also highlights how a traditional notion of knowledge has inspired researchers in the field of strategic management to develop a strong conceptual notion of literature on the development of organizational knowledge. (Please do have in mind that the properties of the cognitivist epistemology discussed below, are implicitly or explicitly in Part I of this book.)

Since the mid 1950s the ideas of Herbert Simon, Noam Chomsky, Marvin Minsky, John McCarthy and others have inspired the growth of cognitive science where human knowledge holds a particular position (Gardner, 1985; Varela, 1992; see for example Newell and Simon, 1972; Minsky, 1975; Simon, 1989). Varela (1992) calls the perspective which builds on the ideas of these scientists the 'cognitivist' perspective. In this perspective, cognition is to a large extent seen as information processing and rule-based manipulation of symbols (like words). Knowledge is abstract, task-specific and oriented towards problem solving.

At the very heart, the cognitivist perspective assumes that the world is pre-given, and that the goal of any cognitive system is to create the most accurate representation of this world (Varela, 1992). Representations (e.g. of persons, things, events) can be stored in and retrieved from schemata of the individual (Anderson, 1983; Bartlett, 1932; Schank and Abelson, 1977), and if events represented frequently recur, their representations are stored in scripts (Schank and Abelson, 1977). Nisbett and Ross (1980) coined the term 'knowledge structures' to cover both schemata and scripts. An important finding of Nisbett and Ross's work is that the individual frequently develops rudimentary knowledge structures by resolving ambiguity, making guesses about unobservable events, and inferring about causal relationships (Bruner, 1964; Nisbett and Ross, 1980; Tversky and Kahneman, 1973). Learning in the cognitivist perspective means that the individual more accurately obtains representations of the world through assimilating new experiences, for example, 'a person actively constructs knowledge . . . by relating incoming information to a previously acquired psychological frame of reference' (Bruner and Anglin, 1973: 397).[7]

The cognitivist perspective has inspired substantial theory development in strategic management, related to both the social cognition of organizations and the cognition of individual managers. At a very general level, several contributions assume that managers and organizations create representations of their environment through processing information available to them in this external environment (e.g. March and Simon, 1958; Argyris and Schön, 1978; Ginsberg, 1990; Gioia and Manz, 1985; Daft and Weick, 1984; Weick, 1979; Huff, 1983; Hedberg 1981).[8] These representations are storable and retrievable in organization-wide knowledge structures that give organizational members a shared perception of the world (Prahalad and Bettis, 1986; Lyles and Schwenk, 1992; Walsh and Ungson, 1991). The evolution of these structures is dependent on the experiences gained.

Further, the strategic management literature frequently assumes that organizations are problem seekers and solvers, and that they develop some task-specific knowledge (Cyert and March, 1963; Lant and Mezias, 1990; Lant et al., 1992). In fact, Prahalad and Bettis take this argument a step forward by claiming that problem-solving behavior ingrained in knowledge structures may be a potential source of a dominant general management logic, that is, 'the way in which managers conceptualize the business and make critical resource allocation decisions' (1986: 490). Such conceptualizations and resource allocation decisions may be sustained in organizations and develop into 'cognitive rigidities' due to conventional wisdom and past experiences. The strategic management literature here demonstrates that novel problems may be approached with old representations of the world. Several authors suggest that until a major crisis occurs, or new top management replaces the old team, a change in rigid knowledge structures cannot be expected (e.g. Hedberg et al., 1976; see also Grinyer et al., 1988). However, one of the central problems identified by Prahalad and Bettis (1986) and Lyles and Schwenk (1992) is that little is known about *how* knowledge structures actually develop. As previously stated, this is one of the central questions in any corporate epistemology.

In summary, two issues come forth from the cognitivist notion of knowledge:

1 The cognitivist perspective is concerned with how representations of the world are created by information processing. In turn, these representations are stored in knowledge structures.
2 Much literature in strategic management builds on this information processing assumption.

The Notion of Knowledge in Autopoiesis Theory

Evoking autopoiesis theory implies rethinking some of the very basic assumptions behind the previous contributions on how and why organizations know. We want to speculate on what happens if one relaxes some of the assumptions of the cognitivist perspective and replaces them with the assumptions of autopoiesis theory. In doing this we believe that autopoiesis theory emerges as an important contribution to these previous works in strategic management.

Unlike the cognitivist perspective, autopoiesis theory suggests not that the world is a pre-given state to be represented, but rather that cognition is a creative act of bringing forth a world. Knowledge is a component of the autopoietic (self-productive) process; it is history dependent, context sensitive, and, rather than being oriented towards problem solutions, enables problem definition (Maturana and Varela, 1987; Varela, 1992; Varela et al., 1992). Moreover, at the individual level, knowledge is not abstract but rather is embodied in the individual. How does this alter our conceptions of managerial cognition? There are at least two important implications of claiming that cognition is autopoietic: (1) knowledge is intimately connected to observation, and (2) the notion of information becomes redefined.

First, the proposition of 'embodied knowledge' suggests that all know-ledge is dependent on the manager, or everything known is known by somebody. More importantly, however, knowledge depends very much on the 'point of observation' of the manager. Where you stand or what you know determines what you see or what you choose to be relevant. In autopoiesis theory 'knowledge' and 'observation' are closely related, since observing systems are autopoietic systems.[9] To be more precise, in autopoiesis theory distinctions and norms are two central categories (Luhmann, 1986; 1988; Varela, 1979). Knowledge is what makes managers able to make *distinctions* in their observations (for example between themselves and others) and, based on their *norms*, determine what they see. The distinctions made reveal the knowledge of the distinguisher. For example, in reading a management book, a manager first isolates the book from the background, like a table. Next, she has to make a distinction between print and paper, or even between different fonts, like Times or Geneva. In reading the book she can distinguish the book as a finance or strategy book and, based on her set of norms, decide whether the book is 'good' or 'bad'. She might even, if she is skilled in the analysis of literature, isolate the stream of thinking to which the book was intended to contribute. This is all of her own doing. It would be difficult to predict exactly what kind of knowledge the manager would develop around this book, based on the mere act of giving her a book.

In turn, applying distinctions allows for new knowledge to develop. By isolating a phenomenon, the manager can gain knowledge about it. The term used to describe this process of knowledge development is *self-referentiality*. Self-referentiality means that new knowledge refers not only to past knowledge but *also* to potential future knowledge (Luhmann, 1990; Varela, 1979). Managers use already established knowledge to determine what they see, and they use what they already know to choose what to look for in their environment. Knowledge is therefore highly dynamic as managers make new observations, talk, use their fantasies to envision possible futures, and formulate problems. Increasing knowledge enables managers to make finer and finer distinctions, and, in many ways, a kind of knowledge structure evolves that resembles a 'decision tree'. The tree structure also implies that knowledge is subject to *scaling*. Scaling means similarity transformations (when two objects have the same shape regard-less of their size), i.e. scales of magnification.[10] Here, scaling means moving along the 'distinction tree' or knowledge structure, that is, adapting the distinction level to the circumstances.

To illustrate: by reading technical literature, an R&D manager may use his knowledge to isolate a technical innovation in telecommunications from the bulk of nicely repackaged but old technical solutions. Moreover, he may distinguish a technical innovation of high possible impact from an imitation with no interest. Here the distinction might be 'innovation–imitation' and the norm applied would be 'a high degree of impact'. In reading more about the innovation, the manager may develop increasingly fine distinctions, for example linear versus non-linear mathematics. In proceeding, the resulting knowledge structure evolves into a distinction tree. In this example it is important to note two features. First, the R&D manager, when talking to the CEO, may scale up and again use the distinction imitation–innovation to arouse the CEO's interest. Second, the manager makes distinctions even if the message he conveys does not make this explicit. Even if he only chooses to say 'Fantastic, I have found a new innovation' rather than 'I have found an innovation that is distinct from imitation', his very use of the concept of innovation implies something distinct from imitation.[11]

A second implication of saying that the cognition is autopoietic is that we need to distinguish between data, information and knowledge. In autopoiesis theory, information is not a commodity or a substance, as is often assumed in the cognitivist perspective and the strategic management literature. Rather, information is a process of interpretation, or, to use the words of von Foerster, 'information is the process by which knowledge is acquired' (1984: 193). Literally, information means 'to put' data 'in form' (Latin *in* in plus*form* form plus *are* doing). Books, movies, lectures, papers, computer programs, memos, etc., are *data* in the environment of the manager – *not* information. They are simply fractions and may be vehicles for potential information. Information is dependent on the manager who makes use of it to create knowledge. The only way to describe this process is to say that the manager is *simultaneously open and closed*. He or she is closed with respect to knowledge (also knowledge about the environment) but open with respect to data from the outside.

Further, the manager is open with respect to data of different degrees of latency. A high degree of latency means that the data are unclear and ambiguous and may appear to be disturbances or noise in the environment. Such data are not immediately presented to the manager as information. These data may indicate areas where the manager has little or no knowledge. More manifest data, i.e. data with a low degree of latency, are lucid, clear, unambiguous, and meaningful to the system, and as such can easily be converted to information. The manager's response to such data may be to make increasingly fine distinctions.

In summary, in autopoietic theory:

1 The world is not pre-given to be represented.
2 Knowledge is connected to observation.
3 The notion of information is redefined.

The Notion of Organizational Knowledge

Previous contributions in organizational behavior and strategic management literature have attempted to bridge individual cognition with social cognition of the organization (e.g. Prahalad and Bettis, 1986; Lyles and Schwenk, 1992; Argyris and Schön, 1978; Weick and Bougnon, 1986; Daft and Weick, 1984; Ginsberg, 1990).

Individuals have private knowledge that can be a basis for organizational knowledge when conveyed through speaking, gesturing, writing, etc.[12] Knowledge *of* the organization is shared knowledge among organizational members. Organizational knowledge allows for shared distinction making in observations made by organizational members on events, situations and objects that are internal and external to the organization. These distinctions are created and maintained in conversations between organizational members and hence allow for new knowledge to develop in a self-referential manner. A prerequisite for organizational knowledge to develop in the organization is the cardinal distinction between the organization and its environment, e.g. 'What do we know about our environment?' Social norms are necessary to coordinate the opinions of organizational members as to what they observe. They also highlight conflict regarding observations and provide guidelines when organizational members need to negotiate on the content of observations (e.g. Daft and Weick, 1984).

Like individual knowledge, organizational knowledge is also scalable. In conversations, managers move up and down the distinction tree depending on the situation at hand. Perhaps this could be stated in the following way. Organization, when developing knowledge for its own strategic decision making (and hence direction for action), is thinking at a scale that encompasses all other scales of knowledge that would be found in other parts of the corporation (the equivalent of flying at 30,000 feet). This level of thought, however, is useless unless it is logically linked to all the other lower scales of understanding (flying at 3,000 feet; 2,000 feet; 1,500 feet, etc.) so that, as decisions are made, the corporate entity can be assured of the reliability of the eventual implementation of decisions at lower scales of the organization, like marketing or manufacturing. This form of 'high-altitude' thinking would indeed be very cumbersome if the corporate entity had to structure a contiguous pyramid of detailed information connecting all of its various activities throughout the corporation. Instead, the corporate entity needs only to deal with the understanding of the process of subsequent distinction making that may occur at each scale of knowledge development (seeing the differences, not trying to manipulate the whole) and take these into account in its own high-level knowledge development process.

Autopoiesis theory also requires a rethinking of what is seen as information available to the organization. Normally, memos, letters, reports, etc. produced by the organization are seen as pieces of information (e.g. Sproull and Kiesler, 1991). A consequence of an autopoietic epistemology is that documentation, even if produced by the organization, is data and these data fuel organizational knowledge development. The process of creating information based on data requires that organizational members not only read data, but also discuss and file them for later use. A report written in one office by a certain team of specialists may be sent by internal mail to another team of specialists out of the country. The team members become informed through the data, and, by discussing their observations of the report, they participate in developing organizational knowledge. Some data have a manifest character and little conversation is needed for these data to become a source of information and knowledge among organizational members. Latent data, on the other hand, may need extensive discussion before they can be converted to information and thereby become a source of new knowledge. Organizations' response to such data may be to adjust distinctions, or alternatively make increasingly fine distinctions. The whole process of organizational knowledge development makes the organization simultaneously open, with respect to data, and closed, with respect to knowledge.

According to the traits of autopoiesis theory, history provides an important starting point for knowledge development. The stapler industry, for instance, that grew from needs in the automotive industry in the 1930s, triggered development of wound closure technologies in the 1980s. The knowledge needed for this new technology stems from the profound knowledge of fastening various materials that has been developed since the 1930s, for instance metallic and non-metallic materials, staplers for fastening such materials, technologies for shifting types of nails without shifting equipment, as well as technologies for powering the nailing process. As seen from this example, organizational knowledge developed and allowed for new types of activities in the organizations.[13] Here, we propose that a key concept to understanding development of organizational knowledge is *languaging*. For the social system it is by languaging that knowledge brings forth a world (Maturana and Varela, 1987; Becker, 1991). Distinctions like strategic/operational, production/marketing, and norms like good/bad, new/old, happy/sad, are maintained in conversations among organizational members. But because individuals differ in their knowledge and observations, discussions frequently uncover differences in distinctions, distinctions at diverse scales, renamings, finer or broader distinctions, etc. For example, the corporate strategist may experience a trauma by listening to the happy sales manager talking about 'the strategy of telephone sales'. Thus, it is perhaps overly restrictive to conceptualize organizational language as a static body of syntax, signs and codes subject to consistent use over time and place. As an alternative, languaging refers to the process in which language is not only maintained but constantly being created, based on previous language. Managers frequently discard distinctions, introduce new distinctions, use old distinctions on new situations, put words in new contexts, use distinctions in a metaphorical sense, etc. In the words of Maturana and Varela, 'because [he has] language there is no limit to what [the manager] can describe, imagine, and relate' (1987: 212). In this process of languaging some distinctions are maintained, discussed and built on by others and thereby form the basis for developing organizational knowledge and finer distinctions; while other distinctions, because they are not understood, are forgotten, are disagreed on by others, or are discarded.

Maintaining distinctions, however, becomes crucially important to the inventor of the distinction because it frequently relates to the role and identity that person has within the organization. Returning to the example of the R&D manager: when he has singled out an invention from the technical magazine, this is done in his position as an R&D manager. It would represent a serious threat to his position should an engineer from production point out to him that the technical solution was based on an imitation of old technology in an adjacent form. Further knowledge development and distinction making based on the isolation of the product as a technical innovation might also be constrained.

In summary, the notion of organizational knowledge has the following properties:

1 It is shared among organizational members.
2 It is scalable and connected to the organization's history.
3 It both demands and allows for languaging.

Conditions for Autopoiesis

If the manager's cognition is the unit of analysis, the conditions for autopoiesis are biologically given and relatively unproblematic: he must be alive and the brain as well as the senses must be functioning. However, when the organization is the unit of analysis, organizational knowledge is highly dynamic, 'fragile', and developed through a self-referential, simultaneously open and closed process. Given this, how do organizations ensure that the autopoietic process continues and, hence, that knowledge develops? One answer is that unless there are *knowledge connections* available, knowledge at one point in time does not connect with new knowledge at a later point in time. Should this occur the autopoietic process, and therefore knowledge development, stops.[14] Knowledge connection is defined as the potential for individuals to convey messages about their observations.

There are two conditions that need to be satisfied for knowledge to connect in the organization over time: (1) the availability of relationships, and (2) a self-description.[15] First, the organization consists of a set of *relationships* that may create immediate knowledge connections. Organizational members develop informal relationships over time that can ensure that the distinctions they convey are further built on and developed by others. Organizational members are also related to one another through organizational structures and reporting relationships. These facilitate communication among individuals and may therefore allow for organizational knowledge to develop. For example, individuals working on developing a new design on a graphical product may be structurally related with those studying new applications of multi-media. Product developers may also be structurally related to the marketing department. Moreover, the organizational structures function as a set of 'expectations' (Deggau, 1988). Individuals, groups, or subunits meet with structurally defined expectations to create or re-create the organizational knowledge, based on what they know or what others in the organization tell them.

Second, knowledge connections require an adequate *self-description* of the organization (Luhmann, 1990). A self-description results from an 'observation' by the organization of itself. In fact, a 'self-description formulates the identity of the [organization]' (Luhmann, 1990: 253). This provides criteria for selecting what passes for 'knowledge', and, as such, should be further connected, as opposed to 'noise' that should not be connected. In many organizations, descriptions of the organization's identity include business ideas, mission statements, strategy documents, vision statements, management principles, guiding values, etc.

For knowledge to connect with other knowledge it requires, in general, that it passes for organizational knowledge as defined by the self-descriptions. Findings that are not related to current businesses may be discarded, customers that ask for other types of services than those provided by the organization may be ignored, scientific findings that are not relevant for the line of business of the organization are not interesting, and so on. Self-descriptions, therefore, have a *legitimating function* in defining adequate behavior. In the words of Maturana and Varela: 'We admit knowledge whenever we observe an adequate behavior in a given context, i.e., in a . . . domain we define by a question' (1987: 174). The result of these self-descriptions of the organization is a focused development on knowledge through knowledge connections. This is in contrast to totally random knowledge development constantly increasing in variety. Self-description prevents the organization from drowning in 'knowledge complexity'.

In summary, we have discussed the conditions for autopoiesis in terms of knowledge connections. There are two prerequisites for knowledge connections, namely:

1 relationships
2 self-description.

Discussion

In a conventional theory-building paper, implications of theoretical propositions would be presented. As the reader has noted, we have chosen a presentation form which is more like an essay. In the essay form the point is to give extensive discussions of surfacing issues. The corporate epistemology in this chapter does not constrain but merely broadens the tasks and increases the importance of strategic management. The following is a list of questions that might fuel further discourse.

*How Does the Corporate Epistemology Shed Light on How
Knowledge Develops in Organizations?*

As indicated above, a central issue raised by previous works in strategic
management is the problem-solving behavior of firms, that is, how
knowledge structures evolve and change. Two issues seem to emerge from
this work. First, there seems to be some consensus as to the role of
experiences in forming knowledge structures (e.g. Prahalad and Bettis,
1986; Lyles and Schwenk, 1992). Knowledge structures evolve and change
as organizational members reach agreement on interpretations of their
individual and shared common experiences (Daft and Weick, 1984;
Hedberg, 1981; Weick, 1979). Second, as Lyles and Schwenk (1992) point
out, only in rare instances will organizational members question core
elements as opposed to the peripheral elements of the knowledge structure, like clients served, the scope of businesses, and management
philosophies. Eventually, however, massive criticism may also lead to
changes in the core of the knowledge structures of the organization.

In our attempt to develop the corporate epistemology, we have put
particular emphasis on languaging. As organizational members observe
events and situations, and as they engage in languaging, that is, apply and
invent distinctions, phrases, sentences, etc., they participate in developing
organizational knowledge. Agreement and disagreement are apparent at
many levels of the organization at all times, and as organizational members
strive towards agreement (or settle for disagreement) they continue to
develop organizational knowledge, enabling finer and finer distinctions.
What Lyles and Schwenk (1992) call a core set of knowledge structure, we
would refer to as a set of fundamental distinctions. Sometimes organizational members invent new fundamental distinctions pertaining to
organization–environment, strategic–operational, innovation–imitation,
etc. In other words, they scale towards the 'root' of the distinction tree.
This scaling has seriously challenged existing organizational knowledge
and current distinction making. The reaction of other organizational
members is often apparent: they do not recognize these new distinctions as
advancing the knowledge of the organization. Why? Perhaps not so much
because they *disagree* with the new distinctions, but rather because they do
not *understand* the distinctions, i.e. they lack knowledge.

In the strategic management literature agreement on knowledge structures typically assumes a shared understanding. However, because people
might say yes to something they do not understand and no to something
they understand, this assumption does not always hold (Luhmann, 1990).
Organizational members frequently introduce new ideas, new concepts,
and new experiences. The key question is to what extent new distinctions
are 'languaged' in the organization, and how long they are sustained. New
distinctions often vanish simply because they are not understood or further
debated.

A key concept in understanding the sustainability of organizational knowledge, therefore, is knowledge connectivity. Consequently, organizations that ensure knowledge connectivity even in the face of non-understanding will allow for the development of new distinctions and organizational knowledge over time. Self-description allows for 'experimentation in the realm of the unknown' and organizational structure and informal relationships bring people together. Therefore, organizational members may recognize new knowledge (distinguish it from old knowledge) even when they do not completely understand it.

This chapter has not developed sufficiently possible patterns of languaging as they pertain to the development of organizational knowledge. In the strategic management literature the role of language and conversations has attracted relatively little interest, with some insightful exceptions (Fiol, 1991; Westley, 1990; Fletcher and Huff, 1990; Nonaka, 1988). However, as Westley (1990) points out, conversations are interesting to study for three reasons: they are discrete, ritualistic and observable events that help to ground empirically strategic management research; they contain elements of authority; and they uncover cultural vocabularies. In addition to this, *our perspective stresses that languaging is the nexus of organizational knowledge development*.

Future research in strategic management would benefit from studying languaging as such, the period of time in which organizational knowledge is sustained, and the conditions under which the autopoiesis is broken (knowledge ceases to be a basis for further organizational knowledge). The studies should attempt to map distinction trees employed, as well as registering agreement, disagreement, understanding and non-understanding. Such studies would uncover both incremental drifts and drastic shifts in organizational knowledge. Given the interest in knowledge structures and 'dominant logics', we suggest that languaging research should isolate the conceptualizations of businesses and critical resource allocation decisions. In doing this we would be able to find out how and why dominant logics may become an impediment. Of special interest is languaging pertaining to latent data. It would be interesting to understand the languaging involved in making data manifest, the difference in languaging on latent and manifest data, and its possible impact on the dominant logic.

How Does Our Corporate Epistemology Help Us Rethink Strategic Management?

When it comes to rethinking strategic management the following feature surfaces from the corporate epistemology presented in this chapter: a fundamental distinction between advancement and survival activities.

There is a painting by Raphael in the Gallery of the Vatican City that reveals to us fundamental distinctions in Western civilization. The picture is dominated by two figures, Plato pointing to the sky, giving us a symbol of speculative thought,[16] and Aristotle pointing to the ground, providing a

Table 8.1 *Advancement and survival activities*

Advancement activities	Survival activities
Developing distinctions and norms	Production–market positioning
Scaling knowledge	Planning and deciding
Processing data	Organizing
Ensuring knowledge connectivity	Resource development and allocation
Self-referencing	Routinization
Languaging	Controlling

symbol of knowledge on matter, substance, and nature. The mastery of nature is necessary for the *survival* of the human race. Speculation, however, is needed for the *advancement* of human existence.

The corporate epistemology outlined in this chapter implies that the organization is simultaneously subject to survival *and* advancement needs. Although not a novel distinction in principle,[17] separating advancement and survival activities may be critical for organizations, groups and individuals alike. Whereas advancement emerges from knowledge development, which in turn can be seen as developing options for the organization,[18] survival activities mean engaging in some of these options. Linking this fundamental distinction to the realm of strategic management, an interesting picture emerges. The list in Table 8.1 is not complete by any means, but it illustrates the differences in strategic management tasks.

The objectives of strategic management are threefold: it must ensure survival, advancement and balance between these two activities. The overall goal of survival activities, e.g. product–market positioning, resource allocation, planning, organizing, human resource management, routinization, and controlling, is to manage the input–output relationship between the firm and its environment. Survival activities pertain to traditional theories of strategic management and organizing. There are many guidelines for how to address methodologies to research them, and outlets to publish the findings. The key is to manage the firm's survival in a way that makes it able to engage in advancement activities.

Advancement activities, e.g. development of distinctions and norms, processing data, scaling knowledge, ensuring knowledge connectivity, languaging, self-referencing, represent new activities for many organizations. There are few theories explaining them, limited knowledge on how to address them, and few outlets to publish in. Consequently, advancement activities represents challenging research topics and methodologies. Balance between the two activities pertains to both attention and time devoted.

Why is this distinction important? If there is a tremendous transformation in society there are also transformations on the corporate level. There are many conflicting pieces of knowledge coexisting in organizations and people are exposed to data originating in many epochs. Fundamental transformation is manifested in contemporary languaging. New perspectives and solutions to managerial problems will emerge, which are concerned with subjective knowledge as opposed to objective truth; with unrepeatable and unique experiences rather than recurring, general lessons; with intertextual relations instead of temporal causality; with richly personal complexity over inert impersonal simplification. Distinguishing between advancement and survival activities allows researchers to develop ways for the advancement of organizational knowledge, inspired by the languaging mentioned above.

A number of questions arise which need to be addressed by future research in the strategic management field. The recent discussion about the 'resource-based' perspective of the firm (e.g. Barney, 1991; Dierickx and Cool, 1989; Wernerfelt, 1984; Mahoney and Pandian, 1992) poses the question of *why* firms differ (e.g. Nelson, 1991; Carroll, 1993; Schendel, 1991). Lyles and Schwenk (1992) suggest that firms differ due to their individually developed knowledge structures. The corporate epistemology goes beyond this and suggests that firms can be less different in terms of their survival activities and more different in terms of their advancement activities.

Future research should attempt to establish not only why, but *where* and *how much* firms differ with respect to advancement and survival activities. What are the management characteristics in the survival and advancement realm? What is the balance between advancement and survival activities? How are advancement activities measured? What management structures are found in the advancement versus the survival mode? What do conversations in successful organizations center around – survival or advancement activities? What is the linkage between 'core competence' and 'advancement activities'?

How Does Autopoietic Epistemology Help Us to Rethink Research Methodologies in the Strategic Management Field?

In fact, autopoietic epistemology forces us to rethink the use of research methodologies. A 'scientific' description of organizational knowledge implies the use of scientific methods. The corporate epistemology highlights a fundamental dimension in research methodology, namely *observer dependency*. An observer-independent perspective implies that there is a domain of consensus shared by the observers, that is, the individual observer's role is not taken into account. The traditional description of scientific method (e.g. observation, model generation, prediction, observation of results) presupposes an observer-independent perspective (Hejl, 1980). From our perspective, a scientific description of organizational knowledge must always take the role of observer into account.[19] Such observer dependency means that only the reality of two strategy professors and one senior executive is presented in this chapter. Still, our construction of reality is *not* meant to be pushed through as the 'generally valid one' in the field.

Another important dimension in research methodology concerns the *distance of observation*. There are two principal ways of studying organization knowledge: system-distant and system-close. As system-distant observers, researchers draw distinctions that isolate streams of knowledge of the organization. Very often there are implicit criteria of what passes for knowledge, often related to a particular kind of behavior (Maturana and Varela, 1987). What is needed for a study of organization knowledge to be valid is not only a definition of the generic characteristics of knowledge, e.g. naming a knowledge base 'core competence', but *also* a clarification of what kind of behavior is associated with knowledge of the organization, e.g. that core competence is associated with consistent investment across businesses (see Hamel and Prahalad, 1989). The main reason for this is that in very few cases can you directly access the knowledge of individuals or teams by asking questions (Prahalad and Bettis, 1986; Argyris and Schön, 1978). The researcher has to rely on observable behavior. For example, when do researchers admit knowledge in a study of corporate acquisitions and performance? Does one admit that the management team of the acquiring organization is knowledgeable of the acquired organization when they choose to intervene in managerial practices of the acquired organization? Does one admit that the acquiring management team has knowledge only when they are successful? If yes, would this not ignore the knowledge gained by the experiences with the new company, and, in cases of diversification, a new business or industry? Such questions can best be answered by conveying the criteria of what passes for organizational knowledge.

Autopoietic epistemology also helps us to address the recent concern about relevance among strategic (process) researchers (e.g. Chakravarthy and Doz, 1992; Van de Ven, 1992). Let us assume that researchers, not only practicing managers, are encapsulated in an autopoietic epistemology, which we think they (we) are. As system-distant observers, perhaps even with an observer-independent perspective, will all of our theorizing be self-referent, running the risk of becoming less and less relevant to practice? From our perspective the risk is substantial. We suggest that the closure of this epistemology may be overcome through a system-closed and observation-dependent methodology, with a bearing on the process of languaging.

Languaging in strategic management research means that researchers and practicing managers co-speculate, co-study, and co-write. In doing this, new phenomena pertaining to strategic management can be effectively isolated and named. Previous distinctions in strategic management, on various scales, can also be reviewed and new distinctions developed. Fantasy might be the only impediment to the development (of finer and more rudimentary distinctions) of the field.

This chapter resulted from a theoretical discourse between researchers and a practitioner. Results followed from a deeply immersed process of matching the practitioners' local theory and the researchers' grand theory of autopoiesis. Therefore, this chapter illustrates a principle of developing knowledge (that is, data for others!), *merging* grand and grounded theory by the process of matching.

In addition to this particular approach to languaging, at least two more ways of languaging can be identified in the realm of strategic management. One is journals and other research outlets in the field asking model-strong, practicing managers to take an active part in the traditional peer review process, including bringing them into editorial boards. Practicing managers may also be used to provide commentaries to papers published within the realm of strategic management, putting each potential contribution in 'their' form.

Two methodologies surface as particularly appropriate for languaging: ethnographies and action research. First, by doing organizational ethnographies, researchers enter the organization, learn the distinctions and norms pertaining to the knowledge of the organization, study self-descriptions in the organization, and establish and enter relationships necessary for the continuous knowledge development of the organization. The criterion of a valid study is whether or not the researcher in his or her descriptions of the organization uses a language (distinctions) that is meaningful to organizational members (see Joergensen, 1989; Geertz, 1973).[20]

Second, action research seems to be a promising research strategy to increase validity and relevance. In action research, both the researcher and the practicing managers develop their mutual knowledge about each other's knowledge. However, we are not advocating action research in which the researcher has questions which are less interesting for the manager. As stated before, we envision a type of action research in which both the researcher and the manager jointly formulate questions about 'how we know what we know' as well as jointly try to answer these questions. A typical action research project (Susman and Evered, 1978) would mean spending considerable time on defining a common problem and extracting the general findings from the research.

All of this should contribute to unifying (dominant) languages from academia and practice into a sole legitimate language for the realm of strategic management – a language that carries data that is more manifest to *both* parties than to either one of them separately. In conventional terms, it will increase both validity and relevance. We believe that languaging, in particular, will result in strong signals that might bring together current autopoietic processes in individuals, groups, organizations and societies. Hopefully, this may yield not only new shared agreement between managers and strategic management researchers, but also increase insights from the perspective of both parties.

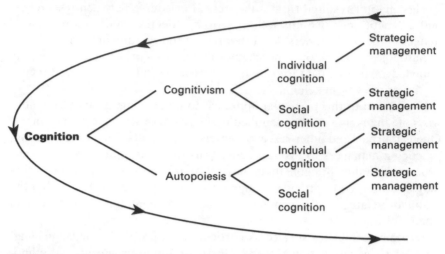

Figure 8.1   *The quest for a new strategy paradigm*

A Final Self-Reference

In our perspective the only way to rethink a certain domain is to (1) move towards the roots of the distinction tree, (2) make new rudimentary distinctions, and (3) make increasingly finer distinctions referring to the rudimentary ones. This is what we have tried to do in this chapter. We have examined some of the fundamental assumptions of the strategic management field by moving towards the domain of cognition. Our new rudimentary distinctions included individual versus social cognition. From here we were able to make increasingly fine distinctions between 'cognitivism' and autopoiesis, and subsequently between social and individual autopoiesis. The quest for a new strategy paradigm is illustrated in Figure 8.1.

This leads us to a brief discussion of the presentation form of strategic management research. We believe that the conventional article form found in most journals in the field is most appropriate for research on what we have labeled survival activities. Here, the crucial task of the claimant of new insights is to gain the acceptance of the scholarly community. For research regarding advancement activities, i.e. knowledge development, perhaps the essay form is better suited to both readers and writers (e.g. Nelson, 1991; Rumelt et al., 1991)?[21] Perhaps the essay could even be written as a dialogue?[22] After all, it is our obligation to present data as lucidly as possible.

Finally, as noted by Calás and Smircich (1988), the credibility and 'goodness' of research depend on *both* the writers *and* the activities of the reader. *Therefore, dear reader, consistent with the autopoietic perspective, we urge you to begin to read this chapter again!*

When you have decided to read further, you will find more insights derived from the autopoietic perspective in the context of organizational cooperation, globalization and conversation.

Notes

This chapter was previously published as a paper in the *Strategic Management Journal*, 1994, 15: 53–77. Reprinted by permission of John Wiley & Sons Ltd.

1 Montague defined epistemology as the extent to which 'the things and qualities of the world are dependent upon their being related as objects to a knower or subject' (1962: 82).

2 Underlying our arguments is the notion of knowledge as being socially constructed; the environment which managers respond to is determined by previous experience, not by observable 'objective' facts (c.g. Weick, 1979). Although the setting described here is strategic management, we have chosen to include all sorts of purposive organizations rather than restricting our discussions to firms.

3 The uncertainty principle, or principle of indeterminism, was discovered (or rather, it was a reaffirmation of the Greek Zeno of Elea's proposition that an object cannot occupy a given place and be moving at the same time) when Heisenberg was struggling to rethink the boundaries of the quantum world that would accord with the new quantum mechanics (for a fuller discussion, see Heisenberg, 1971).

4 See also the discussion in Chakravarthy and Doz (1992).

5 The theory was originally meant for understanding cell reproduction. In cell reproduction, not only are the cells reproducing themselves, but they are also reproducing their own capacity to reproduce. Further, all metacellulars reproduce themselves through the coupled cells that they are composed of. Ongoing interaction between metacellulars, i.e. individuals, has not been discussed by Maturana and Varela in terms of autopoiesis. They speak only of structural coupling of autopoietic systems. However, other authors, e.g. Luhmann, have argued that there are general principles of autopoietic organization in social systems. For a fuller discussion of this see van Twist and Schaap (1991).

6 Several important contributions towards a better understanding of organizational learning are based on cybernetics and general systems theory (e.g. Argyris and Schön, 1978; Senge, 1990). Hence, it may be of interest to some readers to relate autopoiesis theory to more traditional general systems theories. This is done by Bensler (1980), Goguen and Varela (1979), and Varela (1979). Here, we should mention that autopoietic systems can be described as complementary open (with respect to data) and closed (with respect to information). The systems theoretical notion of 'control' exercised by the external environment, contingent on the input–output of information, is supplemented with the notion of 'autonomy' of the system.

7 This frame of reference, e.g., cognitive structure or theory, gives meaning and organization to the regularities in experience, and allows the individual to 'go beyond the information given'.

8 In these works knowledge has often been substituted by other and less troublesome notions, like information, data, resources, reputation, etc. This has also led to a view of organizations as 'non-trivial machines' or computers (Kilduff, 1993), based on basic principles of information science (e.g. Resnikoff, 1989). The *process* by which firms develop, sustain, improve or utilize knowledge has not been subject to extensive study.

9 This resembles very much the ideas of Piaget (1936) that the child constructs a reality through perceptual and conceptual experiences.

10 The consequences of scaling in science were discussed earlier by Galilei (1638). See Bonner (1969) and Morrison and Morrison (1982) for a discussion of scaling in nature and the universe respectively.

11 In fact, here Derrida (1981) and Varela (1979) go so far as saying that no concept can exist without its opposite.

12 A considerable amount of this private knowledge may be difficult or impossible to convey linguistically or in writing. This is what Polanyi (1958) called tacit knowledge.

Nevertheless, tacit knowledge may find other ways of becoming social, for example the imitation of body language. For a fuller treatment, see Spender (1993), Nonaka (1991), and Polanyi (1958; 1962).

13   A final point: since knowledge *of* the social system is shared knowledge, it is no longer entirely dependent on specific individuals (see also Argyris and Schön, 1978). Individuals may leave the group (for example a physicist may retire from his department and field) but the knowledge of the group does not (if there are knowledge connections, see below) vanish. The same is the case when parts of the social system spin off. For example, a medical venture division of a pharmaceutical firm may sell off a high-tech organization that has taken years to establish. The knowledge that resides in this organization, however, may not be lost but can form a basis for further corporate knowledge development (given the knowledge connections). That is why this first type of knowledge conversion process is so important to understand.

14   According to Maturana and Varela (1987) autopoiesis theory is a theory of life. When the individual organism no longer continues the knowledge creation process, its life comes to an end. Thus, for the organism the most important process to maintain over time is the autopoietic process whereby knowledge is created and re-created.

15   This is different from the notion of 'organizational memory' for knowledge (see Walsh and Ungson, 1991; Weick, 1991), including individuals' memory, documents, data and systems. From our autopoietic perspective, such an organizational memory stores and retrieves only *data*, not knowledge.

16   In many of his dialogues, Plato often posed puzzles without solving them and the reader is left aware of his ignorance of important issues.

17   We are referring to the distinction between the natural world (body) and the spiritual world (soul).

18   From our perspective 'new firm knowledge' is knowledge that extends beyond the 'limits' of existing firm knowledge. The limits of knowledge are determined by the autopoietic process in the development of the corporate knowledge base (due to self-reference). The critical distinctions are between what the firm *knows* it knows and what the firm *knows* it does not know, and between what the firm *does not know* it knows and what the firm *does not know* it does not know. See also von Foerster's (1982) identification of the 'blind-spots' in the epistemology of a (living) system. A social system cannot see that it is unable to see what it cannot see. Luhmann (1990) however suggests that an external observer can see precisely this blind-spot, and help the system to realize its weakness. Latent data are of great value here because they indicate areas where the firm has a lack of knowledge (also of its own knowledge).

19   An extreme position on this matter was taken by Hejl, who stated that: 'Any description [of society] which does not allow for the precise specification of the role of the observer is not a scientific one . . . though it may be accepted by a great number of participants in the social process who call themselves "scientists" ' (1980: 160).

20   For examples of organizational ethnographies, see Gioia and Chittipeddi (1991), Rosen (1991), and Pettigrew (1979).

21   Invented by Michel de Montaigne in the sixteenth century, the essay is a particular literary composition dealing with a few subjects in an easy way. Very often an essay represents a writer's personal experiences and perspectives, kept in a vivid and direct style. For a fuller discussion of research as literature, stories and fiction, see Latour and Wolgar (1979).

22   As a literary form, dialogue is an organized exposition of contrasting philosophical or intellectual attitudes.

References

Anderson, J.R. (1983). *The Architecture of Cognition*. Cambridge, MA: Harvard University Press.

Argyris, C. and Schön, D. (1978). *Organizational learning*. Reading, MA: Addison-Wesley.
Argyris, C., Putnam, R. and McLain Smith, D. (1985). *Action Science*. San Francisco: Jossey-Bass.
Arthur, W.B. (1990). Positive feedback in the economy. *Scientific American*, February: 92–9.
Badaracco, J.L. (1991). *The Knowledge Link: How Firms Compete through Strategic Alliances*. Boston, MA: Harvard Business School Press.
Barney, J. (1991). Firm resources and sustained competitive advantage. *Journal of Management*, 17: 99–120.
Bartlett, S.C. (1932). *Remembering: a Study in Experimental and Social Psychology*. Cambridge: Cambridge University Press.
Becker, A. (1991). A short essay on languaging. In F. Steier (ed.), *Research and Reflexivity*. London: Sage. pp. 226–34.
Bensler, F. (1980). On the history of system thinking in sociology. In F. Bensler, P.M. Hejl and W.K. Köck (eds), *Autopoiesis, Communication and Society: The Theory of Autopoietic System in the Social Sciences*. Frankfurt: Campus Verlag. pp. 33–43.
Bonner, J.T. (1969). *The Scale of Nature*. New York: Pegasus.
Bourdieu, P. (1991). *Language and Symbolic Power*. Cambridge, MA: Harvard University Press.
Bruner, J.S. (1964). Going beyond the information given. In H.E. Gruber, K.R. Hammond and R. Jesser (eds), *Contemporary Approaches to Cognition*. Boston, MA: Harvard University Press.
Bruner, J.S. and Anglin, J.M. (1973). *Beyond the Information Given*. New York: W.W Norton.
Calás, M.B. and Smircich, L. (1988). Reading leadership as a form of cultural analysis. In J.G. Hunt, B.R. Baliga, H.P. Dachler and C.A. Schriesheim (eds), *Emerging Leadership Vistas*. Lexington, MA: Lexington Books. pp. 201–28.
Carroll, G.R. (1993). A sociological view on why firms differ. *Strategic Management Journal*, 14, 237–49.
Chakravarthy, B.S. and Doz, Y. (1992). Strategy process research: focusing on corporate self-renewal. *Strategic Management Journal*, 13: 5–14.
Chronbach, L.J. and Meehl, P.E. (1955). Construct validity in psychological testing. *Psychological Bulletin*, 52: 281–302.
Cyert, R.M. and March, J.G. (1963). *A Behavioral Theory of the Firm*. London: Blackwell, 1992.
Daft, R.L. and Weick, K.E. (1984). Toward a model of organizations as interpretation systems. *Academy of Management Review*, 9(2). 284–95.
Davidow, W.H. and Malone, M.S. (1992). *The Virtual Corporation*. New York: Harper Business.
Deggau, H.G. (1988). The communicative autonomy of the legal system, In G. Teubner (ed.), *Autopoietic Law: a New Approach to Law and Society*. Berlin: Walter de Gruyter. pp. 128–51.
Derrida, J. (1981). *Dissemination*. Chicago: University of Chicago Press.
Dierickx, L. and Cool, K. (1989). Asset stock accumulation and sustainability of competitive advantage. *Management Science*, 35: 1514–30 .
Drucker, P.F. (1990). The emerging theory of manufacturing. *Harvard Business Review*, May–June.
Eisenhardt, K.M. (1989). Building theories from case study research. *Academy of Management Review*, 14(4): 532–50.
Elden, M. and Levin, M. (1991). Cogenerative learning: bringing participation into action research. In W.F. Whyte (ed.), *Participatory Action Research*. Newbury Park, CA: Sage. pp. 127–42.
Fiol, C.M. (1991). Managing culture as a competitive resource: an identity-based view of sustainable competitive advantage. *Journal of Management*, 17: 191–211.
Fletcher, K.E. and Huff A.S. (1990). Argument mapping. In A.S. Huff (ed.), *Mapping Strategic Thought*. Chichester: Wiley. pp. 355–75.

180   *Managing Knowledge*

Fombrun, C.J. (1992). *Turning Points: Creating Strategic Change in Corporations*. New York: McGraw-Hill.

Galilei, G.L. (1638). *Discorsi e Dimostrazioni Matematiche, Intorno à Due Nuoue Scienze*. Leida, Holland: Appresso gli Elsevirii.

Gardner, H. (1985). *The Mind's New Science: a History of the Cognitive Revolution*. New York: Basic Books.

Geertz, C. (1973). *The Interpretation of Cultures*. New York: Basic Books.

Ginsberg, A. (1990). Connecting diversification to performance: a socio-cognitive approach. *Academy of Management Review*, 15: 514–35.

Gioia, D.A. and Chittipeddi, K. (1991). Sensemaking and sensegiving in strategic change initation. *Strategic Management Journal*, 12: 433–48.

Gioia, D.A. and Manz, C.C. (1985). Linking cognition and behavior: a script processing interpretation of vicarious learning. *Academy of Management Review*, 10(3): 527–39.

Glaser, B.G. and Strauss, A.L. (1967). *The Discovery of Grounded Theory*. Chicago: Aldine.

Goguen, J.A. and Varela, F.J. (1979). Systems and distinctions: duality and complementarity. *International Journal of General Systems*, 5: 31–43.

Goshal, S., Arnzen, B. and Brownfield, S. (1992). Learning alliance between business and business schools: executive education as a platform for partnership. Working paper, INSEAD, Fontainebleau.

Grinyer, P., Mayes, D.G. and McKiernan, P. (1988). *Sharpbenders*. Oxford: Blackwell.

Habermas, J. (1984). *The Theory of Communicative Action*. Boston, MA: Beacon.

Habermas, J. (1992). *The Philosophical Discourse of Modernity*. Cambridge: Polity Press.

Hage, J. and Powers, C.H. (1992). *Post-Industrial Lives: Roles and Relationships in the 21st Century*. Newbury Park, CA: Sage.

Hamel, G. (1991). Competition for competence and interpartner learning within international alliances. *Strategic Management Journal*, 12: 83–103.

Hamel G. and Prahalad, C.K. (1989). Strategic intent. *Harvard Business Review*, May–June: 63–75.

Hamel, G. and Prahalad, C.K. (1993). Strategy as stretch and leverage. *Harvard Business Review*, March–April: 75–84.

Hamel, G., Doz, Y. and Prahalad, C.K. (1988). Collaborate with your competitors – and win. *Harvard Business Review*, January–February: 133–9.

Hedberg, B. (1981). How organizations learn and unlearn. In P.C. Nystrom and W. Starbuck (eds.), *Handbook of Organizational Design*, vol. I. New York: Oxford University Press. pp. 3–27.

Hedberg, B., Starbuck, W. and Nystrom, P. (1976). Camping on the seesaws: prescriptions for designing self-designing organizations. *Administrative Science Quarterly*, 21: 41–65.

Heisenberg, W. (1971). *Physics and Beyond*. New York: Harper & Row.

Hejl, P.M. (1980). The problem of a scientific description of society. In F. Benseler, P.M. Hejl and W.K. Köck (eds), *Autopoiesis, Communication, and Society*. Frankfurt: Campus Verlag. pp. 147–62.

Huff, A.S. (1983). Industry influence on strategy reformulation. *Strategic Management Journal*, 3: 119–31.

Johnson, H.T. (1992). *Relevance Regained: from Top-Down Control to Bottom-Up Empowerment*. New York: Free Press.

Johnson, H.T. and Kaplan, R.S. (1987). *Relevance Lost: the Rise and Fall of Management Accounting*. Boston: Harvard Business School Press.

Joergensen, D.L. (1989). *Participant Observation: a Methodology for Human Studies*. Newbury Park, CA: Sage.

Karlsen, I.J. (1991). Action research as method: reflections from a program for developing methods and competence. In W.F. Whyte (ed.), *Participatory Action Research*. Newbury Park, CA: Sage. pp. 143–58.

Kilduff, M. (1993). Deconstructing organizations. *Academy of Management Review*, January: 13–31.

Kodoma, F. (1991). *Analyzing Japanese High Technologies: the Techno-Paradigm Shift.* London: Pinter.

Lant, T.K. and Mezias, S.J. (1990). Managing discontinuous change: a simulation study of organizational learning and entrepeneurship. *Strategic Management Journal*, 11: 147–79.

Lant, T.K., Milliken, F.J. and Batra, B. (1992). The role of managerial learning and interpretation in strategic persistence and reorientation: an empirical exploration. *Strategic Management Journal*, 13: 585–608.

Latour, B. and Wolgar, S. (1979). *Laboratory Life: the Social Construction of Scientific Facts.* Beverly Hills, CA: Sage.

Lawson, H. and Appignanesi, H.L. (1989). *Dismantling Truth: Reality in the Post-Modern World.* London: Weidenfeld & Nicolson.

Lorange, P. (1992). Note regarding the strategy of the Norwegian School of Management. Unpublished paper, Norwegian School of Management.

Lorange, P., Chakravarthy, B., Roos, J. and Van de Ven, A. (1993). *Implementing Strategic Processes: Change, Learning and Co-operation.* London: Blackwell.

Luhmann, N. (1982). *The Differentiation of Society.* New York: Columbia University Press.

Luhmann, N. (1986). The autopoiesis of social systems. In F. Geyer and J. van der Zouwen (eds), *Sociocybernetic Paradoxes.* Beverly Hills, CA: Sage. pp. 172–92.

Luhmann, N. (1988). The unity of the legal system. In G. Teubner (ed.), *Autopoietic Law: a New Approach to Law and Society.* Berlin: Walter de Gruyter. pp. 12–35.

Luhmann, N. (1990). *Essays on Self-Reference.* New York: Columbia University Press.

Luhmann, N. (1992). *Ecological Communication.* Cambridge: Polity Press.

Lyles, M.A. and Schwenk, C.R. (1992). Top management, strategy and organizational knowledge structures. *Journal of Management Studies*, 29 (March): 155–74.

Lyotard, J.F. (1984). *The Postmodern Condition: a Report on Knowledge.* Minneapolis: University of Minnesota Press.

Mahoney, J.T. and Pandian, J.R. (1992). The resource-based view within the conversation of strategic management. *Strategic Management Journal*, 13: 363–80.

March, J.G. and Simon, H.A. (1958). *Organizations.* New York: Wiley.

Maturana, H. (1991). Science and daily life: the onthology of scientific explanation. In F. Steier (ed.), *Research and Reflexivity.* London: Sage. pp. 30–52.

Maturana, H. and Varela, F. (1980). *Autopoiesis and Cognition: the Realization of the Living.* London: Reidl.

Maturana, H. and Varela, F. (1987). *The Tree of Knowledge* (in Danish). Copenhagen: Ask.

Minsky, M.A. (1975). A framework for representing knowledge. In P.H. Winston (ed.), *The Psychology of Computer Vision.* New York: McGraw-Hill. pp. 211–77.

Montague, W.P. (1962). *The Ways of Knowing or the Methods of Philosophy.* London: George Allen & Unwin.

Morgan, G. (1986). *Images of Organization.* Beverly Hills, CA: Sage.

Morrison, P. and Morrison, P. (1982). *Powers of Ten: about the Relative Size of Things in the Universe.* New York: Scientific American Library.

Nelson, R.R. (1991). Why Do Firms Differ, and How Does It Matter? *Strategic Management Journal*, 12: 61–74.

Newell A. and Simon, H. (1972). *Human Problem Solving.* Englewood Cliffs, NJ: Prentice-Hall.

Nisbett, R. and Ross, L. (1980). *Human Inference: Strategies and Shortcomings of Social Judgement.* Englewood Cliffs, NJ: Prentice-Hall.

Nonaka, I. (1988). Creating organizational order out of chaos: self-renewal in Japanese firms. *California Management Review*, Spring: 57–73.

Nonaka, I. (1991). The knowledge-creating company. *Harvard Business Review*, November–December: 96–104.

Pettigrew, A. (1979). On studying organizational culture. *Administrative Science Quarterly*, 24: 570–81.

Piaget, J. (1936). *La Naissance de l'intelligence chez l'enfant.* Neuchâtel and Paris: Dechau et Nieste.

Polanyi, M. (1958). *Personal Knowledge*. Chicago: University of Chicago Press.
Polanyi, M. (1962). *Personal Knowledge: towards a Post Critical Philosophy*. London: Routledge.
Prahalad, C.K. and Bettis, R. (1986). The dominant logic: a new linkage between diversity and performance. *Strategic Management Journal*, 7: 485–501.
Prahalad, C.K. and Hamel, G. (1990). The core competence of the corporation. *Harvard Business Review*, May–June: 79–91.
Reason, P. (1988). *Human Inquiry in Action*. London: Sage.
Resnikoff, H.L.(1989). *The Illusion of Reality*. New York: Springer.
Rosen, M. (1991). Coming to terms with the field: understanding and doing organizational ethnography. *Journal of Management Studies*, 28: 1–24.
Rumelt, R.P., Schendel, D. and Teece, D.J. (1991). Strategic management and economics. *Strategic Management Journal*, Special Issue, Winter: 5–29.
Sakaiya, T. (1992). *The Knowledge-Value Company*. London: Bellew.
Schank, R. and Albelson, R.P. (1977). *Scripts, Plans, Goals, and Understanding: an Inquiry into Human Knowledge Structures*. Hillsdale, NJ: Lawrence Erlbaum.
Schendel, D. (1991). Editor's comments on the Winter Special Issue. *Strategic Management Journal*, Special Issue, Winter.
Senge, P. (1990). *The Fifth Discipline*. New York: Doubleday Currency.
Simon, H.A. (1989). *Models of Thought*, vol. 2. New Haven, CT: Yale University Press.
Smith, K.K. (1982). Philosophical problems in thinking about organizational change. In P.S. Goodman and associates (eds), *Change in Organizations: New Perspectives on Theory, Research, and Practice*. San Francisco: Jossey-Bass. pp. 316–74.
Spender, J.C. (1993). Paper presented at the Conference on Distinctive Competences and Tacit Knowledge, Rome, 15 April.
Sproull, L. and Kiesler, S. (1991). *Connections: New Ways of Working in the Networked Organization*. Cambridge, MA: MIT Press.
Susman, G.I. and Evered, R.D. (1978). An assessment of the scientific merits of action research. *Administrative Science Quarterly*, 23 (December): 582–603.
Teubner, G. (1988). Evolution of autopoietic law. In G. Teubner (ed.), *Autpoietic Law: a New Approach to Law and Society*. Berlin: Walter de Gruyter. pp. 217–41.
Teubner, G. (1991). Autopoiesis and steering: how politics profit from the normative surplus of capital. In R.J. in 't Veld, L. Schaap, C.J.A.M. Termeer and M.J.A.W. van Twist (eds), *Autopoiesis and Configuration Theory: New Approaches to Social Steering*. Dordrecht: Kluwer. pp. 127–43.
Tversky, A. and Kahneman, D. (1973). Availability: a heuristic for judging frequency and probability. *Cognitive Psychology*, 4: 207–32.
Van de Ven, A.H. (1992). Suggestion for studying strategy process. *Strategic Management Journal*, Special Issue, Summer: 169–88.
van Twist, M.J.W. and Schaap, L. (1991). Introduction to autopoiesis theory and autopoietic steering. In R.J. in 't Veld, L. Schaap, C.J.A.M. Termeer and M.J.A.W. van Twist (eds), *Autopoiesis and Configuration Theory: New Approaches to Social Steering*. Dordrecht: Kluwer. pp. 31–44.
Varela, F.J (1979). *Principles of Biological Autonomy*. New York: Elsevier North-Holland.
Varela, F.J. (1992). Whence perceptual meaning? A cartography of current ideas. In F.J. Varela and J.P. Dupuy (eds), *Understanding Origins: Contemporary Views on the Origin of Life, Mind and Society*. Dordrecht: Kluwer. pp. 235–64.
Varela, F.J., Thompson, E. and Rosch, E. (1992). *The Embodied Mind*. Cambridge, MA: MIT Press.
Vicari, S. (1991). *The Living Firm* (in Italian). Milan: EtasLibri.
von Foerster, H. (1982). *Observing Systems*. Seaside, CA: Intersystems.
von Foerster, H. (1984). Principles of self-organization in socio-managerial context. In H. Ulrich and G.J.B. Probst (eds), *Self-Organization and Management of Social Systems*. Berlin: Springer. pp. 2–24.
von Krogh, G. and Vicari, S. (1993). An autopoiesis approach to experimental strategic

learning. In P. Lorange, B. Chakravarthy, J. Roos and A. Van de Ven (eds), *Implementing Strategic Processes: Change, Learning and Co-operation*. London: Blackwell. pp. 394–410.

Walsh, J.P. and Ungson, G.R. (1991). Organizational memory. *Academy of Management Review*, 16: 57–91.

Weathly, M.J. (1992). *Leadership and the New Science*. San Francisco: Berrett-Koehler.

Weick, K.E. (1979). *The Social Psychology of Organizing*. New York: Random House.

Weick, K.E. (1991). The nontraditional quality of organizational learning. *Organization Science*, February: 116–24.

Weick, K.E. and Bougnon, M.G. (1986). Organizations as cognitive maps. In H.P. Sims Jr and D.A. Gioia (eds), *The Thinking Organization*. San Francisco: Jossey-Bass. pp. 102–35.

Wernerfelt, B. (1984) A resource-based view of the firm. *Strategic Management Journal*, 5: 171–80.

Westley, F.R. (1990). Middle managers and strategy: microdynamics of inclusion. *Strategic Management Journal*, 11: 337–51.

Whyte, W.F. (1991). *Social Theory for Action: How Individuals and Organizations Learn to Change*. Newbury Park, CA: Sage.

Winograd, T. and Flores, F. (1987). *Understanding Computers and Cognition*. Norwood, NJ: Ablex.

Wold, H. (1969). Mergers of economics and philosophy of science: a cruise in shallow waters and deep seas. *Synthese*, 20: 427–82.

Yin, R.K. (1984). *Case Study Research*. Beverly Hills. CA: Sage.

9

Knowledge Creation through Cooperative Experimentation

*Salvatore Vicari, Georg von Krogh, Johan Roos
and Volker Mahnke*

The Challenge of Knowledge Development

This chapter deals with knowledge development through experimental approaches to interfirm cooperation. The focus is on the process of new knowledge generation. The following questions will be addressed: what is the role of experimentation in organizations? How can organizations overcome inertia through cooperative experimentation? How can managers understand and stimulate the process of knowledge development through cooperative experimentation? And finally: how can organizations balance knowledge development with knowledge exploitation through cooperative experimentation?

The concept of 'cooperative experimentation' is essentially concerned with the management of different experimental forms of cooperations and their impact on knowledge development. A key claim is that the overall level of disturbances released through experimental cooperative arrangements is influential for the knowledge development process across organizational states. Organizational states describe (1) the ability of the organizational cognitive system to cope with the current overall level of 'disturbances' released through cooperative experiments, (2) the relation between 'survival' and 'advancement' activities (see Chapter 8), and (3) the relation between knowledge development and knowledge exploitation in the organization.

The management of cooperative experimentation concerns when and how additional cooperative experiences should be triggered in order to fuel knowledge development and to advance strategically. The process of cooperative experimentation will be depicted as a means to stimulate knowledge development, which may push organizations from states of inertia to states of extension. This is the realm of knowledge development and this is where it is balanced with knowledge exploitation. Cooperative experimentation typically questions existing distinctions in the organization and invites the creation of new distinctions deployable in strategic processes.

Building on von Krogh and Vicari (1993) and von Krogh and Roos (1995) the objectives of this chapter are to (1) demonstrate that the theory of autopoiesis could provide a new understanding of knowledge development through experimental approaches to interfirm cooperation, and (2) develop the new concept 'management of cooperative experimentation' (MCE) in knowledge management. In pursuit of this objective we first highlight selected insights from autopoiesis theory applied to knowledge management and extract propositions for the management of *cooperative* experimentation. Second, based on our propositions, the concept of MCE will be introduced and discussed. Third, we distinguish between three organizational states: the states of inertia, extension and dissolution. Disturbances originating from different cooperative experiments have different impacts on knowledge development, given an organizational state. Finally, we put the management of cooperative experimentation in a larger context, and discuss implications for managerial practice and further research efforts.

The Implications of Autopoiesis Theory

The theory of autopoiesis (Maturana and Varela, 1987) is a theory of cognition originating in the realm of neurobiology. This theory states that human cognitive systems are simultaneously open and closed, and that they construct their own reality through making distinctions in observation. This process is self-referential. In the following we draw upon Maturana and Varela (1987) and von Krogh and Roos (1995a). The main differences between an autopoietic and a traditional view of knowledge are summarized in Table 9.1.

Table 9.1 *Assumptions: the autopoietic vs. the traditional view of knowledge*

Autopoietic view	Traditional view
Knowledge is creational and based on distinction making in observation	Knowledged is representation of a pre-given reality
Knowledge is history dependent and context sensitive	Knowledge is universal and objective
Knowledge refers to information inside the system as opposed to data outside the cognitive system	Knowledge, information and data are used interchangeably
Knowledge is not directly transferable	Knowledge is transferable

Sources: von Krogh and Roos, 1995a; see also Chapter 8 in this book

Knowledge is What Makes an Observer Able to Make
Distinctions in Observation

However, knowledge is, at the same time based on distinctions. Thus, knowledge development takes place through the application of distinctions in a self-referential manner. Self-referentiality means that new knowledge refers not only to past knowledge but also to potential future knowledge. Thus, we use our existing knowledge to determine what we see, and we use what we already know to choose what to look for in our environment. The way to change the environment is to develop knowledge through additional different distinctions (extension) and make new, finer distinctions (refinement). If we imagine the organizational knowledge structure as a tree (see Chapter 8 in this book), the former would represent a different thick branch next to the root, the latter a little thin branch evolving from an existing thick branch. Through the lens of autopoiesis, cooperative strategies look different. We are particulary interested in knowing how and when to encourage the creation of new refining and extensional distinctions. Given that the knowledge development process is self-referential, the answer is not obvious.

Autopoietic Systems are Simultaneously Open and Closed

They are open to data and closed to new information and knowledge. Information and knowledge are exclusively developed within the organizational knowledge process. Data outside the cognitive system may serve as 'perturbations' to the system, which may stimulate new knowledge development. Again, we see different things if we look at cooperative strategies through the lens of autopoiesis. The often used concept of knowledge transfer in strategic cooperations consequently needs to be rethought.

Perturbations Stimulate Knowledge Development

When an autopoietic system interacts in a recurrent manner, signals produced elsewhere reach the autopoietic system as perturbations. Perturbations can trigger knowledge development processes in the receiving, autopoietic system. However, it is important to note that perturbations are interpreted according to the distinction tree (knowledge system) of the receiving system. That means that perturbations can trigger distinction making (knowledge development), but not specify it. The structure of the autopoietic system determines which levels of perturbations are 'allowed' to enter the autopoietic system, how much disturbance it can take before it breaks down, and what changes of states are available at a given point in time.[1] If perturbation levels are too high, the autopoietic system in its current structure is in danger of total dissolution, which means that it cannot maintain its operations. From this perspective, cooperative ventures create perturbations in the organization's cognitive system. Different cooperations, e.g. strategic alliances, joint ventures, coproductions, marketing agreements, therefore will release different levels of perturbations to each party. Which perturbations organizations can use for knowledge development depends on their current cognitive structure. It is well known that cooperative ventures have to be managed carefully. This includes posing the following questions: which cooperations release what levels of disturbances for the partner organizations? What perturbations can be used for knowledge development given a current cognitive structure in an organization?

Organizational Knowledge is Based on Individual Knowledge, When Conveyed through Different Language Systems

Organizational knowledge is based on socially created and maintained distinctions that emerge from conversation between organizational members. It is mainly through language that organizational actions are coordinated. Organizational members interact and live in language. They make sense of situations, events, and objects through language, thereby bringing forth the organizational world through languaging. Languaging refers to both the use of existing language and also innovations in this language (see von Krogh and Roos, 1996a). From this perspective it is important to embody the cooperative experience in stories and narratives and also ensure that these are communicated intensively. Important questions emerge: how do companies use perturbations originating from cooperative ventures for company-wide use? How can this be done in a way that is not limited to parts of the company which actually take part in the cooperation? How are the perturbations stemming from the cooperative venture converted into knowledge by individuals, groups and organizational units? How are discussions managed to make the most of these signals (see von Krogh and Roos, 1995a)?

Based on the autopoietic perspective of knowledge briefly discussed above we start from the following implications to subsequently illustrate how knowledge creation can be managed through cooperative experimentation.

I1 A direct transfer of information or knowledge from one to another company is not possible.
I2 Perturbations released through cooperations become a source of new knowledge for all partner firms in a cooperative venture.
I3 Because of self-reference managers have to consider the current structure of the organization's cognitive system when they manage the knowledge development process.
I4 Languaging is an important vehicle to develop organizational knowledge through cooperations.
I5 Managers confront new cooperative ventures with existing knowledge, and they need a process by which they become open to new signals.

An organization constructs its reality through the making of distinctions. Past distinctions determine future distinction making within the firm. Thus, strategic knowledge development concerns stimulating the natural self-reproductive process of a company to increase its ability to make new distinctions among observations of its environment. In a changing environment, if the firm continues to live by and reinforce the same distinctions over time, it is not developing new knowledge. Three examples may help to highlight this point. First, a joint venture partner finds that the investment does not meet internal requirements of return on investment

(ROI). The joint venture is terminated. Thus, the profitability/non-profitability distinctions and the internal ROI norm have limited the development path. The firm will not gain new distinctions through its cooperative experience. Second, take a pharmaceutical firm that produces ethical drugs. Through one of its many alliances the management team learns about a new word 'nutraceuticals', food with medical effects. A new distinction has been introduced, opening the way to future business. Third, the CEO of a regional newspaper explains: 'Newspapers have existed for a very long time and will continue to do so. There is no need for us to waste time on an electronic version.'

As already stated, strategic knowledge development means to stimulate the cognitive self-production process to increase the ability of the firm to make new distinctions among new observations. But first of all, how can distinction making be stimulated?

Experimentation

Some authors have already stressed the role of experiments with regard to knowledge development in organizations: Argyris and Schön (1978) mentioned the importance of instability in organizations and learning through trial and error; Starbuck and Nystrom (1984) highlighted the role of developing alternatives in organizations; Weick (1979) illustrated self-organization as discovering process through experimentation; Hedberg (1981) suggests making organizations more experimental while unlearning; de Geus (1988) argues that through a process of trial and error organizations discover possible strategic courses of action. In a similar vein, Burgelman (1989) discussed organizations that intentionally create some instability to enable experiments for innovations; Nonaka (1988; 1994) stressed the role of 'creative conflict' in creating variety; Senge (1990) emphasized the willingness to experiment as a condition to enable an organization to learn; Miller (1982) recommends small and independent units to experiment in order to succeed strategically. All these approaches to organizational knowledge development share one assumption: organizations are open systems. What are the consequences if we assume that organizations are simultaneously open (with regard to data) and closed (with regard to information and knowledge)?

The perspective of autopoiesis underlines the need for errors and experimentation as impetus for change and knowledge development. An example may help to highlight this point. According to the 'action learning theory' of Argyris and Schön (1978) errors in the firm are negative because they indicate disequilibrium between firm and environment. A detection of an error is the trigger for organizational inquiry aimed at finding a possible solution that may restore this equilibrium. A very different approach proposes that firms should, to some extent, engage themselves in producing crises and errors in order to bring about changes (Nonaka, 1988; 1994). Thus, we propose that

P1   In order to increase the ability to develop knowledge (new distinctions) in an organization, it becomes necessary to experiment.

This proposition follows naturally from an autopoietic perspective. Self-reference in distinctions and norms, perhaps even in 'organizational culture', restricts the variety of possible goals and strategies pursued. It is difficult to transcend or break this self-referentiality. The way a firm can break this process is to create new distinctions using errors from experiments, and by selecting new data to bring in from the environment. Consequently, a company can cooperate as an experiment to create perturbations, gather new data and increase the ability to develop and apply new distinctions.

Hedberg (1981) suggested experimenting with alternative environments. Although different from the origin of autopoiesis theory, Hedberg calls for planned experiments, i.e. hypotheses to be tested. The basis for the planned experiment is a set of distinctions that allows for a precise articulation for the plan, the intention, or the hypothesis. However, as Runco (1990) observed in his research on creativity, the limitations in language may in themselves prevent possible directions of development. Thus, the planned experiment can at best only lead to incremental improvements in the firm's ability to make distinctions. The solution to this problem is to create random events, errors, crazy ideas, deviation, etc. and develop knowledge around these. Unlike the case of scientific experiments, companies may be without a plan, intention or hypothesis behind the experiment.

Experiments may be planned, but they may also occur spontaneously as 'errors', i.e. perturbations. Leaps in the knowledge development of a company typically stem from events that the firm has neither planned nor hypothesized. The recent introduction of viable digital printing technology into the graphic arts industry may illustrate this. Such events, assuming that the perturbations are picked up by the firm, allow for new distinctions, like cheap, small series of four-colour brochures. These new distinctions may enable a company to create innovative or at least new strategies without explicit intention and planning. What are the implications for the management of 'cooperative experimentation'? We propose that:

P2   Cooperative experimentation includes both *planned* and *spontaneous* experiments.
P3   Given that the survival of the company is ensured, spontaneous experiments have the greatest potential for creating new distinctions.

Based on these propositions we suggest a new managerial responsibility: the management of cooperative experimentation.

The Management of Cooperative Experimentation

It is now time to explore how knowledge development can be stimulated and managed in a cooperative context, and how knowledge development and knowledge exploitation can be managed through 'cooperative experimentation'. We distinguish between experimental forms of cooperations, outline different organizational states, and suggest managerial activities in how to manage cooperative experiments.

Learning and Refinement Cooperations

Cooperative strategies have been discussed under manifold aspects in the literature: between companies and suppliers, customers, financiers (vertical cooperations) and, competitors (horizontal cooperations). Examples concerning types of cooperations range from loosely coupled contracts through inclusive strategic alliances with or without equity stakes.

Contractor and Lorange (1988) outline various goals for interfirm cooperation. These include risk reduction (e.g. lower total capital investment, faster entry and payback), economies of scale and/or rationalization (joint research and/or production efforts), technology exchange, coopting or blocking competition, overcoming government mandated trade or investment barriers, facilitating of international expansion, vertical quasi-integration advantages (e.g. access to material, technology, labor, distribution channels), quick market access, and gaining synergy in operations. Because our main concern here is to explore the management of cooperative experimentation we introduce a new distinction in experimental cooperative strategies: refinement and learning.

Refinement cooperations (R-cooperations) are planned within a well-defined strategic domain. These are the bulk of experimental cooperations. The intent is to deploy validated knowledge to another task.[2] The result is that the task system of the company is extended. In turn this might broaden the base of profitable businesses. The 'organizational distinction tree' (compare Chapter 8) is completed with another branch. The objective may also be to refine distinctions to increase the profitability of existing strategic domains. Cooperative experiments carried out as R-cooperations are designed as *planned experiments*. Two examples illustrate R-cooperations:

1   A pharmaceutical firm used to distribute medicine through wholesalers in a local market. Now it cooperates with a drugstore chain in order to ensure sales and to gain access to new customers for existing products. Together they formed a joint venture to manage stocks and logistics which decreased its fixed costs.
2   The national telecom company of a small European country is worried about the upcoming deregulation in 1998. It negotiated alliances with three other European national telecom companies.

These cooperations are by far the best known, most widely explored theoretically and tested empirically. R-cooperations remain in a well-known strategic domain based on existing distinctions, for instance, the distribution strategy of the pharmaceutical firm and the strategy of the telecom company. Lower-scaled distinctions may be refined, but basic strategic distinctions are assumed to be given (e.g. a novel channel distributing the same product). In the two examples the firms assumed given industries, markets and environments. The decision to cooperate is mainly governed by financial factors. The underlying logic here is to exploit and/or refine existing knowledge by extending the task system in a well-defined, clear line of development.

In contrast, *learning cooperations* (L-cooperations) are those whose specific intent is to experiment in order to create new knowledge which goes beyond existing distinctions. It may also create entirely new tasks to invent future businesses, i.e. new products for new customers (Prahalad and Hamel, 1994). Cooperative experimentation becomes an exploratory discovery process through which the company advances its knowledge base. L-cooperations are designed as *natural* or *spontaneous* experiments. This discovery process demands simultaneous investments in several directions. A proportion of these investments will not be recoverable; some are inevitably destined to fail. Under the conditions of emerging industries and globalization it may be necessary to allow simultaneous cooperative experiments in different strategic domains. However, it is not necessary to know *a priori* which of these experiments is destined to have the greater probability of success.

Let us illustrate this. Within a short time span a major telecommunications firm entered different cooperative ventures to develop new knowledge. They experimented in multi-media including pen-based mobile computers, communication software, on-line networks, video games, and business communication services. The CEO expressed the intent: 'We are willing to seed all sorts of start-ups and new ideas in order to learn, and in the hope that some will flourish.'

The management of L-cooperations is far less explored theoretically. However, L-cooperations do contribute more than R-cooperations to the knowledge development of the company. Basic strategic distinctions, the taken-for-granted knowledge, are typically challenged and questioned. Through the process of cooperative experimentation entirely new strategic domains may be discovered that may evolve into future business. Where the direction and form of strategic development cannot be defined *a priori*, like 'new media', nutraceuticals or biotechnology, cooperative experimentation may serve as a discovery process through which the variety in the company's knowledge may increase.

It follows from our discussion that L-cooperations typically generate stronger signals than R-cooperations. The managerial challenge lies in allowing these signals into the self-referential system of managers, units, and the whole organization. Thus the question is: on what scales are we open (as individuals and the whole system)? Table 9.2 summarizes the main differences between L- and R-cooperations.

We emphasize the differences because behind every cooperation there are multiple objectives. Of course, each experimental cooperation may encompass elements of both types. To distinguish between L- and R-cooperations is not to argue that companies should generally favor

Table 9.2   *R- and L-cooperations*

	R-cooperations	L-cooperations
Strategic intent	Knowledge exploitation and/or knowledge refinement (given a strategic domain)	Knowledge development, exploration and invention of new strategic distinctions (creation of new strategic domains)
Task system	Will be extended quantitatively	Will be extended qualitatively
Knowledge systems	Basic distinctions are given	New basic distinctions are made
Activities	Short-term survival	Long-term advancement
Experimental mode	Planned experiments	Natural, spontaneous experiments

exclusively one or the other form in order to succeed. On the contrary, survival and advancement activities have to be balanced in the organiza-tion. It is a managerial responsibility to combine R- and L-cooperations in cooperative experimentation. To better understand how to manage coop-erative experimentation the following questions need to be addressed:

- How can cooperative experiments be encouraged in the organization?
- Who should trigger cooperative experiments? Why?
- When should a company use cooperative experimentation?
- In which form should cooperative experiments be effected?
- How much natural, spontaneous cooperative experimentation should be encouraged?
- What is the optimal resource balance between R- and L-cooperations? Why?
- How can a company manage perturbations originating from coopera-tive experimentation throughout the company?
- How can the strength of the perturbation be assessed?

Imagine a hardware company that has operated with constantly decreasing returns and profit, despite the fact that the staff consists of highly educated professionals. Still, the company had sufficient free cash flow and its survival was not threatened. The innovation rate of products was low; business was based on hardware technology, mainly in the mainframe business. Technology has been constantly improved, so that the company still can be depicted as a standard bearer in mainframe technology. The organization has been kept constant and operates in a stable manner. Some cooperations exist, e.g. with hard disk producers, in the form of strategic alliances. Recently, management felt that the firm was operating too statically and that the forces of inertia were at work. The company wanted to fuel knowledge development in order to create future business poten-tials and to overcome low innovation rates through cooperative experi-mentation. Three possibilities were discussed: (1) to enable different levels in the organization to experiment through cooperative venturing in different forms and in a self-organizing manner (e.g. marketing and research partnerships as L- and/or R-cooperation), (2) to establish a joint venture with several small creative software producers, and (3) to acquire a major software producer.

Questions like the following concerning the possibilities for knowledge development were posed. *Concerning (1), (2), (3)*: should we favor (1) or (2), a combination of (1) and (2), or (3)? What would be the impact for knowledge development? *Concerning (1)*: to what extent should different levels of the organization be able to trigger and effect cooperations? What would be the impact for organizational knowledge development? How can we manage responsibilities? How can we use experience gained by the experiments? *Concerning (2)*: would it be too confusing for the organization, which has operated for a certain period in a very stable manner, to experiment with several software companies at the same time? How can we manage the different relations concerning speed of interorganizational activities? *Concerning (3)*: would the acquisition of the major software company release disturbances that could exceed the organizational capacity to deal with them?

This example illustrates two crucial points in the pursuit of the management of cooperative experimentation: (1) different forms of experimental cooperation release different degrees of disturbances to the organization's cognitive system, and (2) it depends on the current state of the organization whether and how these disturbances can be used for knowledge development. To address these critical points in a structured way we supplement the management of cooperative experimentation by discerning three organizational states.

Organizational States and Knowledge Development

Organizational states describe (1) the ability of the organizational cognitive system to cope with the current overall level of disturbances released through cooperative experiments, (2) the relation between survival and advancement activities, and (3) the relation between knowledge development and knowledge exploitation in the organization. Depending on the state of the organization and the complexity of the organizational cognitive system, different forms of cooperative experimentations may have different impacts on the knowledge development process. Figure 9.1 illustrates different organizational states: inertia and order; extension; disorder and dissolution.

Companies are theoretically in states of either inertia, extension or dissolution. These states will be described as extreme points in turn. However, it should be noted that the borders between these states are fluid. Therefore it may be a challenging effort for managers to assess the state of the company.

States of Inertia Organizational inertia, a notion borrowed from population ecology (Hannan and Freeman, 1977), limits the ability of the organizations to adapt by stressing stability and order above disorder and

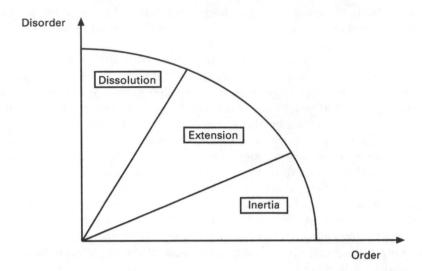

Figure 9.1   *Organizational states*

creativity. Contradictory forces are not sustained; on the contrary, they are dissolved by authority according to a dominant logic of 'whether/or' thinking. Hannan and Freeman argued that organizational norms (read: organizational distinctions) could produce organizational inertia by precluding the consideration of many alternative courses of action. Inertial pressure may arise from stability and an emphasis on survival activities within the firm. The organization runs the risk of reproducing strategic distinctions in a pathological manner while experiments and failure are minimized. In turn, this may diminish the chances for new business options and further advancement of the organizational knowledge base. Authoritative structures that preclude ideas to be uttered, stories to be told, result in normative constraints. For instance, the CEO of Asea Brown Boveri has forbidden his managers to use the word 'foreign' in organizational conversation. In other words: such structures constrain conversation as a vehicle of knowledge development. The level of perturbations released through cooperative experimentation will be low, and not sought after. The organization's ability to deal with perturbations will be equally low.

States of Extension   These may be defined as states where existing distinctions made by and in the organization can be discussed, which in turn will stimulate knowledge development. Contradictory forces within, for instance, a project team or an SBU are sustained and even encouraged through experimentation. The reasoning in the organization follows an 'as well as' logic, where simultaneous courses of actions are reinforced and the tension between them is used as an impetus for conversation. Because there are fewer authoritative structures, normative constraints are less of an issue. Instead, authoritative structures are substituted by self-organization and impediments to knowledge development are overcome by conversation. States of organizational extension may be found between the extremes of complete order and disorder, what in chaos theory is referred to as 'edge of chaos'. In states of organizational extension the organization is exposed to some level of perturbations released through different cooperative experimentations. The organization's ability to deal with perturbations is on some scales matched with the current perturbations released through cooperative experimentation.

States of Dissolution   When contradictory forces and alternative courses of strategic action overbalance order in a bewildering manner we have a state of dissolution. The organization of a group or a whole company cannot be maintained. Over time, the organization reaches a critical point, where there are two alternatives: (1) because not even survival activities can be sustained effectively, the confusion and dissolution lead to ultimate collapse; or (2) the organization tries to create meaning out of emerging ideas and concepts (perturbation) and change the mode and extent of cooperative experimentation. Eventually the latter course might result in terminating existing cooperations. In turn, this may help to effect survival activities and to regain a certain degree of order. In short, the perturbation level released through cooperative experiments is very high and exceeds the ability of the firm to handle it.

Table 9.3 summarizes differences between organizational states and the impact on the knowledge development and exploitation process.

Imagine the hardware company, mentioned above, decided to acquire the major software producer. However, since the company had started from a state of inertia, the disturbance released through the acquisition may have exceeded the ability (cognitive capacity) to cope with it. From this example we see that if order in the knowledge system is not sustained to a certain extent the pendulum may swing to the extreme, where too high a level of

Table 9.3   *States of the organization*

	Inertia	Extension	Dissolution
Match between the ability to deal with perturbation level and current level of perturbation	Match	Simultaneous match on some scales, mismatch on others	Mismatch
Balance between survival and advancement activities	Survival over-balances advancement significantly	Survival is balanced with advancement	Advancement overbalances survival significantly
Knowledge development	Low	Potentially high	High
Knowledge exploitation	High	High	–

disturbances results in confusion and dissolution, and knowledge is generated but impossible to exploit. From the acquisition many ideas emerged for future business exceeding the organization's ability to evaluate them. Hence, it may be wise to increase the level of disturbances in a moderate manner in order to reach states of extension, where knowledge development and knowledge exploitation are balanced. In retrospect the management of cooperative experimentation implies questioning whether it would have been wise instead to experiment with several small cooperative experiments in order to increase continuously the level of disturbances in a step-by-step approach.

Managing Cooperative Experimentation

Five managerial responsibilities surface as particularly important in managing cooperative experimentation: (1) continuously assessing states of the organization, (2) stimulating cooperative experiments, (3) balancing R- and L-cooperations, (4) retaining experience about the experiment, and (5) deciding when and how to disconnect the cooperations.

Assessing states of the organization is a crucial managerial responsibility, because it determines how and how many cooperative experiences should be additionally triggered. Depending on the state (inertia, extension, dissolution) different perturbations released through additional cooperative experiments have different impacts on knowledge development, and on subsequent knowledge exploitation. Perturbations released through additional experience may differ, i.e. an additional equity joint venture may release stronger perturbations compared to a new advertising cooperation for a single product. Table 9.4 relates organizational states, disturbances released through additional cooperative experimentation, their impacts on knowledge development and exploitation, and managerial implications.[3]

Second, cooperative experiments may be triggered at several levels of the organization. Often, however, top management's commitment to carry them out, to promote them and to recognize their occurrence remains important. Given the overall strategy, top management has to provide the frame for cooperative experimentation. Depending on the state of the company we suggest four levers to manage cooperative experimentation: (a) different organizational levels (individuals, departments, divisions) may be enabled to trigger and carry out cooperative experimentation, (b) of different types (e.g. marketing agreements, product and market development, strategic alliances), (c) in different modes (number of cooperative experimentations in a certain time span), and (d) in different forms (L- and/or R-cooperations).

The third managerial responsibility is to balance L- and R- cooperations. Analogous to advancement and survival activities on the organizational scale, the resource balance in terms of allocated time, money, and people has to be found between L- and R-cooperative experiments on the cooperative strategy scale. Knowledge development and knowledge

Table 9.4 *Organizational states, levels, of disturbances and managerial implications*

Organizational states	Levels of perturbations released through additional cooperative experimentation		
	Low	Medium	High
Inertia	Additional knowledge development is incrementally stimulated; the match of knowledge development and exploitation is sustained	Additional knowledge development is stimulated; the match of knowledge development and exploitation is sustained; state of extension may be entered	High rate of additional knowledge development; the match of knowledge development and exploitation cannot be sustained; risk of entering state of dissolution
	Managerial implications	*Managerial implications*	*Managerial implications*
	Increase experimentation; stretch the knowledge development/exploitation balance by cooperative experimentation	Keep marginal level of experimentation	Decrease marginal level of experimentation; relax the knowledge development/exploitation balance
Extension	Additional knowledge development is incrementally stimulated; the match of knowledge development and exploitation is sustained	Additional knowledge development is stimulated on some scales; the balance between match and mismatch on different scales concerning knowledge development and exploitation is sustained	High rate of additional knowledge development; match with knowledge exploitation cannot be sustained; danger of entering state of dissolution
	Managerial implications	*Managerial implications*	*Managerial implications*
	Increase experimentation; stretch the knowledge development/exploitation balance by cooperative experimentation	Keep marginal level of experimentation; carefully observe the level of perturbation	Decrease marginal level of experimentation; relax the knowledge development/exploitation balance
Dissolution	Enforces mismatch between knowledge development and exploitation; leads to potential cognitive breakdown		
	Managerial implications		
	Stop cooperative experimentation; eventually disconnect cooperations resulting from previous cooperative experimentation		

exploitation have to be balanced to succeed in the long term. Time, money, and people allocated to experimental cooperations may vary from company to company. Thus, each company has to find its individual balance.

The fourth responsibility is to retain experience about the cooperative experiment and to ensure that experience developed through cooperative experimentation is used as a stimulus for knowledge development and advancement. That implies the creation of cooperative conversation (talk *in* cooperation and talk *about* cooperation) as a prerequisite for knowledge development (for a discussion of conversation management see von Krogh and Roos, 1995b). Experiences gained in cooperative experiments should be articulated in language, embodied in stories and conversation which may serve as a source of perturbation, not only limited to the people directly taking part in the experiment. These conversations may help to challenge basic assumptions of currently maintained strategic perspectives and to generate additional distinctions from which new strategic perspectives may arise.

In an experimental form of cooperation two companies (A and B) set out to discuss synergy. Company A had initiated the cooperation since the management felt that they were operating in a declining business and that they urgently needed new ideas for future business. Company A was managed in an authoritative manner. Company B on the other hand was managed in a more self-organized way. As they discussed strategic issues company A members were wondering why company B members did not wait until their CEO developed his ideas. Instead they were freely throwing ideas among one another. What was even more surprising for company A was that the team leader of company B was carefully listening, not interrupting the discussion. In the coffee break the two team leaders and the other members were discussing what they experienced during the session. The team leader of company B explained: 'When we discuss strategy, we do not exercise authority. We respect every individual, everybody taking part in the discussion is encouraged to express his ideas. We regard language as the currency of knowledge development. New ideas and strategic distinctions are brought forth by each one of us. When ideas in the form of concepts and phrases diffuse through the organization, other employees develop meaning around them. This is the way we develop new knowledge.' When the team members of company A returned home after the successful meeting they discussed: what does it really mean to say that language is the currency of knowledge development? The CEO of company A said: 'The discussion has to be continued. We should tell our story to other people in our company and ask them what the phrase "language is the currency of knowledge development" means for them.'

Finally, depending on the state of the company and the outcome of the cooperative experiment, a decision will have to be made whether to continue the experiment (through a natural experiment a new strategic perspective could arise which may be followed up by a planned experiment) or to stop the cooperation. Of course this depends on whether the outcome of the experiment is unsatisfactory or the amount of disturbances originating from the sum of cooperations exceeds a certain critical level. The critical level may be reached where disturbances push the organization from states of extension to states of dissolution. To illustrate, assume the hardware company, mentioned above, decided to establish several small L-cooperations with creative software companies at the same time. Project groups were established, generating a high number of new ideas. New distinctions were carried through the company via phrases like quantum electronics, cyberlife, compuware and infonaut. However, nobody in the hardware company knew how to evaluate and give meaning to all these new concepts. No doubt knowledge development took place, but at the same time the question remained: how can one make sense of it and use it?

To sum up: the 'management of cooperative experimentation' offers a new lens to knowledge development in the cooperative context. Cooperative experimentation is based on autopoiesis theory and 'organizational epistemology' (Chapter 8). It includes distinguishing between experimental forms of cooperation (L and R) and between different states (inertia, extension, dissolution), and suggests managerial responsibilities. Figure 9.2 summarizes the management of cooperative experimentation and related managerial responsibilities.

Managerial Implications

To fuel the knowledge development process every company has to experiment by itself or with a partner. Managers can use L- and R-cooperations, where L-cooperations refer to strategic advancement and are of most interest if the intent is to advance strategically and to create new strategic domains for future business. However, knowledge development and advancement have to be balanced with knowledge exploitation and survival. If companies intend to stimulate knowledge development through cooperative experimentation they have therefore to consider the state of the organization (inertia, extension, dissolution) when they change levels, form and type of cooperative experimentation. The management of cooperative experimentation helps managers to relate organizational states, disturbances released through additional cooperative experimentation, and the impacts on knowledge development and exploitation. To manage cooperative experimentation, five managerial responsibilities can be identified: (1) continuously assessing states of the organization, (2) stimulating cooperative experiments, (3) balancing R- and L-cooperations, (4) retaining experience about the experiment, and (5) deciding when and how to disconnect the cooperations.

Given the new insight in this chapter, managers should be open to making use of new conceptual lenses, like autopoiesis theory and organizational epistemology. These offer new perspectives. Cooperative strategies looks different than those previously discussed. Cooperative experimenta-

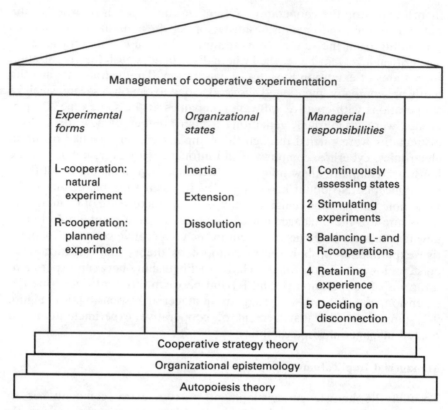

Figure 9.2   *MCE and managerial responsibilities*

tion is one way to knowledge development and organizational advancement. L-cooperations may be the faster way, but they cannot be installed: they need to occur spontaneously. The management has to provide the frame and the commitment to 'cooperative experimentation'; it should carefully observe the level of perturbation released through experimentation. Too much perturbation may be risky, especially in states of organizational extension. The dissolution of an organization may happen quickly.

Implications for Future Research

This work has suggested a new understanding of knowledge development through cooperative strategies: cooperative experimentation. Based on autopoiesis theory and organizational epistemology we have made new distinctions in this field. Of course these distinctions are only a set of perturbations to the reader, which you may or may not allow to enter into your self-referentiality. To fuel the scientific discussion we offer some additional questions:

- What are some further characteristics of L- and R-cooperations?
- What other distinctions should be made in this domain?
- What other theoretical foundations can shed light on this phenomenon?
- What are the different management systems needed to manage R- and L-cooperations?
- How can levels of disturbances (perturbations) be monitored in an organization?
- How can we view cooperations and perturbations on many scales simultaneously?
- How can we distinguish different sources of disturbances (perturbations)?
- How can we recognize them?
- How can we classify different types of disturbances (perturbations), e.g. psychological, technical, cultural, political, structural perturbations?
- Which processes can managers use to assess states in the organization?
- How can we create and encourage cooperative conversation (talk in and about cooperation)?

Notes

1 In the terms of Maturana and Varela (1987) structure denotes the components (strategic distinctions) and relations that actually constitute a particular unity (the company's cognitive system) and make its organization real. The term 'organization' denotes those relations that must exist among the components (strategic distinctions) of a system for it to be a member of a specific class (Maturana and Varela, 1987).

2 The company's competence can be conceived as a combination of the company's task system and knowledge system. Compare, for further explanation, von Krogh and Roos (1995).

3 From the perspective of autopoiesis theory everything is observed by someone. Thus, organizational states and perturbation levels can only be measured in relation to the observing system. Hence, the reader should read this table as a result of what is externalized after a process of self-assessment by an organization (read: observing system).

References

Argyris, C. and Schön, D. (1978). *Organizational Learning*. Reading, MA: Addison-Wesley.

Burgelman, R.A. (1989). Intraorganizational ecology of strategy making and organizational adaptation: theory and field research. *Organization Science*, 2: 239–62.

Contractor, F.J. and Lorange, P. (eds) (1988). *Cooperative Strategies in International Business*. Lexington, MA: D.C. Heath.

de Geus, A. (1988) Planning as learning. *Harvard Business Review*, March–April: 70–4.

Hannan, M.T. and Freeman, J. (1977). The population ecology of organization. *American Journal of Sociology*, 82: 929–40.

Hedberg, B.L.T. (1981). How organizations learn and unlearn. In P.C. Nystrom and W.H. Starbuck (eds), *Handbook of Organizational Design*. London: Oxford University Press. pp. 3–27.

Lorange, P. and Roos, J. (1992). *Strategic Alliances. Formation, Implementation and Evolution*. Cambridge, MA: Blackwell.

Maturana, H. and Varela, F.J. (1987) *The Tree of Knowledge*. Boston, MA: Shambhala.

Miller, D. (1982). Evolution and revolution: a quantum view of structural change in organizations. *Academy of Management Journal*: 131–52.

202   *Managing Knowledge*

Nonaka, I. (1988). Creating organizational order out of chaos. *California Management Review*, Spring: 57–73.

Nonaka, I. (1994) A dynamic theory of organizational knowledge creation. *Organizational Science*, 5(1): 14–37.

Prahalad, C.K. and Hamel, G. (1994). Strategy as a field of study: why search for a new paradigm? *Strategic Management Journal*, 15: 5–16.

Runco, M.A. (1990). Implicit theories and ideational creativity. In R.S. Alberts and M.A. Runco (eds), *Theories of Creativity*. Beverly Hills, CA: Sage.

Senge, P.M. (1990). *The Fifth Discipline: the Art and Practice of the Learning Organization*. New York: Doubleday/Currency.

Starbuck, W.H. and Nystrom, P.C. (1984). To avoid organizational crises, unlearn. *Organizational Dynamics*, 12(4): 53–65.

Varela, F.J., Thompson, E. and Rosch, E. (1992). *The Embodied Mind: Cognitive Science and Human Experience*. Cambridge, MA: MIT Press.

Vicari, S. (1994). Acquisitions as experimentation. In G. von Krogh, A. Sinatra and H. Singh (eds), *The Management of Corporate Acquisitions*. London: Macmillan. pp. 337–58.

von Krogh, G. and Roos, J. (1995a). *Organizational Epistemology*. London: Macmillan. New York: St Martin's Press.

von Krogh, G. and Roos, J. (1995b). Strategic conversations. *European Management Journal*, December: 390–4.

von Krogh, G. and Roos, J. (1996a). Talking about strategy: towards a phraseological view of strategic management. In A. Huff and J. Walsh (eds), *Advances in Strategic Management*. Greenwich, CT: JAI Press.

von Krogh, G. and Roos, J. (1996b). Conversation management. *European Management Journal*, forthcoming.

von Krogh, G. and Vicari, S. (1993). An autopoiesis approach to experimental strategic learning. In P. Lorange, B. Chakravarthy, J. Roos and A. Van de Ven (eds), *Implementing Strategic Processes: Change, Learning and Co-operation*. London: Blackwell. pp. 394–410.

Weick, K.E. (1979). *The Social Psychology of Organizing*. Reading, MA: Addison-Wesley.

10

A Note on the Epistemology of Globalizing Firms

Georg von Krogh, Johan Roos and George Yip

This chapter addresses knowledge development in globalizing firms. The concept of globalizing firms encompasses international, multinational and/ or global firms. The objective is to contribute to a theory of knowledge in globalizing firms, that is, to an epistemology of globalizing firms. This chapter represents a snapshot of an ongoing knowledge development process and is primarily aimed at fueling the discourse in the realms of management and organizational studies. The reader will find that the epistemology of globalizing firms that is being brought forth here is distinct from conventional organizational epistemologies. We also aim to shed light on some of the questions raised in Chapter 1 of the book.

Why is it important to understand knowledge development in firms? There are many arguments in the literature stressing that, today, knowledge is *the* thing for companies to focus on. For instance, Badaracco said that: 'In classical economics, the sources of wealth are land, labor, and capital . . . Now, another engine of wealth is at work. It takes many forms: technology, innovation, science, know-how, creativity, information. In a word, it is knowledge' (1991: 1). Numerous efforts have tried to link competence, firm strategy and performance, as well as to define, identify, analyze and exploit 'knowledge' and 'competence'. A manifestation of this recognition is perhaps the numerous concepts that have surfaced in the strategic management and organizational studies literature helping us to better understand knowledge in firms.[1]

Others have pointed at the shift from decreasing returns to increasing returns on resources in many industries ('positive feedbacks'), and the key role of knowledge in this shift (Arthur, 1990; Stinchcombe, 1990). Also, the tremendous transformations in contemporary society and economics and in the phenomenon we call the firm, which have been labeled the postmodern condition, point to the importance of understanding knowledge development in society and business (Lyotard, 1984; Lawson and Appignanesi, 1989; Hage and Powers, 1992). Thus, there seems to be little doubt that knowledge development is a substantive managerial *and* theoretical problem within the realm of strategic management and organization studies in general.[2] As argued by von Krogh and Roos (1995) knowledge enables us to perceive, act, and move in the world, and as we perceive, act and move the world comes forth as a result of our actions and observations. In the words of Maturana and Varela (1987) knowledge is what brings forth a world.

What are globalizing firms? In the process of becoming increasingly international, many firms follow a developmental path from 'international' to 'multinational' to 'global'. Briefly, the international stage is character-ized by an increasingly autonomous international division, separate from domestic business; the multinational stage is characterized by an increasing duplication of the value chain across countries and local autonomy;[3] and the global stage is denoted by the increasing geographic integration of activities and strategies. As noted by Yip: 'Multinational companies know well the first two steps. What they know less is the third step. In addition, globalization runs counter to the accepted wisdom of tailoring for national markets' (1992: 6). Thus, our concern with globalizing firms both includes and goes beyond the traditional issues discussed within the realm of 'international business', e.g. internationalization processes (Johanson and Vahlne, 1977; Buckley and Casson, 1976; Dunning, 1977), the theory of the multinational firm (Hymer, 1960; Kindleberger, 1969; Knickerbocker, 1973), and foreign direct investment processes (Aharoni, 1966; Stopford and Wells, 1972; Carlson, 1975).

Focusing on knowledge development in globalizing firms at the interna-tional stage many companies accept the wisdom that foreign activities exist to supplement *domestic* capacity utilization and profits. The process of internationalization will, however, give rise to new distinctions and norms, for instance, that each foreign activity is important in its own right, commonly argued by companies at the multinational stage. Again, the process of 'multinationalization' will give rise to new distinctions and norms, and, when reaching a global stage, many companies believe, first, that there should be no distinction between domestic and foreign, and, second, that each country activity exists to serve the greater global good. This knowledge development process is exactly what we are trying to better understand here.

This chapter consists of three core sections. In the first section we discuss how knowledge has been dealt with in the literature on globalizing firms, in the light of a conventional epistemology. In the second section we suggest two properties of an emerging epistemology of globalizing firms: language games and self-similarity. Finally, we discuss some implications of the epistemology and its properties for future research.

Conventional Epistemology of Globalizing Firms

Knowledge, as such, seems to be an important issue in the literature on globalizing firms. Traditional foreign direct investment theory takes as its starting point the concept of firm-specific advantages, a kind of comparative advantage of the multinational firm that needs to be internalized.[4] According to this theory the primary reason for a firm to go multinational is its knowledge, often being monopolistic in nature.[5]

Bartlett and Ghoshal (1987) stressed the need to manage the flow of 'intelligence, ideas and knowledge'; Yip (1992) claimed that an important dimension of being able to manage globally is the balance between autonomy in one country and global integration, and the ability to 'develop learning' across borders; Kogut and Zander, for instance, define information as 'knowledge which can be transmitted without loss of integrity once the syntactic rules required for deciphering it are known' (1992: 386). For the purpose of analysis these authors subdivide knowledge into information and know-how, the latter being 'a description of knowing how to do something' (1992: 386).

In their study of the organizational and administrative tasks facing managers in international, multinational, and global firms in the telecommunications switching industry, Bartlett and Ghoshal found that: 'the ability to learn and to appropriate the benefits of learning in multiple national markets differentiated the winners from the losers' (1989: 24). In fact, to ensure competitiveness this 'learning capability' had to be simultaneously developed with global competitiveness and multinational flexibility, a notable organizational challenge. As a solution, they recommended that globalizing firms break away from traditional management and adopt a new, 'transnational' management model. Although the authors neither define nor discuss knowledge as such, they have defined 'ability to learn' as 'to transfer knowledge and expertise from one part of the organization to others world-wide' (1987: 7).

Gupta and Govindarajan (1991; 1993) studied knowledge flows in multinational firms. More precisely, in their 1991 paper they studied the extent to which subsidiaries used knowledge from the rest of the firm, and the extent to which the subsidiary was a provider of such knowledge to the rest of the firm. Based on their empirical findings they developed a conceptual framework for how such differences are reflected in strategic processes. In their 1993 paper, the authors studied co-alignments between a subsidiary's strategic roles, based on knowledge flows, and strategic processes linking it with the rest of the firm. Knowledge flow is conceptualized as analogous to capital and product flows, 'e.g., technology and/or skill transfer' (1993: 330).[6]

Hedlund and Nonaka (1993) developed models of knowledge creation and discussed the differences and implications of these in Western and Japanese firms. These authors ground their theoretical claims on the belief that 'more encompassing theories of management and organization have not, in our view, really taken the appreciation of the importance of information, and particularly of knowledge, to heart' (1993: 117). Hedlund and Nonaka see knowledge as 'highly structured, complex assemblages of data, whereas information is reserved for simple and more discrete data'

(1993: 121). Their model included both the interplay between tacit and articulated knowledge and knowledge transformation processes between individuals, groups, firms and the environment.

Although the above examples of contributions have provided much insight into knowledge *per se* in globalizing firms, they reveal very little about *how* knowledge actually develops in globalizing firms. As previously discussed, this is a central problem in any corporate epistemology. Even more important, as in most of the literature within the realms of management and organizational studies, these contributions rest on the same assumptions regarding cognition, and, therefore, 'knowledge'.

Much of theory development in strategic management, related to both the social cognition of organizations and the cognition of individual managers, has roots in what Varela et al. (1992) call the 'cognitivist' perspective, captured in Part I of the book. As pointed out in earlier chapters, knowledge has been taken for granted, often as a decomposable, fuzzy, and substitutable concept (von Krogh and Roos, 1995), and the concept of 'knowledge' is often used interchangeably with the concept of 'information'.[7] At the heart of the cognitivist epistemology is the idea that the mind has the ability to represent reality in various ways, that is, creating inner representation that partly or fully corresponds to the outer world, be it objects, events, or states, by processing information available in this external environment (March and Simon, 1958; Argyris and Schön, 1978; Weick, 1979; Huff, 1983; Gioia and Manz, 1985; Ginsberg, 1990). Accordingly, knowledge has, as in the above examples, often been substituted for information, data, resources, skills, reputation, etc. Further, these representations are storable and retrievable in firm-wide knowledge structures that give firm members a shared perception of the world (Prahalad and Bettis, 1986; Lyles and Schwenk, 1992; Walsh and Ungson, 1991; see Chapter 4 of this volume). Thus, learning in the cognitivist epistemology means to improve representations of the world through assimilating new experiences.[8] To sum up, the cognitivist epistemology has had a great influence on our conceptions of organizational epistemology.[9]

Two Properties of a New Epistemology of Globalizing Firms

Based on autopoiesis theory (Maturana et al., 1974; Maturana and Varela, 1987; Luhmann, 1986), we have developed an alternative organizational epistemology in Chapter 8.

From this *Weltanschauung* presented in Chapter 8, two properties surface as particularly interesting for understanding knowledge development in globalizing firms: language games and self-similar processes. We do not claim that these are the only two properties of such an epistemology. Still, we judge them to be the most interesting for globalizing firms.

Language Games

Over time, firms develop their own distinct domains of language (von Krogh and Roos, 1995). Why? Because firms may be understood as systems of language. By introducing the concept of 'the firm', we linguistically distinguish it from something else. Hence, the emergence of an organization presupposes languaging. Concepts like 'the organization', 'the firm', 'the plant', and so on are conserved as concepts over time as organizational members continue to bring them up in their conversations (or writings). Also, over time organizational members make finer linguistic distinctions: from rudimentary distinctions to more fine-grained ones, for instance, of the implications of a new technology (high impact versus low impact on company performance). Therefore, a domain of language can be seen as tradition and this tradition will affect languaging: 'A lawyer speaks from the tradition of his law firm and the legal society; a production engineer speaks from the tradition of his manufacturing organization; a doctor speaks from the tradition of his professional organization; an Eskimo speaks from his "Arctic" tradition' (von Krogh and Roos, 1995: 101).

Language games refer to the process by which language is not only maintained but constantly being created within the firm, based on previous language (in a self-referential manner). Rather than representing a section of the world a particular word acquires its meaning by its very use (Wittgenstein, 1958; Astley and Zammuto, 1992).

There are rules for the usage of certain words that give the words meaning.[10] These rules are dependent on the social context in which the word appears. For example, in some organizations the formal use of the word 'strategy' is limited to the discussions and documents produced by the top management team. An extreme proponent of such rules is the CEO of Asea Brown Boveri, Percy Barnevik, who fines headquarters executives for using the word 'foreign'.[11] But Barnevik also sees a need for 50 or so 'global' managers, while the rest should be 'local'. On the other hand, in some firms all managers (should) speak the same (global) language.

Rules for the usage of words are very seldom static, especially in business organizations where little formal control is exerted. In the globalizing firm managers face a great opportunity in language games, finding new rules and inventing new concepts. One type of language game concerns how the acceptability of phrases changes. At the multinational stage, the utterance 'you can't do it in that way in this country' is a powerful mantra capable of stopping dead any undesired headquarters initiative. But in the era of globalization, those managers making such national distinctions should perhaps be forced to reveal the rules they are applying consciously, or more likely unconsciously, to the claim, i.e. their language games.

Von Krogh and Roos (1995) suggested an observational scheme for understanding language games, encompassing words, concepts and their

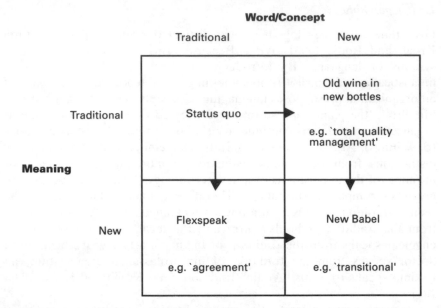

Figure 10.1   *Meaning matrix for language games*

meaning. This conceptual scheme shows that language games may take three forms: (1) the meaning of traditional words and concepts can be changed, for example 'an agreement' in the home country may mean something less binding in a country with more relaxed attitudes; (2) new words and concepts can be invented for traditional meanings, like 'total quality management'; or (3) new words and concepts can be invented carrying new meanings, like 'transnational'.

We further develop the von Krogh and Roos scheme into a 'meaning matrix' in Figure 10.1, where every position, except the top left quadrant, manifests some kind of innovation in language games. Typically changes occur in the directions of the arrows, not directly from 'Status quo' to 'New Babel', but via 'Flex speak' or 'Old wine in new bottles'. Eventually, when no words or concepts are invented and/or introduced, and when the meanings of these existing words and concepts do not change, the languaging of the organization stabilizes. The rules get set and a linguistic tradition is brought forth.

What about language games in globalizing firms? A firm at the international stage may undergo a period of 'language confusion' as its managers struggle with the new demands of operating in foreign environments. This is the period of greatest culture shock; for example, 'brand loyalty' will take on different definitions, 'authorization' will vary in interpretation, and so on. At this internationalization stage, the company may go through language games along both the word/concept and the meaning dimensions. At the multinational stage, the company, again, passes through the turbulent waters of language games. Subsidiaries are started up in several countries with different linguistic traditions: the company is exposed to new words and concepts with traditional and new meanings. Still, a common language may have been developed. For example, every subsidiary may use and comprehend the same term for gross margin, return on investment, and the like. At the global stage, the language ambiguity returns and different kinds of language games proliferate to establish new meanings for new words and concepts, for instance, 'global strategy', 'global career', and 'market dominance'.

The globalizing firm passes through a cycle of linguistic tradition. As it passes through each of the international, multinational, and global stages, the company gets exposed to new lingusitic domains, along the dimensions and directions in the meaning matrix. The resulting language games are dealt with through discussion and other forms of communication, bringing forth a firm-specific, linguistic tradition: the world of the globalizing company. In turn, this (new) tradition is exposed to new words and concepts with or without new meaning, and so on in an ongoing knowledge development process.

Self-similarity

According to von Krogh and Roos (1995), knowledge is what brings forth a world, but the world is also what brings forth knowledge. In addition, knowledge is a process brought forth by individuals, groups, departments, organizations, and so on. Thus, it may be meaningful to discuss knowledge at various organizational *scales*. This is the second property of our epistemology of globalizing firms. As stated by von Krogh and Roos: 'A theory of scaling may help us to understand the relations between individual and social knowledge development, the dynamics of individual and social autopoietic systems' (1995: 71). Although the most intuitive scale in many organizations is 'hierarchical level', in globalizing firms it might be useful to discuss 'degree of' internationalization, market orientation, technological depth, or other scales. 'Scales on the divisional or departmental level might include, for instance, degee of project organization versus operations management, perspectives on time, socialisation among employees. On the individual level, we find scales like level of education and experience, work morale, degree of political or religious beliefs, environmental awareness, sense of urgency, and so on' (1995: 76). Scaling (up or down) simply means moving along such scales.

'Globalization' is typically a scaled concept. At the international stage, the concept of being an 'international' company typically requires a larger and larger percentage of revenues being foreign as the company gains experience. Initially, any overseas revenue allows the company to define itself as 'international'. Over time the self-defined scale is changed until, for instance, 50 per cent becomes the qualifying mark, at least for many American companies. Many European companies increasingly discount intra-European sales as international, again scaling up on the 'globalization' dimension. At the multinational stage, the number of countries and the amount of the globe or its markets that must be served in order to be truly 'global' gradually increase. As companies progress in globalizing, managers gradually scale up: more and more strategies, activities, products, and so on need to be globally integrated for the company to qualify as global.

A special case of scaling is self-similarity, which means *similarity across scale*. The theoretical basis of self-similarity is derived from chaos theory (Lorenz, 1963; Mandelbrot, 1977), where self-similarity is a distinct property of 'fractals', a term invented by Mandelbrot (1977). Thus, self-similarity is about patterns not at one scale or another, but across scale, at all possible scales. Self-similar processes occur everywhere in nature, in many parts of society, and in many organizations. More importantly: 'scaling, and in particular, self-similarity, provides a language for, and a lens through which we may advance our understanding of the dynamics of organizational knowledge, individualised and socialised' (von Krogh and Roos, 1995: 96).

Self-similarity can be seen in practice in many organizational processes, perhaps most easily detected on the organizational-level scale, which is our focus in this chapter. No matter where they are, when they are or what scope they have, when the scale of observation is changed (for instance, at the individual, group or SBU level), new processes, routines, and principles are revealed, each resembling the overall process. Self-similar processes are recognized as always being similar, but not necessarily identical across scale.

Self-similar organizational processes and principles may be more effective, relatively less complex and easier to design and enact than processes that are not self-similar. If we recognize a vision statement embodying the ethical principles of a firm, for instance, we might suspect that it is self-similar in nature on many levels in an organization. Of course, this is an unusual situation because many vision statements are not perceived as meaningful below the top management level; they are *different* across scale.

We do not want to pursue this line of reasoning so far as to suggest that *all* processes *ought* to be self-similar. Rather, we confine ourselves to suggesting that there is a *potential* benefit from the reduction in complexity that results from having processes, principles, working modes, and so on, that are similar across scale. It is up to the reader to decide to what extent this is meaningful for him/her. Many organizational processes, however, already are or might easily be made self-similar. Examples include information systems, power structures, strategic planning, control, and human resource procedures which may be developed at the headquarters and pursued in a similar form throughout a global firm. This concerns the international, multinational, and global firm alike.[12] However, there is often a practical limit to the 'degree' of self-similarity in globalizing organizations. There are just so many organizational levels, countries in which the firm is present, and different meanings given to certain concepts like 'global strategy' in a given organization.

We suggest that the degree of *potential self-similarity* follows an inverse-U trajectory as firms progress through the stages of globalization: being low at the international stage, high at the multinational stage, and moderate at the global scale. This is because a firm at the international stage often maintains a strong distinction between the domestic and international divisions, and also tends to operate with a strong hierarchy within the international division. So the application of management processes, such as planning, budgeting, performance review and compensation, will tend to be different. In contrast, a firm at the multinational stage often operates with a 'United Nations' mentality, whereby each subsidiary is given equal treatment.[13] Therefore, it is more likely that processes will be more self-similar in multinational firms.[14] Lastly, as a firm moves into the global stage, a degree of differentiation will return as different subsidiaries take on different roles,[15] and as the value chain is allocated out to a limited number of countries. So, for example, 'profit responsibility' will have a different scope for the global headquarters of a business unit, for a country that has both manufacturing and selling activities, and for a country that has selling only.

To sum up, we have suggested that (1) two important properties of an epistemology of globalizing firms are language games and self-similarity, and (2) knowledge development differs as companies evolve across three stages of globalization: international, multinational, and global. The reason is that the nature of language games and the formation of a linguistic tradition change, as does the potential for self-similarity, manifested in organizational knowledge development, or understanding of what constitutes 'good strategy and practice'. Consequently, knowledge development in globalizing firms can perhaps be better understood through these two properties.

Discussion

The epistemology of globalizing firms discussed in this chapter has important implications for both research and practice. We would like to fuel further discussion by posing and trying to answer a few questions pertaining to this epistemology.

How Can We Understand Knowledge Development in Globalizing Firms?

The cognitivist-based perspective has led to many insights regarding knowledge in globalizing firms. Nonetheless, the ease by which knowledge is equated with, for instance, information or technology in many cognitivist-based studies has unfortunately created ambiguities for researchers trying to theorize around the substantive problems discussed in this chapter. This is illustrated by the following quote: 'Social scientists of various persuasions wrestle with the terms [knowledge and information], but we have not been able to extract clear or commonly shared definitions' (Hedlund and Nonaka, 1993: 121). In this respect, international studies do not differ significantly from globalizing firms in the types of challenges faced. In any context, when you cross national, historical, intellectual, political or cultural boundaries, definitions will be hard to fix. In fact, some words, like 'knowledge' and 'information', acquire their meaning not by being clearly defined, transparent to any speaker or listener, but rather by the rules for their usage (Wittgenstein, 1958). Like managers of the global firm, it is we, as researchers, who develop such rules through the way we use the words. International studies have the potential to be innovative with respect to language games, attracting researchers from many countries and studying phenomena in diverse cultural contexts.

The attempts to shed light on knowledge development in globalizing firms from a cognitivist perspective will result in increasingly finer distinctions, that is, more knowledge will be developed but *only in the cognitivist stream of knowledge development*. This knowledge will *not* automatically be plausible from another perspective of knowledge, such as the epistemology discussed in this chapter.

The implication is that in order to truly advance our knowledge of knowledge development in globalizing firms, we need to go 'backwards' to make a new, more rudimentary distinction, and (in a self-referential manner) begin to make increasingly finer distinctions again.[16] The epistemology of globalizing firms represents an attempt to make precisely this type of advancement.

What Are the Implications for Future Research?

Our thesis has put strong emphasis on the two properties of self-similarity and language games. These are natural areas for developing increasingly finer distinctions, that is, areas for future research. Still, because these properties concern management, international *and* organization studies alike, they are on a higher scale than any of these areas in themselves.

Language games are only one property of knowledge development. Studies are needed that highlight the complexity of language games faced by global firms (even if the corporate language is English), and the possible impact that languages have on the development of knowledge in globalizing firms. An important field to study would be the 'journey of concept' in globalizing firms, like the many varieties of meaning assigned to 'scenario planning' in Royal Dutch/Shell, or the 'networked organization' in Digital.

To further fuel the discourse, we suggest five such 'what' and 'how' questions pertaining to language games:[17]

'What' questions

- What are the rules for globalizing firms in the usage of specific words and concepts?

- What are the implications of variety in rules for the development of knowledge in the globalizing firm?
- What are the emerging new words and concepts and their respective meaning?
- What are the associations between a corporate language and knowledge development in globalizing firms?
- What are the linguistic obstacles to knowledge development in globalizing firms?

'How' questions

- How can managers learn and affect rules of languages in globalizing firms?
- How can managers stimulate language games in globalizing firms?
- How can managers facilitate the development of a linguistic tradition in globalizing firms?
- How can managers become increasingly sensitive to the relationship between language games and knowledge development in globalizing firms?
- How do language games evolve in globalizing firms?

Please note that some of these questions will be addressed in Chapter 11.

Self-similarity of knowledge development is a particular branch of knowledge development that is just beginning to unfold in the realm of management and organizational studies, implying that there is much potential not only for theory testing, but also for theory development. Still, many issues surface as potentially interesting in connection with self-similar knowledge development in globalizing firms.

To fuel the discourse we suggest another set of 'what' and 'how' questions, this time pertaining to future research on self-similarity:

'What' questions

- What dimensions are or could be made self-similar in globalizing firms?
- What are the potential effects from geographical, cultural, political, social, demographical and financial factors on self-similarity in knowledge development in globalizing firms?
- What are the dynamics of self-similar knowledge development in globalizing firms?
- What are the implications of self-similar knowledge development for different performance dimensions in globalizing firms?
- What are the limitations for self-similar knowledge development in globalizing firms?

'How' questions

- How can global, self-similar knowledge development processes be designed in globalizing firms?
- How 'many' self-similar knowledge development processes are appropriate in what situation?

- How can self-similar knowledge development be managed over time in globalizing firms?
- How many levels of self-similarity are plausible for knowledge development in globalizing firms?
- How can self-similar knowledge development be self-organized in globalizing firms?

In addition to the above sets of questions, numerous 'who' questions can be posed for both properties, e.g. who should be responsible for addressing issues of self-similar processes and language games? Here it seems to us that some questions relating to human resource management in globalizing firms may be redirected and focused on the two properties (self-similarity and language games) discussed in this chapter.

What Does the Epistemology of Global Firms Imply for Studying Globalizing Firms?

Lastly, the two properties of the epistemology discussed in this chapter, namely self-similarity and language games, also have implications for research methodology. The inherent complexity of the two properties makes it hard to conceive meaningful quantitative research techniques. How can one, for instance, adequately capture aspects of language games in a questionnaire to all middle managers in a global firm? Still, we do not want to rule out quantitative approaches in general. It might be useful to experiment with simulation techniques on these phenomena, which probably are far from linear in nature. Still, it appears to us that long-term, in-depth methodological approaches are more respectful to the process *per se*, and also allow for scaling of data collection.

Notes

This chapter was previously published as the article 'An Epistemology of Globalizing Firms', *International Business Review*, 1994, 3: 395–411. Reprinted by permission of Elsevier Science Ltd.

1   Some examples include: distinctive competence (Andrews, 1971; Ansoff, 1965), dominant logic (Prahalad and Bettis, 1986), internal capabilities (Barney, 1986), invisible assets (Itami, 1987), absorptive capacity (Cohen and Levinthal, 1990), migratory and embedded knowledge (Badaracco, 1991), managerial, resource-based, transformation-based, and output-based competencies (Lado et al., 1992), core capabilities (Stalk et al., 1992), underlying capabilities (Williams, 1992).

2   This has also been underscored by the works of Prahalad and Bettis (1986) and Lyles and Schwenk (1992). In the same line, but from a different perspective, this has been underscored by von Krogh et al. (1994) and von Krogh and Roos (1995).

3   In consequence, this stage has been renamed 'multidomestic' by Hout et al. (1982) and 'multilocal' by Yip (1992). Other authors have used different connotations, e.g. Perlmutter (1965).

4   See Hymer (1976) and his many followers.

5   The theory of the multinational firm defines three types of knowledge: technical (expertise in producing goods and services), marketing (expertise in selling and purchasing), and managerial (expertise in administration, delegation and decision making) (Casson, 1987).

6 See Kogut and Zander (1993) for an extensive treatment of knowledge seen as technology.

7 For a recent example, see Cyert et al. (1993).

8 von Krogh et al. (1994); von Krogh and Roos (1995).

9 It should be noted that there is another perspective of cognition and therefore another epistemology, which Varela et al. (1992) labeled 'connectionism'. Although they differ with respect to how they view learning, the connectionist and the cognitivist perspectives see information processing as the basic activity of the brain. See von Krogh and Roos (1995) for a fuller treatment of these epistemologies.

10 Wittgenstein (1958) (*Sprachspiele*).

11 Talk by Percy Barnevik at the Academy of International Business Annual Conference, Brussels, November 1992.

12 Similarly, *distinctions* made by one influential organizational member may carry similar or different *meanings* across countries and levels in the organization.

13 See Bartlett and Ghoshal (1989).

14 A counter-argument for this can be found in Gupta and Govindarajan (1993).

15 Bartlett and Ghoshal (1989) identify at least four different roles for subsidiaries: lead countries, contributors, implementors, and black holes.

16 As suggested by von Krogh et al. (1994).

17 Major 'why' questions have been addressed in this chapter.

References

Aharoni, Y. (1966). *The Foreign Investment Decision Process*. Boston: Harvard University Press.

Andrews, K.R. (1971). *The Concept of Corporate Strategy*. Homewood, IL: Dow Jones Irwin.

Ansoff, H.I. (1965). *Corporate Strategy*. New York: McGraw-Hill.

Argyris, C. and Schön, D. (1978). *Organizational Learning*. Reading, MA: Addison-Wesley.

Arthur, W.B. (1990). Positive feedback in the economy. *Scientific American*, February: 92–9.

Astley, W.G. and Zammuto, P. (1992) Organization science, managers, and language games. *Organization Science*, 3: 443–61.

Badaracco, J.L. (1991). *The Knowledge Link: How Firms Compete through Strategic Alliances*. Boston: Harvard Business School Press.

Barney, J. (1986). Types of competition and the theory of strategy: toward an integrative framework. *Academy of Management Review*, 11: 791–800.

Bartlett, C.A. and Ghoshal, S. (1987). Managing across borders: new organizational responses. *Sloan Management Review*, Fall.

Bartlett, C.A. and Ghoshal, S. (1989). *Managing across Borders: the Transnational Solution*. Boston: Harvard Business School Press.

Buckley, P.J. and Casson, M. (1976). *The Future of the Multinational Enterprise*. London: Macmillan.

Carlson, S. (1975). How foreign is foreign trade? A problem in international business research. Studie Oeconomica Negotiorum, 11, Uppsala.

Casson, M. (1987). *The Firm and the Market*. UK: Butler & Tanner.

Cohen, M. and Levinthal, D. (1990). Absorptive capacity: a perspective on learning and innovation. *Administrative Science Quarterly*, 35: 128–52.

Cyert, R.M., Kumar, P. and Williams, J.R. (1993). Information, market imperfections, and strategy. *Strategic Mananagement Journal*, 14 (Special Issue, Summer): 14: 47–59

Dunning, J.H. (1977). Trade, location of economic activity and the multinational enterprise: a search for an eclectic approach. In B. Ohlin, P.O. Hesselbom and P.J. Wiskman (eds), *The International Allocation of Economic Activity*. London: Macmillan.

Ginsberg, A. (1990). Connecting diversification to performance: a socio-cognitive approach. *Academy of Management Review*, 15: 514–35.

Gioia, D.A. and Manz, C.C. (1985). Linking cognition and behavior: a script processing interpretation of vicarious learning. *Academy of Management Review*, 10(3): 527–39.

Gupta, A. and Govindarajan, V.J. (1991). Knowledge flows and the structure of control within multinational corporations. *Academy of Management Review*, 16(4): 768–92.

Gupta, A. and Govindarajan, V.J. (1993). Coalignment between knowledge flow patterns and strategic systems and processes within MNCs. In P. Lorange, B. Chakravarthy, J. Roos and A. Van der Ven (eds), *Implementing Strategic Processes*. Oxford: Basil Blackwell.

Hage, J. and Powers, C.H. (1992). *Post-Industrial Lives: Roles and Relationships in the 21st Century*. Newbury Park, CA: Sage.

Hedlund, G. and Nonaka, I. (1993). Models of knowledge management in the West and Japan. In P. Lorange, B. Chakravarthy, J. Roos and A. Van der Ven (eds), *Implementing Strategic Processes*. Oxford: Basil Blackwell.

Hout, T., Porter, M.E. and Rudden, E. (1982). How global companies win out. *Harvard Business Review*, September–October: 98–108.

Huff, A.S. (1983) Industry influence on strategy reformulation. *Strategic Management Journal*, 3: 119–31.

Hymer, S.H. (1960). *The International Operations of National Firms*. Cambridge, MA: MIT Press.

Hymer, S.H. (1976). *The International Operations of National Firms: a Study of Direct Foreign Investments*. Cambridge, MA: MIT Press.

Itami, H. (1987). *Mobilizing Invisible Assets*. Cambridge, MA: Harvard University Press.

Johanson, J. and Vahlne, J.E. (1977) The internationalization process of the firm. *Journal of International Business Studies*, Spring/Summer.

Kindleberger, C.P. (1969). *American Business Abroad: Six Lectures on Direct Investment*. New Havem, CT: Yale University Press.

Knickerbocker, F.T. (1973). *Oligopolistic Reaction and the Multinational Enterprise*. Boston: Harvard University Press.

Kogut, B. and Zander, U. (1992). Knowledge of the firm, combinative capabilities, and the replication of technology. *Organization Science*, 3(3): 383–97,

Kogut, B. and Zander, U. (1993). Knowledge of the firm and the evolutionary theory of the multinational corporation. *Journal of International Business Studies*, 24(4): 625–45.

Lado, A.A., Boyd, N.G. and Wright, P. (1992). A competency-based model of sustainable competitive advantage: toward a conceptual integration. *Journal of Management*, 18: 77–91.

Lawson, H. and Appignanesi, H.L. (1989). *Dismantling Truth: Reality in the Post-Modern World*. New York: ECA.

Lorenz, E.N. (1963). Deterministic non-periodic flows. *Journal of Atmospheric Sciences*, 20: 130–141.

Luhmann, N. (1986). The autopoiesis of social systems. In F. Geyer and J. Van der Zouwen (eds), *Sociocybernetic Paradoxes: Observation, Control, and Evolution of Self-Steering Systems*. London: Sage. pp. 172–92.

Lyles, M.A. and Schwenk, C.R. (1992). Top management, strategy and organizational knowledge structures. *Journal of Management Studies*, 29 (March): 155–74.

Lyotard, J.F. (1984). *The Postmodern Condition: a Report on Knowledge*. Minneapolis: University of Minnesota Press.

Mandelbrot, B.B. (1977). *The Fractal Geometry of Nature*. New York: W.H. Freeman.

March, J.G. and Simon, H.A. (1958). *Organizations*. New York: Wiley.

Maturana, H. and Varela, F. (1987). *The Tree of Knowledge*. Boston: Shambhala.

Maturana, H., Varela, F. and Uribe, R. (1974). Autopoiesis: the organization of living systems, its characterization and a model. *BioSystems*, 5: 187–96.

Perlmutter, H.V. (1965). L'entreprise internationale – trois conceptions. *Revue Economique et Sociale*, 23.

Prahalad, C.K. and Bettis, R. (1986). The dominant logic: a new linkage between diversity and performance. *Strategic Management Journal*, 7: 485–501.

Stalk, G., Evans, P. and Schulman, L.E. (1992). Competing on capabilities: the new rules of corporate strategy. *Harvard Business Review*, March–April: 57–69.

Stinchcombe, A. (1990). *Information and Organizations*. Berkeley, CA: University of California Press.

Stopford, J.M. and Wells, L.T. Jr (1972). *Managing the Multinational Enterprise*. New York: Basic Books.

Varela, F.J., Thompson, E. and Rosch, E. (1992). *The Embodied Mind*. Cambridge, MA: MIT Press.

von Krogh, G. and Roos, J. (1995). *Organizational Epistemology*. London: Macmillan.

von Krogh, G., Roos, J. and Slocum, K. (1994) An essay on corporate epistemology. *Strategic Management Review*, 15 (Special Summer Issue): 33–71.

Walsh, J.P. and Ungson, G.R. (1991). Organizational memory. *Academy of Management Review*, 16: 57–91.

Weick, K.E. (1979). *The Social Psychology of Organizing*. New York: Random House.

Williams, J.R. (1992). How sustainable is your competitive advantage? *California Management Review*, Spring: 29–51.

Wittgenstein, L. (1958). *Philosophical Investigations*. New York: Macmillan.

Yip, G. (1992). *Total Global Strategy: Managing for World-Wide Competitive Advantage*. Englewood Cliffs, NJ: Prentice-Hall.

11

Conversation Management for Knowledge Development

Georg von Krogh and Johan Roos

The Importance of Conversations

It is obvious that without language, knowledge could not flow from person to person within a company. It is equally obvious that if two people speak different languages, then communication is stifled. What is not always obvious is that people are constantly in the process of creating new language and new meanings, even if they share the same mother tongue. On the high value-added boundaries of knowledge creation, the ability to 'make' new language – and rapidly diffuse it through a company – is a strategic advantage. The aim of this short chapter is to create awareness of the need for managing conversations in organizations. It should be noted that the following discussions are based on the concept of languaging, presented in Chapters 8 and 10.

Part of understanding a company is learning the phrases and their usage as they occur through the practice of the organization's language. Every company has its own unique set of concepts and phrases and usage of concepts and phrases, as well as potential for creating new concepts and phrases and new usage of them.

Concepts and phrases from one company are, in principle, not translatable into the culture of another organization. Such a translation would presuppose that the *meaning* of a concept or a phrase in company A can be reproduced by a concept or a phrase in the language, tradition or culture of company B, which is rarely possible. Just think of the many different meanings that the concepts 'strategy', 'core-competence' or 'competitive advantage' or the phrase 'we are a learning organization' have to people in the same company!

The *meaning matrix* (see von Krogh and Roos, 1995) in Figure 11.1 illustrates the dynamics of meaning and concepts. Existing concepts can be used in a way that conveys known or new meaning. A new concept can be used to reinforce existing meaning, or express new meaning.

The organizational world, in this sense of evolving meaning and concepts, is brought forth in language and in conversations. Yet, given its importance, many businesses are still sloppy in the way they invest in

Word/Concept

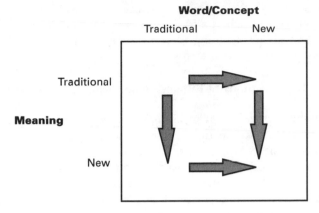

Figure 11.1　*Meaning matrix*

conversations. Most managers use phrases like 'we are a global company', 'the customer is king', 'our company is a learning organization', 'related diversification' without much reflection. Because their use of this language is not seen as a strategic concern, few spend time giving meaning to the new language people are exposed to every day.

There are numerous examples in the business literature where a new word or phrase has brought forth new companies, new jobs and new competition and/or led the strategic repositioning of a company (see von Krogh and Roos, 1996). Such concepts are, for instance, advertorial, hollywired, legolization, edutainment, infomercials, femidom, netsurfers, nanotechnology, personal contract purchase, packet sniffers, technopreneur, wankware, nutraceuticals, freedom food, Web aware, quantum electronics, edusprectum and cyberlife. Also just think of the financial equity invested in phrases such as 'to fly to serve', 'computers and communication', 'integrated technology conglomerate', 'from chips to ships', and 'built for the human race'.

This is why we urge managers to develop systematic processes that stimulate 'languaging' throughout the company so that over time an internal company lexicon is formed. This requires careful attention to the concepts used and the way they acquire meaning. Rather than simply imposing borrowed words, concepts and phrases on the rest of the organization, this means spending time and resources discussing new meanings that reflect where the current state of the company is compared to the historical conditions. Concepts are used in a dynamic way, and frequently, concepts used in the past do not fit with the current situation of the company. For example, the way 'long-range planning' was used in the 1960s does not necessarily correspond well to the dynamic strategy processes of the 1990s where core competence creation, rather than learning curves, is the essence of strategy work.

Language and knowledge go hand in hand. If the currency of business operations is money, *the currency of knowledge development is language* (see Roos and von Krogh, 1995). The more time and resources spent on developing and giving meaning to concepts and phrases, the 'richer' the company is, – 'in knowledge terms'.

Engaging in Conversations to Enhance Knowledge Development

Due to the sheer pressure of modern business, most managers typically seek a fast resolution to any discussion. Under considerable time pressure people advocate their own versions of 'the truth', almost like in a court of justice, and then engage in a contest to resolve whose version will prevail. This push for early closure in discussions acts as a barrier to the development of knowledge. Instead of allowing this adversarial form of decision making to continue, and even encouraging it as happens in some companies, companies need to stimulate and foster conversations, at all levels of the organization. Such conversations should aim at promoting a *dialogue for understanding rather than advocacy for agreement*.

Key questions most managers should ask themselves are: how do we develop knowledge that is relevant for the formation of successful strategies? How do you assist members of a management team to convey their own observations of the company and its environment, and moreover, how do you provide the conditions that stimulate further knowledge development? What kind of conversations will help us develop successful strategies? Or in other words, to paraphrase Prahalad and Hamel (1994), what kind of conversations does it take to invent the future of a company? The role of conversations needs increasing attention. As managers talk they shape their understanding of strategic issues, challenges, and opportunities. A good conversation can turn a strategic challenge into a strategic opportunity. From experience, each one of us also knows that a thorough dialogue can turn a limited awareness of an issue into broad understanding of that issue and a clear direction for further action. Hence, the kind of process that happens as managers devote time to sit down and discuss the future of the company will probably have far-reaching consequences. The strategic management field, however, has almost overlooked the role of conversations. Conversation has been treated as a 'default value'; it's just there, and there is nothing you can do about it (see also von Krogh and Roos, 1996; 1995). When we examine the practices of many companies and managers today, we believe that 'conversation by default' is based on the wrong assumptions. You can do something about it. We see some companies that nurture a 'conversation culture'; some that invite researchers from completely different fields, like brain science, to talk about their own research findings; and others that have 'discussions for knowledge development'. Common for these players is a belief that if you can manage your company's conversations on a variety of levels, you will simply run faster (and perhaps better) than your opponent. You will get a host of new ideas for your business operations, and you will come to see other patterns that you can act on. Good conversations can also make strategic decision making faster and more effective. The trickiest parts, however, are precisely those conversations that are associated with strategic management of a company.

The good news is that *conversation management* is not costly or fad oriented. The bad news is that it requires discipline, mastery, and subtlety. Most managers are not used to getting the most out of their conversations. And it requires a completely new skill set. As a starting point, you might want to *assume that conversations are your company's vehicle for knowledge development*!

Managing Conversations

While most companies are proficient in carrying out operational conversations, they lack the mastery of strategic conversations. *Operational conversations* are oriented towards the survival of the company, the day-to-day operation of the business. People on all levels in the organization meet to discuss a variety of operational issues: how to bring down the maintenance costs of a production line; what salary and benefits packages to include in an employment contract; which clients to approach with a proposal for a new project; which new switchboard to select; how to build up an archive; how to renegotiate a deal with a supplier; how to decrease the shutdown time of a plant; and so on. As a manager, you allocate a substantial part of your available work time to discussing these issues with a variety of people in the company. If you think about it, you normally have no problem allocating time to operational conversations.

Strategic conversations, on the other hand, are oriented towards the advancement of the company, to the creation of the future for the business. You (in theory) meet with other people in the organization to discuss issues of a different nature than operational issues: the nature of emerging technologies; the structural changes in the industry; what competencies the company should build in order to remain competitive in this changing industry; what values should guide the company in the future; what kind of cooperative arrangements would be needed in order to secure the company's technological developments in the future; and so on. Strategic conversations are also about the creation and acquisition of resources for the future, and how these resources should be allocated in the future. In short, strategic conversations are the cradle of a company's strategy. However, how much time do you really allocate to discuss strategic issues? Perhaps too little, and if you spend considerable time, perhaps it is not sufficiently well used.

The reason why most companies are not proficient in strategic conversations lies in the anatomy of such conversations. In many companies conversations about strategies are either *ad hoc*, over-structured, boring or political. Often these discussions happen in remote places, far away from the company's reality. Traveling time is seen as a nuisance, and once you get there you normally spend considerable time on your cellular, keeping in touch with the operation.

Frequently discussions of strategy happen at weekends, competing with time you could have allocated to your family, and showing how much the company really cares about your input to strategies. Most of the participating managers are haunted by a feeling that they waste time. As a strategic business unit manager, you are measured on the sales of your unit, not on your appearance as business poet, creating 'stories' using words like 'core competence', 'strategic intent', 'business portfolios', 'market growth and share', 'corporate identity', 'corporate culture', etc. But, your boss said you had to be there.

In our experience, many participants in such sessions participate with their bodies, not with their minds. The mind is elsewhere: on getting the next sale, on finalizing this contract, on firing that bloke who didn't deliver. Perhaps this is what you keep to yourself: 'Let us keep this strategy thing as fluffy as possible, throw in some great words here and there, and we can get on with doing our business. Then at least, nothing changes!' This is the *insipidity* of strategic processes.

There is yet another problem tied to the anatomy of strategic conversations. Managers frequently apply the same rules to these conversations as they do to operational conversations, especially those of authority, intimidation and closure. In order to get things done, in a company, these three rules are frequently applied. Let us first start with an example of conversational patterns.

Operational Conversation

> *John [CEO]*: Sue, what has happened to that offer we made to the Swiss client? Did you get an answer from Mr Lipton?
>
> *Sue [Marketing director]*: No, John. I've been trying to call him, but he's on vacation.
>
> *John*: Sue, you know that your ass is on the line here. You've been trying to sell this project now for a long time. Let's conclude this now. Either you fix this deal, or you'd better start looking for some other employer. I'll give you my own personal contact. You can call the top executive there, Mr Gilbert. Ask him for a quick reply.
>
> *Sue*: OK, John, I'll do it at once.

This example has all three ingredients. *First*, John threatens Sue with the possibility of losing her job. *Second*, John uses authority to tell Sue to call Mr Gilbert. *Third*, John pushes for closure both in the relationship with Sue and in the relationship with the client. Now consider these rules of intimidation, authority, and closure directly transferred to a strategic conversation on a possible acquisition strategy.

Strategic Conversation

> *John*: Sue, you tell us that we should buy the company PLX Ltd.
>
> *Sue*: Yes, John. I believe this company has a great asset reserve, some excellent

clients, and some of the best managers in the business. The question is, however, can we integrate it into our business?

John: Well, hm, yes . . . well, you should know Sue. It's your call. You'd better make sure we can integrate so that we achieve the synergies *you* expect.

Sue: Hm, yes, John. I'll do my best.

John: I want to close this thing now. Far too much time has been spent on strategy today. We need to get moving on this deal. Sue: you set up the practicalities with the lawyers. And by the way, Sue, you'd better make sure to integrate, or else . . .
Sue: Sure, I was just . . .Well, I'll do my best.
John: Let's hope that's good enough, Sue. Let's really hope that's enough.

As you may have noticed, the strategic conversation is carried out exactly according to the same pattern. *First*, John uses authority to order Sue to set up the deal with the lawyers. There was at no time any question about whether John was perhaps better suited to manage the details of the acquisition. *Second*, John uses intimidation, connecting Sue's position to the success of the acquisition. There are two clear effects of this. John believes he will make Sue work even harder on the strategic acquisition. Moreover, John will always have a potential scapegoat in Sue if the acquisition should go wrong. *Third*, John pushes for closure. Sue does not get the chance to explain her fear to John that synergies perhaps are difficult to achieve. There is no dialogue on John's potential role in creating these synergies. There is no knowledge developed on the managerial responsibilities that the acquisition involves.

There are two lessons from these considerations. *First*, in order to make your company master strategic conversations you have to make strategic conversations pungent. *Second*, you have to abandon the old rules of steering your operational conversations and adopt a completely new set of rules for strategic conversations. Table 11.1 summarizes the main issues and differences between strategic and operational discussions.

To Get Going

What does it take for a management team to have some real conversations about the future of their company? What typically happens parallels what we have seen in a number of organizations.

We will give you one story that might illustrate this. The management team in a newspaper had decided to set aside three hours for a strategy meeting. They met at 11.00 a.m. in the boardroom of the company, a very prestigious and beautiful room. At 11.10, everybody had arrived – well, almost everybody. The editor in chief was still missing. The managing director of the newspaper suggested starting the meeting, and getting on with discussions of the strategic issues confronting the newspaper. The director of personnel, a smooth shaven and careful personality, suggested waiting for the editor. More small talk. Even more coffee. Everybody

Table 11.1 *Characterization of operational and strategic conversations*

Operational conversations	Strategic conversations
Discussing future	
Focused on present	Focused on future
Facts	Fictions
'Real'	'Play'
Focused on 'hows'	Focused on 'whys'
Scope of issues	
Limited impact	Unlimited impact
Limited scope of issues	Unlimited scope of issues
Solving issues	Understanding issues
Knowledge development	
Knowledge confirmation	Knowledge development
Static language	Dynamic languaging
'Solid'	'Fragile'
Given industry	Creating industry
Implicit, covering grounds	Explicit, challenging grounds
Rules for conversations	
Clear-cut	Ambiguous
Advocacy	Dialogue
Authoritative exposition	Hypothetical exposition
Strategy of intimidation	Strategy of emboldment
Reach for closure	Open for new conversations
Fixed roles	Dynamic roles
Need for expertise	Need for generalists
Power linked to expertise	Power fluid
Event based	Continuous

looks at their watches. At 11.20 the editor in chief arrives, red-eyed, furious, and with a puff of cigar smoke following in his wake. He slams the newspaper of today onto the table and exclaims: 'Have you seen this?!? Pages two and five are completely missing. Our best stories have vanished. Our best advertisers have had their expensive advertisements erased. *Who* is responsible?' And then it was done. The remaining two hours and thirty minutes were spent discussing issues like: who was responsible, what to do with the advertiser, where to stack the newspapers that could not be sent out, how to tell the readers that they had missed out on what the headlines promised, how to make sure that the printer worked reliably.

You might think that this was an accidental event, one of a kind. Wrong, we are sad to say. In another company having the same intention, the management team drifted away in their conversations and started to talk about fixing the doorbell at the headquarters, choosing a new secretary, and buying a new coffee machine for their management meetings.

This is unfortunately the fate of most supposedly strategic conversations in many companies. Considering that these conversations are the cradle for what should eventually grow into successful and winning strategies, we believe that management teams must come to terms with the way they discuss the future. That is, they must educate themselves in conversation management. Perhaps it would be useful to start with the following:

1   Discuss your current rules for strategic conversations. As a starting point, use Table 11.1 to identify what kind of rules you normally apply to your current strategic activities.
2   Identify a new set of rules for strategic conversations. Use Table 11.1, and pay particular attention to the rules of 'authority', 'intimidation', and 'closure'.
3   Reflect on the rules in practice. How do your strategic conversations emerge?
4   Use the meaning matrix to innovate in language. Think about the strategic issues, externally or internally, that will affect the performance of your company over the coming years. Can you invent new concepts that express what you know about existing strategic issues in a better way? Can you develop new meaning around existing strategic issues? Can you identify new strategic issues? Can you find new concepts that describe these issues more clearly?

Notes

This chapter is based on an article previously published in the *European Management Journal*, December 1995.

References

Prahalad, C.K. and Hamel, G. (1994). *Competing for the Future*. Boston: Harvard Business School Press.
Roos, J. and von Krogh, G. (1995). What you see and understand depends on who you are. *IMD Perspectives*, September, International Institute for Management Development, Lausanne.
von Krogh, G. and Roos, J. (1995). *Organizational Epistemology*. London: Macmillan.
von Krogh, G. and Roos, J. (1996). A phraseologic view of organizational learning. In A.S. Huff, and J. March (eds), *Advances in Strategic Management*. Greenwich, CT: JAI Press.

Afterword: an Agenda for Practice and Future Research

Georg von Krogh and Johan Roos

In this book we have tried to shed light on a number of theoretical and managerial issues in the realm of knowledge management. In a world where business to an ever increasing extent is seen as 'knowledge-driven', and where many employees are referred to as 'knowledge workers', the topics discussed in the book are central to competitive and corporate strategy. Knowledge is and will be *the* most important source for building a sustainable competitive advantage. Few management teams, however, have discussed questions such as: what is our company knowledge? How does this knowledge come about? What partners are attractive for our own knowledge development? How can we develop knowledge in cooperative settings? How can we measure knowledge? We argue that managers who have the ability to address, challenge and reflect on the issue of knowledge management will be of more value to their companies than those who do not. Only a few companies, or better managers, have begun this process – but the number is increasing!

The Swedish insurance company Skandia for instance, is exploring ways to extend its knowledge. This company has recently pioneered a new and unconventional way to measure and extend its 'intellectual capital'. Through its 'business navigator' model Skandia has decided to manage and measure its intellectual capital in terms of four distinct dimensions: customer relationship, people, infrastructure and renewal efforts. Sencorp, a *Fortune* 1000 US company, has perhaps the most unconventional and innovative way to manage its knowledge resources. It follows the anti-representationism perspective on knowledge development described in Part II of this book and has introduced management responsibilities to encourage self-referencing, to initiate language games in discussions and to stimulate self-similar organizational processes. Sencorp's fractal 'ABC model' is designed to allow for replication on all levels throughout the company. Swiss pharmaceutical company Hoffman La Roche has developed a catalogue of knowledge – the 'yellow pages' – comparable to a telephone book. This book lists the 'knowledge resources' of each employee and therefore enhances the knowledge transfer and exchange in the company.

Examples of joint knowledge development in organizational cooperation can be seen in very dynamic and fast changing industries such as the
pharmaceutical, telecommunications and media industry. Swiss drug giant
Sandoz has purchased the food company Gerber in order to develop new
innovations for the fast growing market of nutraceuticals, i.e. supplements
that are halfway between a nutrient and a pharmaceutical. Many drug and
food companies build alliances and share their knowledge resources to
enter this market. The global telecommunications industry is changing
almost every day. A simple two-dimensional plot of the alliances of, for
instance, Cable and Wireless looks like a spider's web: Petersburg Long
Distance, Tele 2, Bell Cablemedia, Mercury Communications, Hong Kong
Telecom, Digital, Oceanic Wireless and so on. Of course, each of these
partner companies, in turn, is intertwined with numerous other companies
that are not necessarily telecommunication companies. The aim of this
complex web of interorganizational cooperation is to develop and transfer
knowledge. The media industry is another example of joint knowledge
development efforts to explore the huge existing business opportunities.
Deutsche Telekom entered an alliance with Microsoft to jointly develop
services and applications in the field of electronic media: they develop new
knowledge together!

These examples demonstrate how the issue of knowledge management
has caught the interest of business. Hence, we do encourage any manager
reading this book to create awareness of the 'knowledge challenge' in his/
her company.

Besides the practical implications of managing knowledge it is our strong
conviction that there remains an increasing need for further research into
the relatively new area of knowledge management. We have argued that
managers need to be aware of the tremendous 'knowledge challenge', and
to this end they need support and help from academia. It is a major task for
academics to provide reliable, deep and broad insights as well as practical
tools to support managers. At the same time we do recognize conceptual
and methodological difficulties in this research area. However, these
difficulties should be a motivation for academics to focus their research
efforts on the attractive and relatively unmapped area of knowledge
management in cooperation and competition.

Apart from the many research questions addressed in the chapters of this
book we see the need for the following streams of future research in the
realm of knowledge management:

1   *Research into the way strategic intent or motives behind acquisitions and
    alliances shape the subsequent knowledge development and transfer
    between firms.* Given the strategic intent of knowledge development in
    cooperation, how can companies create and sustain knowledge
    alliances and successfully exchange their knowledge resources?

2 *Research into the impact of information communication technologies (ICTs) on knowledge development and transfer within and between firms.* Innovations such as electronic data exchange, internet, world-wide web or videoconferencing are eliminating physical and temporal boundaries. How can companies use these revolutionary inventions of the information age to better manage and develop their knowledge resources?

3 *Research into the way industries transform as an effect of extensive cooperation, joint knowledge transfer and joint knowledge development.* Cooperative linkages between companies from quite different indus-tries are increasing rapidly. For example, how does cooperation of companies in the media industry with the objective of joint knowledge development change the overall industry structure and evolution?

4 *Research into the way societies transform as a result of knowledge-driven strategic cooperation between firms.* What is the role of regulating bodies within and between nations? What are the influences of cooperation between different companies on our everyday lifestyle?

5 *Research into the creation of 'foresight' in management teams within organizations and in organizational cooperation.* A foresight creation process is ideally brought forth through participation on many organ-izational and interorganizational levels. Given this, what is the role of knowledge in the foresight creation process? How can cooperating companies create a common foresight for all partners?

6 *Research into industry-specific barriers to knowledge transfer between cooperating firms.* For example, such boundaries can be created through patenting and channel access in the pharmaceutical industry, client discretion in consultancy, and contents distribution in the media. How can these barriers be overcome?

7 *Research into the way new management recipes, models and tools emerge.* In our opinion the conventional distinction between researchers and practicing managers is an increasingly irrelevant one. Researchers do not have a monopoly on creating knowledge. Pro-fessors are managing numerous students and employees. Likewise, managers develop knowledge through discussion and reflection. Some even write articles and give talks where the audience is academic. Thus, there is a need for further reflection: what are effective ways managers and researchers can jointly develop knowledge? How can this occur on the individual, group, unit or organizational level? What are the obstacles and how can these be overcome?

8 *Research into the characteristics of a 'knowledge manager'.* What are the skills and tasks of a 'knowledge manager': one who is competently equipped to handle organizations of knowledge workers, and to manage knowledge development projects?

Finally, we would like to draw the attention of academics to an important consideration. We do encourage anyone who intends to study the management of knowledge to remember what Henry Mintzberg said: 'relevance counts more than scientific rigor'. But relevance, in turn, depends on the eyes that see, and what you see depends on who you are.

Good luck – whoever you are!

Index